Collins

AQA GCSE 9-1
German

evision Guide

th audio download

Amy Bates,  eely Laycock

About this Revision & Practice book

Revise

These pages provide a recap of everything you need to know for each topic.

You should read through all the information before taking the Quick Test at the end. This will test whether you can recall the key facts.

Quick Test

1. What is 'I play hockey' in German?
2. What is the difference between 'ich laufe Ski' and 'ich bin Ski gelaufen'?
3. Translate into English: **Früher sind wir Skateboard gefahren**.
4. Translate into German: 'Five years ago I used to go to the youth club'.
5. Translate into German: 'I would like to try extreme sports'.

Practise

These topic-based questions appear shortly after the revision pages for each topic and will test whether you have understood the topic. If you get any of the questions wrong, make sure you read the correct answer carefully.

Review

These topic-based questions appear later in the book, allowing you to revisit the topic and test how well you have remembered the information. If you get any of the questions wrong, make sure you read the correct answer carefully.

Mix it Up

These pages feature a mix of exam-style questions for the different topics within a chapter. They will make sure you can recall the relevant information to answer a question without being told which topic it relates to.

Test Yourself on the Go

Visit our website at **collins.co.uk/collinsGCSErevision** and print off a set of flashcards. These pocket-sized cards feature questions and answers so that you can test yourself on all the key facts anytime and anywhere. You will also find lots more information about the advantages of spaced practice and how to plan for it.

Workbook

This section features even more topic-based questions as well as Higher tier practice exam papers, providing two further practice opportunities for each topic to guarantee the best results. Visit our website at **collins.co.uk/collinsGCSErevision** to download listening exercises for every topic and audio tracks to accompany the listening exam paper.

ebook

To access the ebook revision guide visit

collins.co.uk/ebooks

and follow the step-by-step instructions.

Contents

Contents

Contents

Review Questions

Key Concepts from Key Stage 3

1 **Trag die richtigen Wörter in die Lücken ein.** Insert the correct words in the gaps.

Juli	Mittwoch	Dezember	Winter	Dienstag
März	Sommer	Oktober	Donnerstag	Mai

Die Jahreszeiten (seasons)

  der Frühling

a) der ....

  der Herbst

b) der ....

Die Monate (months)

  Januar

  Februar

c) ....

  April

d) ....

  Juni

e) ....

  August

  September

f) ....

  November

g) ....

Die Tage (days)

  Montag

h) ....

i) ....

j) ....

  Freitag

  Samstag

  Sonntag

[10 marks]

2 **Trag die Daten ein.** Write in the dates.

einunddreißigste	Januar	Dezember	November
fünfundzwanzigste	April	erste	Oktober
vierzehnte	erste	Februar	fünfte

a) 14 / 2   **der** ....

b) 31 / 10   **der** ....

c) 25 / 12   **der** ....

d) 5 / 11   **der** ....

e) 1 / 4   **der** ....

f) 1 / 1   **der** ....

[6 marks]

3 **Beantworte die Fragen auf Deutsch.** Answer the questions in German.

a) Wie heißt du?

b) Wie alt bist du?

c) Wann hast du Geburtstag?

d) Wo wohnst du?

e) Hast du Geschwister?

f) Hast du ein Haustier? [6 marks]

4 **Trag die Zahlen ein.** Write in the numbers (in numerals).

a) vier .... vierzehn .... vierzig .... vierundvierzig ....

b) zweiundachtzig .... achtundzwanzig .... achtzehn .... acht ....

c) dreißig .... dreizehn .... dreiunddreißig .... drei ....

d) siebzehn .... siebenundsiebzig .... sieben .... siebzig .... [16 marks]

5 **Schreib die Zahlen in deutschen Wörtern auf**. Write the numbers in German words.

a) 66   **b)** 74   **c)** 23   **d)** 12   **e)** 51   **f)** 11   **g)** 84   **h)** 19   **i)** 47   [9 marks]

6 **Verbinde die Uhrzeiten.** Match up the times.

halb sieben	12.35
Viertel vor acht	5.30
fünf nach halb zwölf	6.30
Viertel nach zwei	9.40
fünf nach halb eins	2.15
halb sechs	11.35
zwanzig vor zehn	7.45

[7 marks]

7 **Schreib die Uhrzeiten in Wörtern auf**. Write the times in German words.

a) 6.45   **b)** 3.30   **c)** 4.30   **d)** 10.35   **e)** 9.25   [5 marks]

My Family

You must be able to:

- Describe appearance and personality
- Say how well you get on with family members
- Apply adjectives.

Family Members

- **mein Vater / Stiefvater** — my father / stepfather
  mein Großvater / Opa — my grandfather / grandad
  mein älterer Bruder / jüngerer Bruder — my older / younger brother
  mein Stiefbruder / Halbbruder — my stepbrother / half-brother
  mein Schwager — my brother-in-law
  mein Onkel — my uncle
  mein Neffe — my nephew
  mein Cousin — my (male) cousin
  meine Mutter / Stiefmutter — my mother / stepmother
  meine Großmutter / Oma — my grandmother / granny
  meine ältere Schwester / jüngere Schwester — my older sister / younger sister
  meine Stiefschwester / Halbschwester — my stepsister / half-sister
  meine Schwägerin — my sister-in-law
  meine Tante — my aunt
  meine Nichte — my niece
  meine Kusine — my (female) cousin
  meine Eltern — my parents
  meine Großeltern — my grandparents

Key Point

Remember to add **–e** to **mein** when used with feminine and plural nouns:
Masculine / Neuter singular — **mein**
Feminine singular — **mein<u>e</u>**
Plural — **mein<u>e</u>**

Key Point

Remember that all German nouns begin with a capital letter.

Describing Appearance

- **Er / Sie ist...** — He / She is…
  Sie sind... — They are…
- **ein bisschen** — a bit
  sehr — very
  ziemlich — quite
  zu — too
- **alt** — old
  dick — fat
  dünn — thin
  groß — big / tall
  gut aussehend — good-looking
  unattraktiv — unattractive
  hübsch — pretty
  jung — young
  klein — small
  schlank — slim
  schön — beautiful

Key Point

No ending is needed on the adjective when it is not placed with the noun:
Mein Opa ist <u>alt</u>.
My grandad is old.
Meine Schwester ist <u>schlank</u>.
My sister is slim.

- **Mein Opa ist ziemlich jung und ein bisschen dick.**
  My grandfather is quite young and a bit fat.
- **Meine Stiefschwester ist klein, schlank und sehr hübsch.**
  My stepsister is small, slim and very beautiful.
- **Meine Eltern sind ziemlich groß und dünn.**
  My parents are quite tall and thin.

Relationships

- **Ich verstehe mich gut mit...**   I get on well with...
- **Ich verstehe mich nicht gut mit...**   I don't get on well with...
- **Ich streite mich mit...**   I argue with...
- **Wir verstehen uns.**   We get on well.
- **Wir streiten uns.**   We argue.
- **...nervt mich.**   ...annoys me.
- **Ich nerve sie / ihn.**   I annoy her / him.

Adjectives of Personality

nett	nice	**nervig**	irritating
großzügig	generous	**laut**	noisy
sympathisch	likeable	**doof**	stupid
glücklich	happy	**egoistisch**	selfish
artig	well-behaved	**frech**	cheeky / naughty
ruhig	quiet	**faul**	lazy
fleißig	hard-working	**peinlich**	embarrassing
intelligent	intelligent	**streng**	strict
freundlich	friendly	**stur**	stubborn
witzig	funny	**traurig**	sad

- **Ich verstehe mich gut mit meiner Tante, weil sie immer sehr großzügig ist.**
  I get on well with my aunt because she is always very generous.
- **Aber ich streite mich oft mit meinem Stiefbruder, weil er so nervig ist.**
  But I often argue with my stepbrother because he is so irritating.

Quick Test

1. Translate into English:
   Ich verstehe mich sehr gut mit meiner Schwester. Sie ist sehr jung aber sie ist sehr nett und großzügig.
2. Translate into German:
   I don't get on very well with my father. He is quite old and very strict. We often argue.

Key Point

Remember to use the dative after **mit**:

Masculine / Neuter	**mit meinem** ...
Feminine	**mit meiner** ...
Plural	**mit meinen** ...

Key Point

To make your language sound more natural and detailed, use expressions of frequency:

immer	always
meistens	mostly
oft	often
manchmal	sometimes
selten	rarely
ab und zu	occasionally
nie	never

Key Vocab

Er / Sie ist...	He / she is
Sie sind...	They are
Ich verstehe mich gut mit...	I get on well with...
Ich verstehe mich nicht sehr gut mit...	I don't get on very well with...

My Friends

You must be able to:

- Describe a friend's appearance
- Explain why you are friends
- Use the **wir** form correctly in the present tense.

Describing a Friend's Appearance

- **Mein bester Freund...** My best friend (male)...
- **Meine beste Freundin...** My best friend (female)...
  heißt... is called...
- **Er / Sie hat...** He / She has...
  blaue Augen blue eyes
  braune Augen brown eyes
  graue Augen grey eyes
  grüne Augen green eyes
  blonde Haare blonde hair
  braune Haare brown hair
  dunkelbraune Haare dark brown hair
  hellbraune Haare light brown hair
  rote Haare red / ginger hair
  schwarze Haare black hair
  kurze Haare short hair
  lange Haare long hair
  mittellange Haare medium-length hair
  glatte Haare straight hair
  lockige Haare curly hair
- **Er / Sie trägt eine Brille.** He / She wears glasses.
- **Er / Sie ist größer / kleiner als ich.** He / She is taller / shorter than me.
- **Er / Sie ist mittelgroß.** He / She is of medium height.
- **Wir kennen uns seit... Jahren.** We have known each other for... years.

- **Mein bester Freund heißt Tim. Er hat blaue Augen und kurze, glatte, blonde Haare. Er trägt eine Brille. Er ist größer als ich.**
  My best friend is called Tim. He has blue eyes and short, straight, blonde hair. He wears glasses. He is taller than me.
- **Meine beste Freundin heißt Tara. Sie hat braune Augen und lange, lockige, dunkelbraune Haare. Wir kennen uns seit vier Jahren.**
  My best friend is called Tara. She has brown eyes and long curly, dark brown hair. We have known each other for four years.

The Qualities of a Friend

- **Er / Sie ist...** He / She is...
  treu faithful, loyal
  ehrlich honest
  schlau clever
  sportlich sporty

> **Key Point**
>
> If you say **mein Freund** or **meine Freundin**, it means 'my friend'. It can also mean 'boyfriend' or 'girlfriend'. If you say **mein bester Freund / meine beste Freundin**, it means 'my best friend'.

> **Key Point**
>
> **Haare** is a plural word. Any adjective that comes before it must end in **–e**:
> **lange Haare** long hair

schüchtern	shy
lustig	amusing
immer gut gelaunt	always in a good mood
• **Er / Sie ist nie…**	He / She is never…
böse	angry
neidisch	envious
schlecht gelaunt	in a bad mood

What You Have in Common

• Wir haben viel gemeinsam.	We have a lot in common.
• **Wir haben den gleichen Humor.**	We have the same sense of humour.
• Wir mögen…	We like…
die gleiche Musik	the same music
die gleiche Fußballmannschaft	the same football team
die gleichen Sportarten	the same types of sport
die gleichen Fernsehsendungen	the same TV programmes

What You Do Together

• **Wir treffen uns immer am Wochenende.**	We always meet up at the weekend.
• **Wir schicken uns jeden Abend SMS.**	We text each other every evening.
• **Wir gehen zusammen einkaufen.**	We go shopping together.
• **Wir gehen zusammen ins Kino.**	We go to the cinema together.
• **Wir spielen zusammen Videospiele.**	We play video games together.
• **Wir hören zusammen Musik.**	We listen to music together.

• **Meine beste Freundin Klara ist ein bisschen schüchtern aber nie neidisch. Wir mögen die gleichen Fernsehsendungen. Wir treffen uns immer am Wochenende und gehen zusammen ins Kino.**
My best friend Klara is a bit shy but never envious. We like the same TV shows. We always meet up at the weekend and go to the cinema together.

• **Mein bester Freund Mehmet ist sehr sportlich. Er ist immer gut gelaunt und wir mögen die gleiche Fußballmannschaft, HSV Hamburg.**
My best friend Mehmet is very sporty. He is always in a good mood and we like the same football team, HSV Hamburg.

Key Point

When you use **wir** (meaning 'we'), the verb will always end in –**en**:
wir gehen…   we go…
wir spielen…   we play…

Key Point

Words that indicate togetherness:
gleich (adjective) the same
zusammen   together

Key Point

Be careful when using reflexive verbs:
wir treffen uns
we meet each other

Key Point

Join sentences together by using words like **und** (and), **aber** (but) and **auch** (too).

Key Vocab

Mein bester Freund…
My best friend (male)…
Meine beste Freundin…
My best friend (female)…
Er / Sie hat…
He / She has…
Wir haben…
We have…
Wir mögen…
We like…

Quick Test

1. Translate into German:
   My best (male) friend has blue eyes and long, straight, brown hair. He is very honest and we like the same types of sport.
2. Choose the correct spelling: **Susanne ist oft neidisch / niedisch.**
3. Choose the correct words and then translate the sentence into English:
   Wir mögen den / die / das gleiche Musik und wir gehen oft in den / in die / ins Kino.
4. Describe your best friend: write about his / her appearance and qualities and describe what you do together and what you have in common.

Marriage and Partnerships

You must be able to:

- Describe people's marital status
- Say whether you want to get married
- Use **seit** with the present tense.

Marital Status

- **der Familienstand** — marital status
- **der Freund** — boyfriend
- **der Hochzeitstag** — wedding anniversary
- **der Mann** — husband
- **der Partner** — male partner
- **der Sohn** — son
- **der Verlobte** — fiancé
- **die Frau** — wife
- **die Freundin** — girlfriend
- **die Hochzeit** — wedding
- **die Liebe** — love
- **die Partnerin** — female partner
- **die Tochter** — daughter
- **die Verlobte** — fiancée
- **das Einzelkind** — only child
- ledig — single / unmarried
- **ein Kind / Kinder haben** — to have a child / children
- **eine Lebenspartnerschaft eingehen** — to be in a civil partnership
- **die gleichgeschlechtliche Ehe** — same-sex marriage
- **einschlafen** — to pass away
- **geboren werden** — to be born
- geschieden **sein** — to be divorced
- getrennt **sein** — to be separated
- heiraten — to marry
- **sich verlieben** — to fall in love
- **sich verloben** — to get engaged
- **sterben** — to die
- **verheiratet sein** — to be married
- **zusammen leben** — to live together
- **Meine Schwester ist ledig.** — My sister is single / unmarried.
- **Mein Opa ist tot.** — My grandad is dead.
- **Meine Eltern sind seit fünf Jahren geschieden.** — My parents have been divorced for five years.

Key Point

Seit means 'since'. Use it with *the present tense* to say how long something has been happening. In English we would use the word 'for'.
Mein Onkel ist <u>seit</u> einem Jahr getrennt.
My uncle has been separated <u>for</u> a year.

Key Point

You often need to deduce the meaning of a word from its context. **Mann** can mean 'man' or 'husband'.
Mein Mann ist ein Mann!
My husband is a man!
It is the same with **Frau** (woman or wife). To make it completely clear, you can use **Ehemann** or **Ehefrau**.

Key Point

Eingeschlafen can mean 'asleep' or 'passed away'. If you saw the sentence: **Meine Oma ist eingeschlafen**, you would have to deduce its exact meaning from the circumstances.

Do You Want to Get Married?

- **Möchtest du heiraten?** — Would you like to get married?
- Ich möchte **eines Tages** heiraten. — I'd like to get married one day.
- Ich möchte nicht heiraten. — I wouldn't like to get married.
- **Ich möchte lieber ledig bleiben.** — I would prefer to remain single / unmarried.
- **Ich würde gern [viele] Kinder haben.** — I would like to have [lots of] children.
- **Ich möchte keine Kinder haben.** — I wouldn't like to have children.
- **Ich weiß noch nicht.** — I don't know yet.

Die Ehe – Pro und Kontra
Marriage – For and Against

Dafür	Dagegen
Die Ehe ist ein Zeichen der Liebe. Marriage is a symbol of love.	**Sie ist altmodisch.** It's old-fashioned.
Sie ist besser für Kinder. It's better for children.	**Zusammenleben ist besser.** Living together is better.
Sie ist sicherer als Zusammenleben. It's more secure than living together.	**Die Ehe endet oft mit** Scheidung. Marriage often ends in divorce.

Quick Test

1. Write the English for these verbs: **sich verloben   heiraten   sterben**
2. Write the German for these words: unmarried   divorced   marriage
3. Translate into English:
   Ich würde gern ledig bleiben. Ich möchte nicht heiraten.
4. Translate into German:
   My aunt has been married for twelve years.
5. Explain whether you would like to get married one day and say why.
   Write your answer and say it out loud.

Social Media

You must be able to:

- Talk about computers and the internet
- Discuss how you use social media
- Use **man muss / man darf nicht.**

Computers and the Internet

der Bildschirm	screen
der Blog	blog
• der Computer	computer
der Drucker	printer
der Laptop	laptop
der USB-Stick	USB stick
• **die E-Mail / Mail**	email
die Maus	mouse
die Startseite	homepage
die Tastatur	keyboard
die Webseite	website
• **das Forum**	forum / chat room
das Internet	internet
das Tablet	tablet
das WLAN	Wi-Fi
soziale Medien (pl)	social media

Online Activities

• **chatten**	to chat
drucken	to print
erhalten	to receive
herunterladen	to download
hochladen	to upload
klicken	to click
schicken	to send
suchen	to search
surfen	to surf
tippen	to type

- **Ich verbringe viel Zeit online.** — I spend a lot of time online.
- **Ich besuche täglich meine Lieblingswebseiten.** — I visit my favourite websites each day.
- **Ich schicke und erhalte E-Mails und Nachrichten.** — I send and receive emails and messages.

> ### Key Point
>
> Note how many words are similar to the English words. This is often true in the world of technology. Sometimes English words are converted into German verbs, e.g. **chatten, klicken**.

Protecting Yourself Online

- **online sicher bleiben** — stay safe online
- **Man muss...** — You must...
  regelmäßig das Passwort ändern — regularly change your password
  sich nur mit bekannten Leuten unterhalten — only converse with people you know
  ein Virenschutzprogramm installieren — install an anti-virus program
  vorsichtig sein — be careful
- **Man darf nicht...** — You mustn't...
  das Passwort verraten — give away your password
  persönliche Informationen teilen — share personal information
  sich mit fremden Leuten unterhalten — converse with strangers

Advantages and Disadvantages of Social Media

- **Das Gute ist, dass man** mit Freunden in Kontakt bleiben **kann.**
  The good thing is that you can stay in contact with friends.
- **Das Schlechte ist Cybermobbing. Das ist gefährlich.**
  The bad thing is cyberbullying. That is dangerous.

Key Point

man muss... (+ infinitive) means 'you must...'
man darf nicht... (+ infinitive) means 'you mustn't...'
Be careful not to say **man muss nicht**... as this means 'you don't have to...'

Key Point

Mobbing (bullying) is an example of a German word, which is taken from the English but given a different meaning.

Key Point

Man is used to mean 'you' as well as 'we'.
Man muss vorsichtig sein. You must be careful.

Key Vocab

der Computer computer
die Webseite website
soziale Medien (pl) social media
surfen to surf the internet
mit Freunden in Kontakt bleiben to stay in contact with friends
sich nur mit bekannten Leuten unterhalten to only converse with people you know
vorsichtig sein be careful
man muss... you must...
man darf nicht... you mustn't...

Quick Test

1. Write down four words of German technological vocabulary that are not adaptations of English words.
2. Complete these sentences with good advice for internet users:
   a) Man muss...
   b) Man darf nicht...
3. Write two sentences about how you use the internet.

Mobile Technology

You must be able to:

- Talk about your mobile phone and what you use it for
- Say what you think about mobile technology
- Use adjectives to give opinions.

Using a Mobile Phone

- **Ich benutze ein Handy.** — I use a mobile phone.
  Ich schicke eine SMS. — I send a text / I text.
  Ich rufe meine Freunde / Freundinnen an. — I call my friends.
  Ich chatte mit meinen Freunden / Freundinnen. — I chat with my friends.
  Ich kaufe online ein. — I shop online.
  Ich höre Musik. — I listen to music.
  Ich lade Apps herunter. — I download apps.
  Ich spiele Online-Spiele. — I play games online.
  Ich lese meine Nachrichten. — I read my messages.
  Das Internet hilft bei meinen Hausaufgaben. — The internet helps with my homework.
  Ich mache Fotos. — I take photos.

Key Point

Handy (mobile phone) is another German word that is taken from the English but given a different meaning.

Giving Opinions

- **Meiner Meinung nach ist er / sie / es...** — In my opinion, it is…
  Ich finde ihn / sie / es / sie... — I find it / them…

Key Point

Be careful with genders. When using the accusative after **ich finde**, you need to know the gender of the word you are talking about, e.g. **Ich finde ihn** (m) / **sie** (f) / **es** (n) **sie** (pl)…

billig	cheap		blöd / doof	stupid
lustig	amusing		furchtbar	awful
nützlich	useful		gefährlich	dangerous
praktisch	practical		langweilig	boring
schnell	fast		schrecklich	terrible
toll	great		teuer	expensive
witzig	funny		uninteressant	uninteresting

- **Ich kaufe online ein. Meiner Meinung nach ist es schnell und billig.**
  I shop online. In my opinion it's fast and cheap.
- **Ich chatte mit meinen Freunden, weil ich sie witzig finde.**
  I chat with my friends because I find them funny.

Key Point

Don't forget that **weil** (because) sends the verb to the end.

Advantages and Disadvantages of Mobile Technology

- **die Vorteile der Mobiltechnologie** — the advantages of mobile technology
- **Man kann...** — You / One can...
  mit anderen in Kontakt bleiben — stay in touch with people
  im Notfall Hilfe rufen — call for help in an emergency
  schnell einkaufen — do the shopping quickly
  sich auf dem Laufenden halten — keep up to date
  sich schnell informieren — quickly find out information
  sich verabreden — organise get-togethers

- **die Nachteile der Mobiltechnologie** — the disadvantages of mobile technology

- **Manchmal gibt es keinen Empfang.** — Sometimes there is no signal.
- **Man muss das Gerät immer wieder aufladen.** — You keep having to charge your device.
- **Die Technologie ändert sich so schnell.** — The technology changes so fast.
- **Es ist teuer, immer die aktuelle Version zu haben.** — It's expensive always having the latest version.
- **Viele Leute sind stundenlang an ihrem Handy.** — Lots of people spend hours on their mobiles.

Key Point

Note the use of reflexive verbs:
sich informieren
to inform oneself
sich verabreden
to arrange a meeting

Key Point

When an adjective doesn't come before a noun, it has no ending:
Ich finde es witzig / doof / teuer.
I find it funny / stupid / expensive.

Key Vocab

Ich schicke	I send
Ich chatte	I chat
Ich höre	I listen to
Ich spiele	I play
Ich lese	I read
Ich nehme	I take
Meiner Meinung nach...	In my opinion...
Ich finde ihn / sie / es / sie...	I find it / them...

Quick Test

1. Translate these adjectives into English:
   billig   nützlich   langweilig
2. Which of these verbs is the odd one out and why?
   chatten   sich informieren   hören   kaufen
3. Translate into English:
   Meine Freundin ist stundenlang an ihrem Handy. Das finde ich blöd.
4. Translate into German:
   In my opinion, mobile technology is practical. You can do the shopping quickly.

Music

You must be able to:

- Discuss musical interests and preferences
- Give your opinions on different types of music and songs
- Talk about a favourite musician or music event you've been to.

Musical Interests and Preferences

ich mag gern...	I like...
Hip-hop	hip-hop
Jazz	jazz
klassische Musik	classical music
Metal	metal
Popmusik	pop music
Rapmusik	rap music
Rockmusik	rock music
Techno	techno

der Chor	choir
der Künstler / die Künstlerin	male artist / female artist
der Sänger / die Sängerin	male singer / female singer
der Schlager	hit song
die Gruppe / die Band	group / band

ich höre gern...	I like listening to...
ich höre nicht gern / ungern...	I don't like listening to...
ich höre lieber...	I prefer listening to...
ich liebe...	I love...
ich spiele gern...	I like playing...
ich bin Fan von...	I'm a fan of...
ich interessiere mich für...	I'm interested in...
singen	to sing
hören	to listen to
Klavier / Gitarre / Schlagzeug spielen	to play piano / guitar / drums
herunterladen	to download

Talking about Music

- **Wir sprechen über Musik.** We talk about music.
  Ich interessiere mich für Musik. I'm interested in music.
  Ich lade Musik herunter und höre sie auf meinem Handy. I download music and listen to it on my phone.
- **Was für Musik hörst du am liebsten?** What kind of music do you most like listening to?
- Ich höre am liebsten **(Rockmusik / klassische Musik usw.)**. I most like listening to (rock music / classical music etc.).
- **Meine Familie hört am liebsten...** My family most like listening to...
- **Meine Eltern hören am liebsten...** My parents most like listening to...
- **Mein Lieblingssänger** (m) / **meine Lieblingssängerin** (f) My favourite singer

Key Point

When talking about types of music you like, no article is needed before the noun, e.g. **Ich mag / ich höre gern Musik / Popmusik.** I like / like listening to music / pop music.

Key Point

To make a word for a person feminine, add **–in** (and sometimes an umlaut): **Künstler – Künstlerin** **Sänger – Sängerin**

Key Point

am liebsten is a superlative. Put it after any verb to indicate that it is something you *most like* doing.

Key Point

The verb **hören** means 'to hear' but also 'to listen to', e.g. **Ich höre gern Jazz.** I listen to jazz.

Key Point

usw. is short for **und so weiter** and means etc (etcetera). It's very useful when listing items.

- **Meine Lieblingsband / Lieblingsgruppe** — My favourite band / group
- **Meine Lieblingsmusik ist...** — My favourite music is…

- **Hast du einen Lieblingssänger / eine Lieblingssängerin?**
  Do you have a favourite singer?
- **Mein Lieblingssänger / meine Lieblingssängerin ist…**
  My favourite singer is…

- **der Rhythmus** — the rhythm
  der Text — the lyrics
- **die Melodie** — melody
  die Stimme — voice

- **ich mag es gern** — I like it
  es gefällt mir — it pleases me
  es nervt mich — it irritates me
  ich finde es beruhigend — I find it relaxing
  es macht mich glücklich — it makes me happy
  es macht mich traurig — it makes me sad

- **Das Lied macht mich glücklich, weil der Text so romantisch ist.**
  The song makes me happy because the lyrics are so romantic.
- **Ich finde die Melodie beruhigend.** — I find the melody relaxing.

Opinions using the Perfect Tense

- **Ich habe immer gern Techno-Musik gehört, obwohl meine Freunde sie doof finden.**
  I've always liked listening to techno even if my friends think it's stupid.
- **Ich habe nie klassische Musik gehört, weil ich sie nicht mag.**
  I've never listened to classical music because I don't like it.

Describe a Music Event

- **der Schlager** — hit song
  der Star — star
- **die Tour** — tour
- **das Konzert** — concert
  das Musikfestival — music festival
  Musiksendungen — music TV programmes

- **Im Sommer war ich auf dem Wacken-Festival in Norddeutschland. Da habe ich meine Lieblingsbands gesehen.** In the summer I was at the Wacken Festival in north Germany. There I saw my favourite bands.

> **Quick Test**
>
> 1. What is the difference between 'ich höre gern' and 'ich höre lieber'?
> 2. What's wrong with this sentence: 'Meine Lieblingssängerin ist Ed Sheeran'?
> 3. Translate into English: **Ich interessiere mich für Rapmusik, obwohl sie oft zu laut ist. Klassische Musik macht mich traurig.**
> 4. Translate into German: I've never been to the Lorelei Festival.

Key Point

Attaching **Lieblings–** to the front of a noun indicates that it is your *favourite*: **Lieblingslied** favourite song.

Key Point

obwohl means 'although'. Like **weil**, it sends the verb to the end.

Key Point

Remember that **Musik** is a feminine noun, so you must use **sie** rather than **es**:
Ich mag klassische Musik, weil sie beruhigend ist.
I like classical music because it is relaxing.

Key Vocab

der Künstler / die Künstlerin
male artist / female artist
der Sänger / die Sängerin
male singer / female singer
die Gruppe / die Band
group / band
der Schlager hit song
ich höre gern...
I like listening to…
ich höre nicht gern / ungern...
I don't like listening to…
ich höre lieber...
I prefer listening to…
ich höre am liebsten...
I most like listening to…
Ich habe... gesehen.
I saw…
weil because
obwohl although
immer always
nie never

Cinema and TV

You must be able to:

- Describe a film or TV programme
- Discuss whether you prefer going to the cinema or watching TV
- Make comparisons.

Describing a Film or TV programme

- **Beschreib einen Film oder eine Fernsehsendung.**
  Describe a film or a TV programme.

der Kriegsfilm	war film
der Krimi	thriller / crime film
der Zeichentrickfilm	cartoon
die Geschichte	story
die Reality-Sendung	reality programme
die Seifenoper	soap opera
die Sendung	programme
die Serie	series
die Spielshow	game show
das Programm	programme listings
die Nachrichten (pl)	news

- **Das bringt mich zum Lachen.** — It makes me laugh.
- **Das bringt mich zum Weinen.** — It makes me cry.
- **Das macht mir Angst.** — It frightens me.
- **stattfinden** — to take place

- **Es ist eine sentimentale Liebesgeschichte, die in Polen im zweiten Weltkrieg stattfindet.**
  It's a sentimental love story that takes place in Poland in the Second World War.
- **Es ist ein lustiger Zeichtrickfilm, der mich zum Lachen bringt.**
  It's a funny cartoon which makes me laugh.

- **Wovon handelt er / sie / es?** — What's it about?
  Er / sie / es handelt von... — It's about…
  der / die / das — who / which

- **Der Film handelt von einem Kommissar, der einen Mörder sucht.**
  The film is about a police inspector who is looking for a murderer.

- **Die Sendung handelt von einem Mädchen, das ihren Bruder verloren hat.**
  The programme is about a girl who has lost her brother.

Go to the Cinema or Watch TV?

- **Ins Kino gehen oder fernsehen?** — Go to the cinema or watch TV?

der Platz	seat
der Filmstar	film star
der Spezialeffekt	special effect

Key Point

Use **beschreib...** when talking to someone you'd call 'du'. Use **beschreiben Sie...** if you are talking to someone you'd call 'Sie'.

Key Point

Die Sendung means 'a programme' (that you might see on TV). **Das Programm** means the programme listings.

Key Point

When using **der**, **die** or **das** as a relative pronoun, make sure the gender is correct:
Der Film, der...
The film which…
Die Krankenschwester, die...
The nurse who…

der Ton	sound
die Eintrittskarte	ticket
die Leinwand	screen
die Werbung	adverts
das Kino	cinema

Ich sehe lieber Filme zu Hause.	I prefer watching films at home.
Meine Clique geht sehr gern ins Kino.	My bunch of friends love going to the cinema.
Wir laden lieber Filme herunter.	We prefer to download films.

Making Comparisons

- **warum?**   why?
- **Die Spezialeffekte sind besser auf der großen Leinwand.**
  The special effects are better on the big screen.
- **Die Plätze sind bequemer.**
  The seats are more comfortable.
- **Der Ton ist lauter im Kino.**
  The sound is louder in the cinema.
- **Die Karten werden immer teurer.**
  The tickets are getting more and more expensive.

Justifying your Argument

- **Man muss...**   You have to…
  Man kann...   You can…
  Man will...   You want to…
  Man sollte lieber...   It's better to…

- **Man muss die langweilige Werbung sehen.**
  You have to watch the boring adverts.
- **Wenn man einen Film sehen will, muss man in die Stadt gehen und teure Kinokarten kaufen. Man sollte lieber zu Hause bleiben, dann kann man den Film sehen, wenn man will.**
  If you want to see a film, you have to go into town and buy expensive cinema tickets. It's better to stay at home, then you can see the film when you want.

- Make some sentences negative:
  Man muss die Werbung nicht sehen!
  You don't have to watch the adverts!

> **Quick Test**
>
> 1. How do you say 'What's it about?' in German?
> 2. Translate into English: **Man sollte lieber Filme herunterladen.**
> 3. Translate into German:
>   a) The seats are not very comfortable.
>   b) You don't want to see the adverts.

Food

You must be able to:

- Buy food in a German-speaking country
- Discuss what you and your family eat at mealtimes
- Use negatives.

Quantities

die Dose	tin / can
die Flasche	bottle
die Scheibe	slice
das Glas	jar
das Kilo	kilo
das Stück	piece
eine Packung	packet
500 Gramm	500 grams

Key Point

In English we say a jar (etc.) 'of' something. In German you just say the amount and the item: **ein Glas Marmelade** a jar of jam

Key Point

Use the polite **Sie** form when buying something at a shop or market.

Shopping at a German Market

Ich möchte…	I would like…
Ich nehme zwei Kilo Kartoffeln bitte.	I will have two kilos of potatoes please.
Gerne. Bitte schön.	Of course. Here you are.
Haben Sie auch Schinken?	Do you have ham as well?
Natürlich. Wie viel möchten Sie?	Of course. How much would you like?
Sechs Scheiben bitte.	Six slices please.
Sonst noch etwas?	Anything else?
Nein danke. Was macht das?	No thanks. How much is that?
Das macht fünf Euro dreißig.	That comes to five euros thirty.

Meals

das Essen	meal
das Frühstück	breakfast
das Mittagessen	lunch
das Abendessen / Abendbrot	supper, dinner
die Kaffeezeit	coffee time (in the afternoon)

Key Point

Always use **Bitte schön** when giving or handing something to someone. The nearest English equivalent is 'Here you are'.

Verbs

essen	to eat
trinken	to drink
nehmen	to take
schmecken	to taste

Key Point

In German, **das Essen** (noun) means 'meal' and **essen** (verb) means 'to eat'.

How Often?

jeden Tag	every day
normalerweise	normally
meistens	mostly
oft	often
manchmal	sometimes

Key Point

Put time expressions straight after verbs: **Ich esse einmal pro Woche Pommes.** I eat chips once a week.

ab und zu	occasionally
selten	rarely
einmal pro Tag / Woche / Monat	once a day / week / month

- **Mein Vater isst zum Frühstück normalerweise Toast mit Butter und Marmelade.**
  Normally my father eats toast with butter and jam for breakfast.
- **Wir essen zweimal pro Woche bei meinem Stiefvater Abendbrot.**
  We eat dinner twice a week at my stepfather's place.

Describing Food and Taste

• **bitter**	bitter
fettig	fatty / greasy
gut durch	well done
lecker	delicious
salzig	salty
sauer	sour
scharf	spicy
süß	sweet
zu	too
• **das Essen**	food
die Küche	cooking / cuisine / kitchen
der Geruch	smell
der Geschmack	taste
• **Vegetarier(in) sein**	to be a vegetarian
Veganer(in) sein	to be a vegan
• **Der Döner ist zu fettig.**	The doner kebab is too greasy.
• **Der Kuchen ist zu süß.**	The cake is too sweet.
• **Das schmeckt!**	That tastes good!
• **Das schmeckt nicht!**	That tastes bad!

Using Negatives

- **Ich nehme nichts.**
  I won't have anything (to eat).
- **Ich esse kein Fleisch mehr, weil ich Vegetarier bin.**
  I no longer eat meat because I am vegetarian.
- **Meine Schwester isst weder Eier noch Käse, weil sie Veganerin ist.**
  My sister eats neither eggs nor cheese because she is vegan.
- **Ich habe noch nie Blutwurst gegessen.**
  I've never eaten black pudding.
- **Opa hat nie türkisches Essen probiert.**
  Grandad has never tried Turkish food.

Quick Test

1. How would you ask for:
   five slices of cheese? a piece of meat? a can of lemonade?
2. Translate into English: **Ich esse selten Kartoffeln und ich habe noch nie Schinken probiert.**
3. Translate into German: I never eat ketchup because it is too sweet.
4. What's the German for: sometimes? occasionally? every day?

> **Key Point**

You can't use **Vegetarier(in)** or **Veganer(in)** as an adjective. In English you can say 'I am vegetarian' or 'I am vegan'. In German you have to say **Ich bin Vegetarier(in) / Veganer(in)** (I am *a* vegetarian / vegan).

> **Key Point**

Don't confuse:
kochen	to cook
Kuchen	cake
Küche	cooking / kitchen

> **Key Point**

Be careful using **kein** (no). It is nearly always used in the accusative and the ending changes: **Ich esse keinen Käse / keine Marmelade / kein Fleisch**. I don't eat cheese / jam / meat.

> **Key Vocab**

nichts	nothing
nie	never
nicht mehr	not any more
noch nie	not yet
kein	no
weder …noch	neither …nor

Eating Out

You must be able to:

- Understand a German menu
- Order a meal in a restaurant
- Describe a meal in a restaurant.

The Menu

- **die Speisekarte** — menu
- **die Vorspeise** — starter
- **die Hauptspeise** — main course
- **der Nachtisch** — dessert
- **der Apfel** — apple
- **der Fisch** — fish
- **der Hamburger** — burger
- **der Kartoffelsalat** — potato salad
- **der Käse** — cheese
- **der Knoblauch** — garlic
- **der Lachs** — salmon
- **der Salat** — salad
- **der Thunfisch** — tuna
- **die Ananas** — pineapple
- **die Apfelsine / Orange** — orange
- **die Banane** — banana
- **die Bockwurst** — boiled sausage
- **die Bratwurst** — fried sausage
- **die Currywurst** — sausage with ketchup / curry powder
- **die Erdbeertorte** — strawberry tart
- **die Forelle** — trout
- **die Frikadelle** — meatball
- **die Pute** — turkey
- **die Suppe** — soup
- **das Eis** — ice cream
- **das Fleisch** — meat
- **das Gemüse** — vegetables
- **das Hähnchen** — chicken
- **das Obst** — fruit
- **das Rindfleisch** — beef
- **das Schweinefleisch** — pork
- **Bohnen** — beans
- **Erbsen** — peas
- **Karotten** — carrots
- **Kartoffeln** — potatoes
- **Nudeln** — pasta
- **Pommes Frites** — chips

Ordering a Meal

- **Haben Sie einen Tisch für drei Personen?** — Do you have a table for three people?
- **Wir möchten bestellen.** — We'd like to order.
- **vorne / hinten / in der Ecke** — at the front / at the back / in the corner
- **Als Vorspeise möchte ich…** — As a starter I'd like…
- **Als Hauptspeise nehme ich…** — As the main course I'll have…
- **Als Nachtisch bestelle ich…** — For dessert I'll order…
- **Zu trinken möchten wir…** — We'd like to drink…
- **Was für Gemüse / Eis (usw) haben Sie?** — What kinds of vegetables / ice cream do you have?
- **Was ist… eigentlich?** — What is… actually?
- **Zahlen bitte!** — Can we have the bill please?

- **der Kellner** — waiter
- **die Kellnerin** — waitress
  die Rechnung — bill
- **das Trinkgeld** — tip
- **Ich habe keinen / keine / kein...** — I don't have a...
- **der Löffel** — spoon
  der Teller — plate
- **die Gabel** — fork
- **das Glas** — glass
  das Messer — knife

der Kellner	waiter
die Kellnerin	waitress
die Rechnung	bill
das Trinkgeld	tip
Ich habe keinen / keine / kein...	I don't have a...
der Löffel	spoon
der Teller	plate
die Gabel	fork
das Glas	glass
das Messer	knife

Describing a Visit to a Restaurant

- To describe an event in the past, use the perfect tense. Use the correct form of **haben** plus the past participle at the end. The past participle will normally end in either **–en** or **–t**.

ich habe... gegessen	I ate
wir haben... gegessen	we ate
...genommen	had
...getrunken	drank
...begonnen	began
...gewählt	chose
...bestellt	ordered
...besucht	went to (an eating place)
...reserviert	reserved
...probiert	tried
...bezahlt	paid
Es hat (gut) geschmeckt.	It tasted good.

- **Wir haben in einem großen griechischen Restaurant gegessen, wo wir Moussaka bestellt haben. Es hat toll geschmeckt.**
  We ate in a large Greek restaurant where we ordered Moussaka. It tasted great.

- To express an opinion, simply use **war** and an adjective:
- **Es war super.** — It was great.
- **Die Suppe war kalt.** — The soup was cold.

Quick Test

1. Write down German words for:
   a) two types of fish   b) two types of meat
   c) two types of sausage d) two types of fruit
2. Translate into English:
   a) **Was für Eis haben Sie?**
   b) **Als Nachtisch möchte ich Erdbeertorte.**
3. Translate into German:
   We ate in a Turkish restaurant. It tasted quite good but the soup was spicy.

Sport

You must be able to:

- Talk about sports and activities you used to do
- Compare past and present activities
- Talk about activities you would like to try in the future.

Sporting Activities

- **Sportarten** — types of sport

- Verbs that take **haben** in the perfect:

- **angeln** — to fish
  spielen... — to play
  - **Basketball** — basketball
  - **Fußball** — football
  - **Handball** — handball
  - **Hockey** — hockey
  - **Volleyball** — volleyball

- Verbs that take **sein** in the perfect:

- **schwimmen** — to swim
  wandern — to hike
  segeln — to sail
  fahren... — to ride
  - **Mountainbike** — mountain bike
  - **Rad** — bike
  - **Skateboard** — skateboard
  gehen... — to go
  - **spazieren** — for a walk
  laufen... — to run
  - **Schlittschuh** — skate
  - **Ski** — ski
  - **Wasserski** — water ski

- To say *what you used to do*, use the *perfect* tense:

- **Früher habe ich oft Volleyball gespielt.**
  I often used to play volleyball.
- **Als ich jung war, bin ich jeden Tag Schlittschuh gelaufen.**
  When I was young, I went skating every day.

Places for Sport

- **der Berg** — mountain
  der Jugendklub — youth club
  der Strand — beach
- **die Eishalle** — ice rink
- **das Rennen** — race

- **das Schwimmbad** — swimming pool
- **das Sportzentrum** — sports centre
- **das Stadion** — stadium
- **das Turnier** — tournament

Key Point

When starting a sentence with **Früher** or **Als ich jung war**, use the perfect tense of **haben** or **sein** + past participle:
ich habe, er / sie / es hat, wir haben, sie haben
ich bin, er / sie / es ist, wir sind, sie sind

Key Point

Examples of past participles:
haben verbs –
geangelt, gespielt
sein verbs –
geschwommen, gewandert, gefahren, gelaufen, gegangen, gesegelt

- To say *where you used to go*, use the *perfect* tense:
- **Als ich jünger war, bin ich ab und zu zum Sportzentrum gegangen.**
  When I was younger, I occasionally went to the sports centre.

Comparing Now and Then

Useful Verbs

Angst haben	to be frightened	**joggen**	to jog
hassen	to hate	**laufen**	to run
hoffen	to hope	**schwimmen**	to swim
können	to be able	**sich für...**	to be interested
lieben	to love	**interessieren**	in...
versuchen	to try	**ein Tor**	to score a goal
wollen	to want to	**schießen**	
Fan sein	to be a fan		

Key Point

To say *where you went to*, use **zum** with masculine and neuter nouns and **zur** with feminine nouns:
zum Stadion to the stadium
zur Eishalle to the ice rink

Key Point

For the past tense of **sein**, simply use **war / waren**:
Als ich dreizehn war...
When I was thirteen...
Als wir im Schwimmbad waren... When we were in the swimming pool...

Useful Adverbs and Connectives

früher	before	**als**	when
jetzt	now	**aber**	but
vor... Jahren	...years ago	**doch**	however
im Moment	at the moment	**also**	so
damals	back then	**obwohl**	although
heutzutage	nowadays	**dann**	then

- **Damals habe ich immer Fußball gespielt, aber heutzutage sehe ich Fußball lieber im Fernsehen.**
  Back then I always played football but nowadays I'd rather watch football on TV.
- **Früher bin ich nie schwimmen gegangen aber jetzt gehe ich jeden Tag ins Schwimmbad.**
  Before, I never went swimming but now I go to the swimming pool every day.

Types of Sport to Try

der Mannschaftssport	team sports
der Wintersport	winter sports
der Extremsport	extreme sports
der Einzelsport	individual sports
der Wassersport	water sports

- **Ich will Wassersport probieren.** I want to try water sports.
- **Ich möchte Karate üben.** I'd like to practise karate.

Key Point

'Sports' (plural) in English are singular in German (**der Sport**).

 Quick Test

1. What is 'I play hockey' in German?
2. What is the difference between '**ich laufe Ski**' and '**ich bin Ski gelaufen**'?
3. Translate into English: **Früher sind wir Skateboard gefahren.**
4. Translate into German: 'Five years ago I used to go to the youth club'.
5. Translate into German: 'I would like to try extreme sports'.

Key Vocab

Ich will...	I want to...
Ich möchte...	I would like to...

Customs and Festivals

You must be able to:

- Know the main festivals in German-speaking countries
- Describe how you spend public holidays
- Explain why you think they are important or not.

Festivals

der Aprilscherz	April Fool's trick
der erste April	April Fool's Day
der erste Weihnachtstag	Christmas Day
der Fasching / Karneval	Carnival (before Lent)
der Heiligabend	Christmas Eve
der Maifeiertag	May Bank Holiday
der Muttertag	Mother's Day
der Neujahrstag	New Year's Day
der Ramadan	Ramadan
der / das Silvester	New Year's Eve
der Tag der Deutschen Einheit	German Unity Day
der Valentinstag	Valentine's Day
der Vatertag	Father's Day
der zweite Weihnachtstag	Boxing Day
das Passah	Passover

Aschermittwoch	Ash Wednesday
Ostern	Easter
Pfingsten	Whitsun
Rosenmontag	Shrove Monday
Weihnachten	Christmas
Yom Kippur	Yom Kippur
der Gottesdienst	(church) service
die Hochzeit	wedding
die Kirche	church
die Messe	mass
die Moschee	mosque
die Tradition	tradition
das Fest	festival
das Geschenk	present
das Kostüm	costume
christlich	Christian
jüdisch	Jewish
muslemisch	Muslim
religiös	religious
traditionnell	traditional

Herzlichen Glückwunsch!	Congratulations!
Herzlichen Glückwunsch zum Geburtstag!	Happy birthday!
Frohe Weihnachten!	Happy Christmas!
Frohe Ostern!	Happy Easter!
Frohes neues Jahr!	Happy New Year!
Viel Glück!	Good luck!
Alles Gute!	Best wishes!

How do you Spend Public Holidays?

an einem Feiertag...	on a public holiday...
das Feuerwerk	firework display
die Kultur	culture
man trifft sich	we meet
der Karnevalszug	carnival procession

> ### Key Point
>
> Carnival is an important festival before Lent in Germany. In the south it is called **Fasching** and in the north it is called **Karneval**. In America and France, celebrations take place on Shrove Tuesday (Mardi Gras) but in Germany the big celebrations are on **Rosenmontag** (Shrove Monday). Fasting then begins on **Aschermittwoch** (Ash Wednesday).

> ### Key Point
>
> To say *when* an event is, you can use **zu** or **am**:
> **zu Weihnachten** – at Christmas, **zu Ostern** – at Easter, **am ersten Weihnachtstag** – on Christmas day, **am Aschermittwoch** – on Ash Wednesday
> The verb comes immediately after the time expression:
> **Zu Weihnachten machen wir Geschenke.** At Christmas we make presents.

Useful Verbs

- **feiern** — to celebrate **sich treffen** — to meet up
  gratulieren — to congratulate **singen** — to sing
  heiraten — to marry **tanzen** — to dance
  lachen — to laugh **verlieren** — to lose
  schenken — to give (a present)

- **Man trifft sich und man feiert. Man isst, singt und tanzt.**
  We get together and celebrate. We eat, sing and dance.

Are Traditional Festivals Important or Not?

- **Sind traditionelle Feste wichtig?** Are traditional festivals important?

- **Für mich...** For me,...
  Für andere... For other people,...
  Meiner Meinung nach... In my opinion...
  Einige Leute finden, dass... Some people think that...
  Andere finden, dass... Others think that...
  Es ist wichtig It's important
  Am wichtigsten ist... The most important thing is...
  Man muss... You have to...
  Man soll... You should...
  Man soll nicht... You shouldn't...
  Man soll nie... You should never...
  Man müsste... You ought to...
  Man könnte... You could...
  Ich glaube, dass... I believe that...
  Viele Leute glauben, dass... Lots of people believe that...
  Auf der einen Seite On the one hand
  Auf der anderen Seite On the other hand

- **Für mich sind die Kostüme faszinierend, weil ich mich für die Tradition interessiere.**
  For me the costumes are fascinating because I am interested in tradition.
- **Einige Leute finden, dass traditionelle Feste sehr wichtig sind, aber andere Leute glauben, dass Feste altmodisch sind.**
  Some people think that traditional festivals are very important and others think that festivals are old-fashioned.

Quick Test

1. What is the German for:
   a) Christmas b) Christmas Eve c) Christmas Day d) Boxing Day?
2. What do these expressions mean in English?:
   a) Viel Glück! b) Herzlichen Glückwunsch! c) Frohe Ostern! d) Alles Gute!
3. Translate this perfect tense sentence into English:
   Wir haben gegessen, gesungen und getanzt.
4. Translate into German:
   'Some people think festivals are very fascinating'.

My Family and Friends & Marriage and Partnerships

1 **Übersetze die englischen Wörter ins Deutsche.** Translate the English words into German.

a) **Meine Schwester** [irritates] **mich und wir** [argue] **uns oft aber ich** [get on] **sehr gut mit meinem kleinen Bruder. Er ist** [well-behaved] **und** [quiet].

b) **Meine Oma hat** [curly] [hair] **und** [grey] [eyes].

c) **Ich möchte lieber** [single] **bleiben und nicht** [marry], **weil meine Eltern** [divorced] **sind.**

[12 marks]

2 **Bring die Wörter in dem zweiten Satzteil in die richtige Reihenfolge. Dann übersetze die ganzen Sätze.** Put the words in the second half of each sentence in the correct order. Then translate the full sentences.

a) **Wir treffen uns immer am Wochenende und** <u>zusammen / Videospiele / spielen / wir</u>.

b) **Wir haben viel gemeinsam, weil** <u>Humor / den / wir / haben / gleichen</u>.

c) **Wir streiten uns nie,** <u>seit / weil / wir / kennen / Jahren / uns / fünf</u>.

d) **Auf der einen Seite möchte ich Kinder haben, aber** <u>Seite / bin / auf / anderen / ich / der / jung / zu</u>.

[8 marks: 4 marks for unjumbling and 4 marks for translation]

3 **Füll die Lücken mit Wörtern von unten.** Fill the gaps with words from below.

verstehen	glücklich	traurig	geschieden
verheiratet	egoistisch	seit	streiten

Meine Eltern sind _____ **über zwanzig Jahren** _____ **und sind**

sehr _____ **. Sie** _____ **sich nie, aber die Eltern von meiner**

Freundin Melissa sind _____ **, weil sie sich nicht gut** _____ **.**

Die Situation ist ziemlich _____ **, aber der Mann ist zu** _____ **.**

[8 marks]

Social Media & Mobile Technology

1 **Übersetze diese technologischen Ausdrücke ins Englische. Die deutschen Ausdrücke sind rückwärts geschrieben!** Translate these technological expressions into English. The German expressions have been written backwards!

a) potpaL

b) suaM

c) nettahc

d) nekcilk

e) gnibboM

f) trowssaP

g) nefrus

h) nedalretnureh

i) etiesbeW

j) NALW

[10 marks]

2 **Vor-oder Nachteil der Technologie? Schreib V (Vorteil) oder N (Nachteil).** An advantage or a disadvantage of technology? Write V (Vorteil = advantage) or N (Nachteil = disadvantage).

a) **Man kann mit Freunden in Kontakt bleiben.** ....

b) **Cybermobbing ist gefährlich.** ....

c) **Man kann sich mit Freunden unterhalten.** ....

d) **Man muss regelmäßig das Passwort ändern.** ....

e) **Man muss vorsichtig sein.** ....

f) **Man kann online einkaufen.** ....

g) **Manchmal gibt es keinen Empfang.** ....

h) **Man kann im Notfall Hilfe rufen.** ....

[8 marks]

3 **Bring die Wörter in die richtige Reihenfolge, um Sätze über Technologie zu machen.** Put the words in the right order to make sentences about technology.

a) **Gerät / Man / das / aufladen / immer / muss / wieder.**

b) **Handy / Viele / stundenlang / Leute / sind / ihrem / an.**

c) **Internet / meinen / Das / hilft / bei / Hausaufgaben.**

d) **Freunden / chatte / mit / Ich / meinen.**

e) **besuche / Ich / oft / Lieblingswebseiten / meine.**

[5 marks]

Music & Cinema and TV

1 **Ergänze die deutschen Wörter.** Complete the German words.

a) **Musiksorten.** Types of music.

i) S _ _ _ _ _ _ r   ii) T _ _ _ _ o

iii) k _ _ _ _ _ _ _ _ e M _ _ _ k

b) **Musikinstrumente.** Musical instruments.

i) S _ _ _ _ _ _ _ _ g   ii) G _ _ _ _ _ e

iii) K _ _ _ _ _ r

c) **Künstler.** Artists.

i) S _ _ _ _ r   ii) S _ _ _ _ _ _ n   [9 marks]

2 **Verbinde die deutschen Ausdrücke mit den englischen.** Match up the German expressions with the English ones.

ich mag es gern	it irritates me
es bringt mich zum Weinen	I find it relaxing
es nervt mich	it makes me laugh
ich finde es beruhigend	it makes me cry
es macht mich glücklich	I like it
es gefällt mir	it makes me happy
es bringt mich zum Lachen	it makes me sad
es macht mich traurig	it pleases me

[8 marks]

3 **Was bedeuten diese Wörter auf Englisch?** What do these words mean in English?

a) Zeichentrickfilm   e) Sendung   h) Kriegsfilm

b) Werbung   f) Spielshow   i) Ton

c) Nachrichten   g) Krimi   j) Geschichte

d) Seifenoper   [10 marks]

4 **Übersetze diese Sätze ins Deutsche.** Translate these sentences into German.

a) The sound is better.

b) The tickets are more expensive.

c) I most like listening to pop music.

d) I prefer watching films at the cinema.

e) It's better to stay at home.   [5 marks]

Food and Eating Out, Sport & Customs and Festivals

1 **Bring die Wörter in die richtige Reihenfolge, um Sätze zu machen.** Put the words in the right order to make sentences.

a) **Schinken / möchte / Scheiben / sechs / Ich.**

b) **Tag / Wir / essen / Kuchen / jeden.**

c) **Onkel / nie / Mein / Fleisch / isst.**

d) **Sie / Suppen / Was / haben / für?**

e) **lecker / Das / hat / Essen / geschmeckt.** [5 marks]

2 **Übersetze die Sätze aus Übung 1 ins Englische.** Translate the sentences from activity 1 into English.

[5 marks]

3 **Übersetze diese Sätze ins Deutsche.** Translate these sentences into German.

a) I don't have a spoon.

b) The soup was cold.

c) What is Döner actually?

d) We'd like to order.

e) Do you have a table for six people?

f) For pudding I'd like strawberry tart. [6 marks]

4 **Trag das richtige Partizip perfekt ein.** Insert the correct past participle.

a) **Wir sind zur Eishalle _____** (went).

b) **Ich bin im kalten Meer _____** (swam).

c) **Papa hat früher Tennis _____** (played).

d) **Wir sind sechs Kilometer _____** (hiked).

e) **Ich habe keine Nachspeise _____** (ordered).

f) **Meine Schwester hat nie Bier _____** (drunk). [6 marks]

5 **Wie sagt man das auf Deutsch?** How do you say these things in German?

a) Mother's Day

b) New Year's Eve

c) Carnival

d) Christmas

e) Christmas Eve

f) Easter

g) April Fool's trick

h) Ramadan

i) Whitsun

j) costume [10 marks]

At Home

You must be able to:

- Describe your house and bedroom
- Say where things are in relation to each other
- Use prepositions.

My House

- **das Haus** — house
  - **das Bauernhaus** — farmhouse
  - **der Bauernhof** — farm
  - **das Doppelhaus** — semi-detached house
  - **das Einfamilienhaus** — detached house
  - **das Reihenhaus** — terraced house
  - **der Wohnblock** — block of flats
- **das Dach** — roof
- **das Gebäude** — building
- **die Treppe** — stairs
- **die Etage** — floor, storey
- **das Erdgeschoss** — ground floor
- **das Zimmer** — room
- **oben** — upstairs
- **unten** — downstairs
- HT **der Wolkenkratzer** — sky scraper
- HT **das Mehrfamilienhaus** — house for several families

- **Ich wohne in einem Doppelhaus.** — I live in a semi-detached house.
- **Es gibt acht Zimmer.** — There are eight rooms.
- **Im Erdgeschoss gibt es die Küche und das Wohnzimmer.**
  Oben findet man drei Schlafzimmer und das Badezimmer.
  On the ground floor there is the kitchen and the living room. Upstairs there are three bedrooms and the bathroom.
- **Es gibt acht Zimmer in meinem Haus.** There are eight rooms in my house.
- **In meinem Haus gibt es acht Zimmer.** In my house there are eight rooms.

Rooms

- **der Dachboden** — attic, loft
- **der Eingang** — entrance
- **der Flur** — hall, corridor
- **der Keller** — cellar
- **der Rasen** — lawn
- **der Wintergarten** — conservatory
- **die Dusche** — shower
- **die Küche** — kitchen
- **die Toilette** — toilet

- **das Arbeitszimmer** — office, study
- **das Badezimmer** — bathroom
- **das Esszimmer** — dining room
- **das Schlafzimmer** — bedroom
- **das Wohnzimmer** — living room
- HT **der Abstellraum** — store room
- HT **die Essecke** — eating area (in the kitchen)

Key Point

Es gibt and **gibt es** mean the same thing (there is / there are). But remember that in German, word order is important. When you start a sentence, you can use **es gibt**. But if you start a sentence with another idea then the order changes to **gibt es** because the verb (**gibt**) must come as the second idea in a sentence.

Prepositions

- **gegenüber**   opposite   **vor**   in front of
  in der Nähe von   near   **hinter**   behind
  neben   next to   **zwischen**   between

My Bedroom

- **der Fußboden**   floor   **die Wand**   wall
  der Kleiderschrank wardrobe   •   **das Bett**   bed
  der Nachttisch   bedside   **das Bild**   picture
                   cabinet   **das Regal**   shelf
  der Schrank   cupboard   •   **die Möbel** (pl)   furniture
  der Spiegel   mirror   •   **(un)ordentlich**   (un)tidy, (not) neat
  der Vorhang   curtain   **putzen**   to clean
- **die Kommode**   chest of   **schmutzig**   dirty
                   drawers   **sauber**   clean
  die Pflanze   plant   HT **geräumig**   spacious, roomy

- **In meinem Zimmer** habe ich **eine große Kommode und andere Möbel.**
  Es gibt einige Bilder an der Wand.
  In my bedroom I have a large chest of drawers and other furniture. There are some pictures on the wall.
- **Mein Zimmer ist manchmal schmutzig.**
  My bedroom is sometimes dirty.

More Prepositions

- **an**   at, to, close by, on   **in**   in
  auf   on, on top of, upon, onto   **unter**   under, below
                                     über   over, above

- Use these prepositions to describe where things are in your room in more detail. You can include the prepositions you also know too:
- **Mein Bett ist unter dem Fenster.**
  My bed is under the window.
- **Über meiner Kommode habe ich ein Regal.**
  Above my chest of drawers I have a shelf.
- **An der Wand hängt ein Spiegel.**
  There is a mirror (hanging) on the wall.

 Key Point

When describing where things are in your home, use prepositions. But make sure that you add the right ending to the gender of the noun:

- **Die Küche ist neben dem Wohnzimmer.**
  The kitchen is next to the living room.
- **Das Schlafzimmer ist neben der Toilette.**
  The bedroom is next to the toilet.
- **Das Esszimmer ist zwischen dem Wohnzimmer und der Küche.**
  The dining room is between the living room and the kitchen.

 Key Point

When describing someone else's room you say **'das Zimmer mein…'** with the correct ending: **das Zimmer meiner Schwester** (f) my sister's room, **das Zimmer meines Bruders** (m) my brother's room, **das Zimmer meiner Eltern** (pl) my parents' room

 Key Vocab

Es gibt…	There is…
Ich habe…	I have…
neben	next to
zwischen	between
gegenüber von	opposite
an (der Wand)	on (the wall)
auf (dem Tisch)	on (the table)
Mein Zimmer ist…	My room is…

Where I Live

You must be able to:

- Describe your local town and its shops
- Say what there is, or isn't, in your town
- Say what you have done in town by using the perfect tense
- Use negatives, quantifiers, and the modal verb **können**.

In the Town

der Dom	cathedral
der Friseur(salon)	hairdresser's
der Hauptbahnhof	main railway station
die Kirche	church
der Kirchturm	church spire/tower
der Laden	shop
der Marktplatz	market place
der Obst- und Gemüseladen	green grocer's
die Apotheke	pharmacy
die Bäckerei	bakery
die Brücke	bridge
die Bücherei	library
die Buchhandlung	bookshop
die Drogerie	chemist's
die Fleischerei	butcher's
die Metzgerei	butcher's
die Konditorei	confectioner's
die Kreuzung	crossroads
die Kunstgalerie	art gallery
die Reinigung	dry cleaner's
das Denkmal	monument
das Elektrogeschäft	shop for electrical goods
das Juweliergeschäft	jeweller's
das Kaufhaus	department store
das Kleidergeschäft	clothes shop
das Lebensmittelgeschäft	grocer's
das Schreibwarengeschäft	stationery shop
das Warenhaus	department store
die Geschäfte (pl)	shops
HT **die Grünanlage**	park
HT **die Sparkasse**	(savings) bank

- **Wir brauchen ein Einkaufszentrum.** — We need a shopping centre.
- **Die Post** befindet sich **neben dem Bahnhof.** — The post office is next to the train station.

Shopping

- **das Sonderangebot** — special offer
- **der Ausverkauf / ausverkauft** — sale / sold out
- **dieses Geschäft ist sehr billig / teuer** — this shop is very cheap / expensive
- **die Wahl** — the choice

Key Point

When using the negative **kein** to say what your town doesn't have, you should always use the accusative ending for the noun. For example, '**es gibt keinen Dom**', '**es gibt keine Reinigung**' and '**es gibt kein Kaufhaus**'.

Key Point

When using quantities such as **viele** and **wenige**, use the plural of the noun. For example, '**wir haben viele Buchhandlungen**' and '**es gibt wenige Grünanlagen in meiner Stadt**'.

- **Es gibt wenige Geschäfte.** There are few shops.
- **Es gibt viele Geschäfte.** There are many shops.
- **Es gibt keine Tankstelle und kein Kino.** There is no petrol station or cinema.

- der Preis ist günstig — the price is good value for money
- Kann ich **mit Kreditkarte** zahlen? — Can I pay by credit card?

HT	der Rabatt	discount
HT	preiswert	good value for money / cheap
HT	Ich bin pleite	I'm broke / skint

- der Einkaufskorb — shopping basket
- der Einkaufswagen — shopping trolley
- der Geldbeutel — purse / wallet
- der Kunde — customer
- der Verkäufer — shop assistant
- die Verkäuferin — shop assistant
- die Einkaufstasche — shopping bag
- die Kasse — till / cash point
- die Marke — brand / make
- die Quittung — receipt
- das Schaufenster — shop window

- ausgeben /ausgegeben — to spend / spent
- einkaufen / eingekauft — to shop / shopped
- verlieren / verloren — to lose / lost

- Ich habe mein ganzes Geld ausgegeben. — I've spent all my money.
- Ich habe **meinen Geldbeutel** verloren. — I've lost my purse / wallet.

In the Clothes Shop

- der Badeanzug — swimsuit
- der Gürtel — belt
- der Hut — hat
- der Mantel — coat
- der Pullover — jumper
- der Rock — skirt
- der Schal — scarf
- der Schmuck — jewellery
- der Schuh — shoe
- der Trainingsschuh — trainer / sports shoe

- die Bluse — blouse
- die Hose — trousers
- die Jacke — jacket
- die Kleidung — clothes
- die Krawatte — tie
- die Socke — sock
- das Hemd — shirt
- das Kleid — dress
- das T-Shirt — T-shirt
- die Kleider (pl) — clothes

- Kann ich dieses Kleid anprobieren? — Can I try on this dress?
- Es ist sehr modisch! — It's very fashionable!

Quick Test

1. Write a description of your town. What is there in your town? What does your town not have?
2. Translate the following sentences into English:
   a) In meiner Stadt gibt es viele schöne Geschäfte, wo man hübsche Kleider kaufen kann.
   b) Kann ich diese Hose anprobieren?
   c) Mein Vater hat mit seiner Kreditkarte bezahlt.
3. What is your favourite outfit? Write a description of the clothes you most like to wear.

Town or Country?

You must be able to:

- Describe your surrounding area
- Compare living in a town with living in the countryside
- Use comparatives along with adjectives.

Where I Live

- Ich wohne... I live...
  - in der Stadtmitte – in the town centre
  - am Stadtrand – on the outskirts of town / in the suburbs

  - **in den Bergen** – in the mountains
  - auf dem Land – in the countryside

- **In welchem** Stadtteil **wohnst du genau?** Which part of town do you live in exactly?

- **Es gibt viele Einwohner.** There are a lot of inhabitants.

- HT **das Stadtviertel** district / part of town
- HT **die Sackgasse** cul-de-sac

In the Town

- Ich wohne gern **in der Stadtmitte.** I like living in the town centre.
- **Meine Mutter arbeitet am Stadtrand.** My mum works in the suburbs.

- **Es gibt viel zu machen / tun.** There is a lot to do.
- **In der Stadtmitte zu wohnen ist sehr praktisch.** Living in the town centre is very practical.
- **Die Stadt ist eine lebhafte Stadt.** The town is a lively town.
- **Dort findet man eine Fußgängerzone.** There you can find a pedestrianised zone.

- **Die Miete ist teuer.** The rent is expensive.
- **Die Straßen sind schmutzig.** The streets are dirty.
- **Es gibt zu viel Lärm.** There is too much noise.
- **Es gibt nicht genug Grünanlagen.** There are not enough parks.

In the Countryside

- **Das Leben auf dem Land ist sehr ruhig.** Life in the countryside is very peaceful / quiet.

- **Ich wohne auf einem Bauernhof.** I live on a farm.
- **Aus dem Fenster kann man Blumen und Hügel sehen.** From the window you can see flowers and hills.

- Ich möchte **aufs Land** umziehen. I would like to move to the country.

- **Ich kann im Wald spazieren gehen.** I can walk in the woods.
- **Das Dorf ist sauberer als die Stadt.** The village is cleaner than the town.

> ### Key Point
>
> Remember that when using a modal verb such as **mögen**, **können** and **müssen**, the second verb in the sentence must be in the infinitive and moves to the end of the sentence.
> For example:
> **Man muss mit dem Auto fahren.** You have to go by car / drive.
> **Ich kann im Wald spazieren gehen.** I can walk in the woods.

- **Es gibt in der Nähe keine Geschäfte**.   There are no shops nearby.
- **Man muss mit dem Auto fahren, wenn man Freunde sehen will.**   You have to drive if you want to see friends.
- **Die öffentlichen Verkehrsmittel fahren nicht häufig genug.**   The public transport is not frequent enough.

- **Wir haben keine Nachbarn.**   We have no neighbours.

der Baum	tree		**arm**	poor
der Fluss	river		**flach**	flat
der Stau	traffic jam		**laut**	noisy
die Hecke	hedge		**lebhaft**	busy / lively
die Landschaft	landscape		**ruhig**	calm / quiet
die Pflanze	plant		**sauber**	clean
die Wiese	meadow		**schmutzig**	dirty
das Feld	field			
HT **die Sicherheit**	safety			

- To compare two things in German, you must do two things:
    - Add **–er** to the end of the adjective to make it mean more/greater.
    - And put the word **als** (than) after the adjective:
- **Das Dorf ist** sauberer als **die Stadt**. The village is cleaner than the town.
- **Die Stadtmitte ist** lauter als **das Land.** The town centre is louder than the countryside.

- There are, of course, some exceptions:
- **Das Leben auf dem Land ist** besser als **in der Stadt**.
  Life in the countryside is better than in the town.
- **Der Wohnblock, in dem ich wohne, ist** höher als **der Kirchturm.**
  The block of flats I live in is higher than the church tower.

Key Point

Adjectives before nouns need the correct adjective ending.
- **Dortmund ist eine schmutzige Stadt (f).**
  Dortmund is a dirty town.
Adjectives after nouns need no adjective endings.
- **Die Stadt ist sehr schmutzig.** The town is very dirty.
- **Auf dem Land ist es ziemlich ruhig.** The countryside is fairly quiet.

Key Vocab

Ich wohne...	I live...
Ich wohne gern...	I like living...
in der Stadtmitte	in the town centre
am Stadtrand	on the outskirts of town
auf dem Land	in the countryside
der Stadtteil	part of town
Ich möchte...	I would like...
umziehen	to move house
besser	better
höher	higher

Quick Test

1. Say the following in German:
   a) Houses in the town are smaller than in the country.
   b) There are fewer shops in the countryside.
2. Translate into English:
   Ich wohne gern in der Stadtmitte, weil ich zu Fuß in die Schule gehen kann. Meine Freundin wohnt am Stadtrand und sie muss mit dem Bus fahren.
3. Do you live in the town or the country? Make a list of some of the benefits of where you live.

Charity and Voluntary Work

You must be able to:

- Describe voluntary work
- Say what you do and what others do using **ich** and **man**
- Use **ich möchte** and an infinitive to say what you would like to do in the future.

Voluntary Work

- **Ich mache Freiwilligenarbeit für eine Wohltätigkeitsorganisation.**
  I do voluntary work for a charity.
- **Ich besuche bedürftige Menschen.** I visit people in need.
- **Wir machen Ausflüge mit Behinderten**.
  We go on excursions with disabled people.
- **Ich möchte Krankenschwester werden.** I would like to become a nurse.

der / die Freiwillige	volunteer
die freiwillige Arbeit	voluntary work
die Hilfe	aid / help
die Wohltätigkeit	charity
der Arzt / die Ärztin	doctor
die Ernährung	food / nourishment / nutrition
die Krankheit	illness
die Mahlzeit	meal
das Medikament	medicine
das Trinkwasser	drinking water
krank	ill
sorgen (für)	to care for
abhängig sein von	to be dependent on

- Ich helfe **Menschen, die krank sind.** I help people who are ill.
- **Man verteilt Mahlzeiten und Trinkwasser an Obdachlose.**
  Food and drinking water are distributed to the homeless.
- **Ich sammle Geld.** I collect money.
- **Ich bringe älteren Menschen Medikamente.**
  I deliver medicines to older people.
- **Man hilft auch Menschen, die deprimiert sind.**
  People who are depressed also get help.
- **Man hilft Leuten, die von Drogen abhängig sind.**
  People who are dependent on drugs get help.
- HT **Schulden können zu Elend führen.** Debt can lead to misery.
- HT **Rauchen verursacht einige ernsthafte gesundheitliche Probleme.**
  Smoking causes some serious health problems.

Key Point

You can use '**man**' to translate 'one' or a passive form in English.
Man hat letzte Woche Mahlzeiten und Trinkwasser an Obdachlose verteilt.
One distributed food and drinking water to the homeless last week.
Man liebt die Arbeit des Roten Kreuzes.
The work of the Red Cross is loved.

Key Point

Impersonal verbs in German use the pronoun '**es**'. The pronoun '**es**' usually means 'it' but it loses this meaning when using impersonal verbs. Impersonal verbs are only used in the third person.
umgehen (to get around / to be about): **es geht um…** (it's about…);
gefallen (to like / be pleasing): **es gefällt mir** (I like it / it's pleasing to me);
fehlen to lack:
Es fehlt mir die Zeit. I don't have time.
Es fehlt mir die Zeit, freiwillige Arbeit zu machen. I don't have time to do voluntary work.

Verbs that Can Follow 'Ich möchte'

- **Nach dem Abitur möchte ich auf die Uni gehen. Ich möchte Arzt werden.**
  After A-levels, I would like to go to university. I would like to become a doctor.
- Another option might be to substitute '**möchte**' with '**würde gern**'.
  - **Ich würde gern in einem Altersheim arbeiten.**
    I would like to work in an old people's home.
  - **Ich würde gern mit benachteiligten Leuten arbeiten.**
    I would like to work with disadvantaged people.

Ich möchte (I would like)	**(den Obdachlosen)** helfen **(als Arzt) arbeiten** **(Geld) sammeln** **(Medikamente) bringen** **(Mahlzeiten und Trinkwasser) verteilen** **(ältere Leute)** besuchen **(Krankenschwester) werden** **(nach Afrika** fahren**, um den Menschen dort zu helfen)** HT **(auf Kinder in einem Kinderheim) aufpassen**	(the homeless) to help (as a doctor) to work (money) to collect (medicines) to bring (meals and drinking water) to distribute (older people) to visit (nurse) to become (travel to Africa, in order to help the people there) (children in a children's home) to look after

Quick Test

1. Translate into English:
   Ich mache freiwillige Arbeit. Im Dorf, in dem ich wohne, bringe ich älteren Menschen Medikamente.
2. Translate into German:
   I distribute meals and drinking water to the homeless in the street. In the future I would like to be a doctor. I would like to help people who are disadvantaged.
3. Is there anything that you currently do that might help with your chosen career? Use the language in this unit to help you say it in German.

Key Vocab

die Wohltätigkeits-organisation	charity
die freiwillige Arbeit	voluntary work
der / die Freiwillige	volunteer
Ich möchte...	I would like...
Er hilft...	He helps...
helfen	to help
arbeiten	to work
fahren	to travel
besuchen	to visit
werden	to become

Healthy and Unhealthy Living

You must be able to:

- Describe your lifestyle choices
- Say whether you live healthily or not
- Use the future tense as well as **man soll**.

Fitness

der Schlaf	sleep
die Bewegung	exercise / movement
die Figur	figure
die Gesundheit	health / fitness
die Gewohnheit	habit
fit sein	to be in good shape
gesund	healthy
gut gehen (es geht mir gut)	to be well (I am well)
sich fühlen	to feel
stark	strong
HT **der Atem**	breath
HT **einatmen**	to breathe in

- **Mir geht's gut / Ich habe gute Gewohnheiten.** I'm well / I have good habits.
- **Ich bleibe fit, weil ich viel Sport treibe.**
  I stay in good shape because I do a lot of sport.
- **Ich fühle mich wohl mit mir selbst.** I feel well in myself.
- **Ich bleibe gesund, weil ich gut esse und genug Schlaf bekomme.**
  I stay healthy, because I eat well and I get enough sleep.

Meals and Diet

die Mahlzeit	meal		**süß**	sweet
das Frühstück	breakfast		**der Rat**	advice
das Mittagessen	lunch			
das Abendessen	dinner / evening meal	HT	**die Süßigkeiten**	sweets
		HT	**die Nahrung**	food / nourishment
der Imbiss	snack			
fettig	fatty	HT	**abstinent**	teetotal
ungesund	unhealthy	HT	**würzig**	spicy
beschäftigt sein	to be busy	HT	**sich betrinken**	to get drunk
eine Diät machen	to go on a diet			

- Man soll **gesund essen.** You should eat healthily.
- **Man soll ungesunde Lebensmittel** vermeiden.
  You should avoid unhealthy foods.
- Ich mache **Diät. / Ich werde Diät** machen.
  I am on a diet / I am going to go on a diet.
- **Ich esse zu viel Fett.** I eat too much fat.
- **Ich werde versuchen, gesünder zu essen.** I will try to eat more healthily.

> ## Key Point
>
> When talking about healthy living, it's very useful to use 'man soll' plus the infinitive to say what we should or should not be doing:
> **Man soll gesund essen.** You should eat healthily.
> **Man soll nicht rauchen.** You should not smoke.
> Remember that like all modal verbs, you use the infinitive after **man soll** and this should go at the end of the phrase / sentence:
> **Man soll mehr Obst und Gemüse essen.** You should eat more fruit and vegetables.
> **Man soll zu viele Süßigkeiten vermeiden.** You should avoid too many sweets.

HT **Man soll versuchen, mehr fettarme Produkte zu konsumieren.**
You should try to consume more low fat products.

HT **Ungesundes Essen ist aber schmackhaft!** But unhealthy food is tasty!

Health

• **der / die Drogensüchtige**	drug addict	**ekelhaft**	disgusting
		erfolgreich	successful
• **die Haut**	skin	**fettleibig**	obese
die Sucht	addiction	**müde**	tired
die Zigarette	cigarette	**süchtig machen**	to be addictive
• **aufhören**	to stop		
rauchen	to smoke	**täglich**	daily
schlafen	to sleep	**töten**	kill
sich entspannen	to relax		
atemlos	breathless		
betrunken	drunk		

HT **vermeiden** — to avoid
HT **der Raucherhusten** — smoker's cough
HT **das Rauschgift** — drug / narcotic
HT **die Entziehungskur** — detox programme for drug and alcohol addicts

- **Meine Mutter hat aufgehört zu rauchen.** My mum has stopped smoking.
- **Zigaretten können töten und sie stinken auch.**
  Cigarettes can kill and they also stink.
- **Man soll sich entspannen, um Stress zu vermeiden.**
  You should relax in order to avoid stress.
- **Ich habe erfolgreich abgenommen.** I was successful in losing weight.
- **HT** **Ich bewege mich mindestens dreimal in der Woche.**
  I take some exercise at least three times per week.
- **HT** **Ich leide an Atembeschwerden.** I suffer from breathing difficulties.

• **der Krankenwagen**	ambulance
der Krebs (Lungenkrebs)	cancer (lung cancer)
der Schmerz	pain
• **die Krankheit**	illness
die Leber	liver
• **das Krankenhaus**	hospital
• **sich besser fühlen**	to feel better
HT **sich erbrechen**	to be sick
HT **der Husten**	cough
HT **die Überdosis**	overdose
HT **magersüchtig**	anorexic

> **Key Point**
>
> Look at the way you can adapt a word like '**gesund**':
> **Ich bin gesund.**
> I am *healthy* – *adverb*
> **Ich esse gesunde Mahlzeiten.** I eat *healthy* meals – *adjective*
> **Meine Gesundheit ist mir sehr wichtig.** My *health* is very important to me – *noun*

> **Key Vocab**
>
> **Ich mache / Ich werde...**
> **machen** I do / I will do...
> **Man soll...** You should...
> **vermeiden** to avoid
> **aufhören** to stop
> **gesund / Gesundheit** healthy / health
> **ungesund** unhealthy
> **fit sein** to be in good shape

> **Quick Test**
>
> 1. Describe what you currently do to be healthy. Now describe an intention of yours to be even healthier.
> 2. Write five sentences beginning with **Man soll**, relating to healthy and unhealthy living.
> 3. Translate into German:
>   I eat quite healthily, but I do not do enough sport. I am going to play tennis and avoid too much fat, in order to stay in good health.

The Environment: Problems

You must be able to:

- Talk about environmental issues
- Express your opinion about the environment
- Use quantifiers.

Environmental Problems

der Abfall	rubbish / waste
der Karton	cardboard box
der Lärm	noise
der Müll	refuse / rubbish / waste
der saure Regen	acid rain
der Treibhauseffekt	greenhouse effect
der Verbrauch	consumption
der Verkehr	traffic
die Dose	can / tin
die Gefahr	danger
die Heizung	heating
die Kohle	coal
die Luftverschmutzung	air pollution
die Ozonschicht	the ozone layer
die Pappe	cardboard
die Spraydose	aerosol
die Überschwemmung	flood
die Umwelt	environment
die Verpackung	packaging
das Altpapier	waste paper
das Kraftwerk	power station
das Öl	oil
das Ozonloch	hole in the ozone layer
gefährdete / bedrohte Arten	endangered species
schädlich	harmful
umweltfeindlich	environmentally hostile
umweltfreundlich	environmentally friendly
weltweit	worldwide
HT die Abholzung	deforestation
HT die Auspuffgase	exhaust fumes
HT die Einwegflasche	non-recyclable bottle
HT die Müllentsorgung	waste disposal
HT schaden	to damage
HT Atembeschwerden	breathing difficulties

Key Point

When expressing quantities in German, we can use the following:

zu viel / viele
too much / many
genug enough
so viel / viele wie
as much / many as
mehr more
weniger fewer / less
kein no
die meisten the most
die wenigsten the fewest

Key Point

Remember to change the endings of your verbs when using them with different people (**ich / man / wir**…). Check what type of verb it is and whether it is regular or irregular.

Key Point

Remember that you can use 'man' when you want to say 'we'.

Which are the Most Important Problems?

- **Ich denke, dass es auf den Straßen zu viel Müll gibt.** I think that there is too much rubbish on the streets.
- **Meiner Meinung nach ist die Luftverschmutzung das größte Problem weltweit.** In my opinion, air pollution is the biggest problem worldwide.
- **Für mich sind die Abholzung und die Wasserverschmutzung die größten Gefahren für die Umwelt.** For me, deforestation and water pollution are the biggest threats to the environment.
- **Soweit es mich betrifft, sind der Treibhauseffekt und das Ozonloch sehr beunruhigend.** As far as I'm concerned, the greenhouse effect and the hole in the ozone layer are very worrying.

Useful Verbs

kein... mehr haben	to run out of	**schaden**	to damage / harm
anmachen	to turn / switch on	**verschmutzen**	to pollute
ausmachen	to turn / switch off	**verschwinden**	to disappear
aussterben	to die out / become extinct	**wegwerfen**	to throw away
		zerstören	to destroy
bedrohen	to threaten	HT **verpesten**	to pollute
benutzen	to use	HT **verschwenden**	to waste

- Using verbs with different persons in the present tense:

man benutzt	one uses	wir benutzen	we use	Leute benutzen	people use
man verschwendet	one wastes	**wir verschwenden**	we waste	**Leute verschwenden**	people waste
man verwertet... wieder	one recycles / reuses	**wir verwerten... wieder**	we recycle / reuse	**Leute verwerten... wieder**	people recycle / reuse

- **Ich finde, dass ich nicht genug recycle und Menschen zu viel verschwenden.** I find that I don't recycle enough and that people waste too much.
- **Meiner Meinung nach ist es wichtig, den Bus und den Zug zu benutzen, anstatt mit dem Auto zu fahren.** In my opinion, it is important to use the bus and the train instead of the car.
- **Ich denke, dass wir heutzutage zu viel Energie benutzen.** I think that we use too much energy nowadays.
- Show that you can use tenses confidently. So, for example, compare now and before using the imperfect tense.
  - **Vorher verbrauchten wir nicht so viel Energie, aber heutzutage verschwenden wir alles!** Before, we didn't consume so much energy, but nowadays we waste everything!

The Environment: Solutions

You must be able to:

- Suggest solutions to environmental issues
- Use a range of modal verbs in the conditional
- Use infinitive constructions such as **um... zu + infinitive** (in order to) and **(an)statt... zu +infinitive** (instead of).

What Should We Do to Protect Our Environment?

Useful Verbs

anbauen	to grow	**sich entscheiden**	to decide
anfangen	to start / begin	**sich schämen**	to be / feel ashamed
aufpassen	to pay attention	**sorgen (für)**	to care for / look after
brauchen	to need		
entsorgen	to dispose of (waste)	**sparen**	to save / to conserve
entwickeln	to develop	**stecken**	to put (something into)
erlauben	to allow		
heizen	to heat	**suchen**	to look for
keine Ahnung haben	to have no idea	**unterstützen**	to support
raten	to advise	**verbessern**	to improve
reinigen	to clean	**versuchen**	to try
sauber machen	to clean	HT **entdecken**	to discover
schützen	to protect	HT **wiederverwerten**	to recycle / reuse

Modal Verbs in the Conditional Tense

- Modal verbs are very useful to express what must / should be done. Here are some useful forms in the conditional tense:

- **Man könnte...**   One / We / You could / might...
- **Ich könnte...**   I could / might...
- **Man sollte...**   One / We / You should / ought to...
- **Wenn ich könnte, würde ich gerne...** If I could, I would like...
- **Es wäre**...   It would be...
- **Es wäre besser, wenn**... It would be better if...
- **Meiner Meinung nach sollten wir mehr auf unsere Umwelt achten.**
  In my opinion, we should pay more attention to our environment.
- **Wir sollten weniger Plastiktüten benutzen.**
  We should use fewer plastic bags.
- **Ich denke, dass wir nicht wiederverwertbare Materialien verbieten müssen.** I think that we should ban non-recyclable materials.
- **Wir müssen weder überfischen noch Fabrikschiffe erlauben.**
  We must neither overfish, nor allow factory ships.
- **Ich finde, es wäre besser, öffentliche Verkehrsmittel zu fördern statt Autos im Stadtzentrum zu haben.**
  I think it would be better to promote public transport rather than having cars in the city centre.

> **Key Point**
>
> Think of **müssen** as a stronger form of **sollen**, i.e. 'must' instead of 'ought to'.

> **Key Point**
>
> Remember that when you use two verbs together, the second verb is always in the infinitive form (the 'to do' form). You will also need to use the infinitive when using common impersonal phrases:
> **Es ist wichtig, den Bus und den Zug zu benutzen, anstatt mit dem Auto zu fahren.**
> It is important to use the bus and the train instead of the car.
> **Es ist schlecht, zu viel zu verschwenden.**
> It is bad to waste too much.

- **Ich weiß, dass ich versuchen sollte, weniger Energie zu verschwenden, und dass ich meinen Stromverbrauch begrenzen sollte. Ich denke auch, dass ich mehr zu Fuß gehen könnte, anstatt das Auto zu benutzen.**
  I know that I should try to waste less energy and limit my power consumption. I also think that I could walk more, instead of using the car.

Useful Grammatical Structures

- These structures are very useful for improving your German:
- **um... zu** + infinitive   in order to...
  um die Umwelt zu schützen   in order to protect the environment
  um... zu verbessern   in order to improve...
  um... zu retten   in order to save / preserve...
- With a negative:
  um die Umwelt nicht **zu zerstören**   in order not to destroy the environment
  um... nicht **zu verschwenden**   in order not to waste...
  um... nicht **zu beschädigen**   in order not to damage...

HT Acting in the same way as **um ... zu** are:
(an)statt... zu...   instead of
ohne... zu...   without

- **Ich verschwende zu viel statt zu** recyceln.
  I waste too much instead of recycling.
- **Ich habe Plastikflaschen weggeworfen, ohne über die Umwelt nachzudenken.**
  I have thrown plastic bottles away without thinking about the environment.

- Using modal verbs, **um... zu** plus infinitive, negatives and opinions together:
- **Meiner Meinung nach, um unsere Umwelt zu verbessern, sollten wir den Menschen empfehlen, nicht mehr zu verschmutzen, sondern weniger Autos zu benutzen und mehr zu recyceln.**
  In my opinion, in order to improve our environment, we should advise people not to pollute anymore, but to use fewer cars and recycle more.
- **Um unsere Umwelt zu schützen, müssen wir unsere Einstellung ändern. Statt Plastik sollten wir recycelbare Materialien verwenden, um sicher zu sein, dass wir die Tier- und Pflanzenwelt nicht mehr bedrohen.**
  To protect our environment, we need to change our attitude. Instead of plastic we should use recyclable materials, to be certain that we no longer threaten the animal and plant world.

 Quick Test

1. Rearrange the words to make sentences and then translate them:
   a) denke / ich / man / mehr / recyceln / könnte / dass
   b) weniger / Meinung / nach / Plastiktüten / meiner / sollten / benutzen / wir
   c) Umwelt / um / müssen / benutzen / öffentliche / die / zu / schützen / wir / mehr / Verkehrsmittel
2. What is the German for:
   a) in order to save? in order to improve? in order to protect? in order not to pollute anymore?
   b) instead of recycling? without thinking about the animal and plant life?

> ### Key Point
>
> Negatives go after a conjugated (changed) verb, e.g. **Ich recycle nicht** (I don't recycle), but go before the **zu** and the infinitive when using **um... zu / (an)statt... zu / ohne... zu**, e.g. **um die Umwelt nicht zu zerstören** (in order not to destroy the environment).

> ### Key Vocab
>
> **verbessern**   to improve
> **schützen**   to protect
> **Man könnte...**
> One / We / You could / might...
> **Ich könnte...**
> I could / might...
> **Man sollte...**
> One / We / You should / ought to...
> **um... zu...**   in order to...
> **recyceln**   to recycle

Poverty and Homelessness

You must be able to:

- Talk about the issues related to poverty
- Talk about the consequences of these issues
- Share your concerns.

Social Problems

Useful Verbs

abhängig sein von	to be dependent on	**missbrauchen**	to abuse
aus sein	to be over / finished	**sauer sein**	to be annoyed
bitten	to beg	**sich streiten**	to argue / quarrel
erfrieren	to freeze to death	**spritzen**	to inject
fliehen	to flee	**stehlen**	to steal
gehören (zu)	to belong (to)	**unterstützen**	to support
keinen festen	to have no fixed	HT **begehen**	to commit / perpetrate
Wohnsitz haben	abode	HT **pleite sein**	to be broke

Useful Nouns

der Ausländer	foreigner	**die Armut**	poverty
der Bettler	beggar	**die Diskriminierung**	discrimination
der Dieb	thief	**die Gewalt**	violence
der Drogenhändler	drug dealer	**die Sorge**	worry
der Einwanderer	immigrant	**das Altenheim**	old people's home
der Flüchtling	refugee		
der Krieg	war	**das Opfer**	victim
der Missbrauch	abuse	**das Verbrechen**	crime
der / die Obdachlose	homeless person	HT **der/die Bedürftige**	person in need
		HT **die Eingliederung**	integration
der Rassimus	racism	HT **Rassenvorurteile** (pl)	racial prejudice
der Streit	argument	HT **die Straftat**	criminal offence
die Arbeitslosigkeit	unemployment		

Useful Adjectives

arm	poor
ernst	serious
gemein	mean
hart	hard
traurig	sad
überbevölkert	over-populated

Useful Phrases

heutzutage	nowadays
jetzt	now
zur Zeit	currently
gegenwärtig	presently

vor kurzem	recently
es gibt immer mehr…	there are more and more…
wir sehen eine Zunahme der Anzahl von…	we see an increase in the number of…
wir sprechen oft über das Problem…	we often talk about the problem…
man hört oft davon	we often hear about it
das wichtigste Problem ist…	the most important problem is…
das bedeutendste Problem ist…	the most significant problem is…
Am beunruhigendsten ist, dass…	The most worrying thing is that…

Which are the Most Important Social Problems?

- **Heutzutage gibt es immer mehr Arbeitslosigkeit und Armut in der Welt.**
  Nowadays, there is more and more unemployment and poverty in the world.
- **Vor kurzem hat man von einem Anstieg der Flüchtlingszahlen gehört.**
  Recently, we've heard about an increase in the numbers of refugees.
- **Es gibt immer mehr Leute, die arbeitslos sind.**
  There are more and more people who are unemployed.
- **Es gibt immer mehr Leute, die stehlen.**
  There are more and more people who steal.
- **Es gibt immer mehr Leute, die obdachlos sind.**
  There are more and more people who are homeless.

Expressing Feelings about these Issues

es ärgert mich, dass	it annoys me that…
wir sollten…	we should…
wir sollten nicht…	we should not…
Ich mache mir Sorgen um …	I'm worried about…
Ich bin besorgt über…	I'm anxious about…
was mich beunruhigt, ist…	what worries me is…
was ich am schlimmsten finde, ist…	what I find the worst is…
Ich befürchte…	I fear…

- **Ich mache mir Sorgen um die Zahl der Obdachlosen in unseren Städten.**
  I'm concerned about the number of homeless people in our towns.
- **Was mich beunruhigt, ist dass immer mehr Leute stehlen.**
  What worries me is that more and more people are stealing.
- **Wir sollten uns um die Anzahl der Arbeitslosen sorgen.**
  We should be concerned about the number of unemployed people.

Quick Test

1. Translate into English:
   a) Es gibt viel Arbeitslosigkeit.
   b) Das wichtigste Problem ist die Zahl der Obdachlosen auf den Straßen.
   c) Heutzutage gibt es zu viele Verbrechen.
   d) Wir hören in den Nachrichten immer mehr von Gewalt.
   e) Ich mache mir Sorgen um die Zunahme der Armut in der Welt.

Key Point

Use relative clauses to make your responses longer; use the definite article for 'who' (e.g. **der, die, das**), and remember to move the verb to the end of the phrase/ sentence.

Key Point

You can use **'immer'** in front of comparatives (**besser, mehr**) to express that something's happening more and more:
Es wird immer besser. It's getting better and better.
Reiche werden immer reicher, und Arme immer ärmer. The rich keep getting richer and the poor keep getting poorer.

Key Vocab

die Arbeitslosigkeit unemployment
die Armut poverty
der / die Obdachlose homeless person
das wichtigste Problem the most important problem
heutzutage nowadays
immer mehr more and more

Travel and Tourism 1

You must be able to:

- Give the main details about a holiday
- Use key verbs in the past, present and future
- Use the prepositions **nach** and **in** with countries and **mit** with transport.

Countries

Belgien (das)	Belgium	**Polen (das)**	Poland
Deutschland (das)	Germany	**Portugal (das)**	Portugal
Frankreich (das)	France	**Schottland (das)**	Scotland
Griechenland (das)	Greece	**Spanien (das)**	Spain
Großbritannien (das)	Great Britain	**Niederlande (die)**	Netherlands
Irland (das)	Ireland	**Schweiz (die)**	Switzerland
Italien (das)	Italy	**Türkei (die)**	Turkey
Österreich (das)	Austria	**Vereinigten Staaten (die)**	United States

Nationalities

amerikanisch	**der Amerikaner**	**die Amerikanerin**	American
belgisch	**der Belgier**	**die Belgierin**	Belgian
britisch	**der Brite**	**die Britin**	British
deutsch	**der Deutsche**	**die Deutsche**	German
französisch	**der Franzose**	**die Französin**	French
griechisch	**der Grieche**	**die Griechin**	Greek
niederländisch	**der Niederländer**	**die Niederländerin**	Dutch
irisch	**der Ire**	**die Irin**	Irish
österreichisch	**der Österreicher**	**die Österreicherin**	Austrian
polnisch	**der Pole**	**die Polin**	Polish
schottisch	**der Schotte**	**die Schottin**	Scottish
schweizerisch	**der Schweizer**	**die Schweizerin**	Swiss
spanisch	**der Spanier**	**die Spanierin**	Spanish
türkisch	**der Türke**	**die Türkin**	Turkish

- **Letztes Jahr** bin ich mit **meiner Familie** nach **Frankreich** gefahren **und ich habe gefunden, dass die Franzosen sehr freundlich waren.**
  Last year I went to France with my family and I found that the French were very friendly.
- **Nächstes Jahr** werde ich **für zwei Wochen** in **die Schweiz** fahren, **um meine Freundin zu besuchen.** Next year I will go to Switzerland for two weeks to visit my friend.
- **Normalerweise verbringen wir unsere Ferien in Spanien, weil wir uns in das Land verliebt haben.** Usually we spend our holidays in Spain because we have fallen in love with the country.

Key Point

When talking about the future, use the correct form of '**werden**' and the infinitive.

Key Point

Most countries and cities are neuter (**das**). You do not need the '**das**' in a sentence: **Deutschland liegt in Europa.** Germany lies in Europe. **Berlin liegt in Deutschland.** Berlin lies in Germany.
Countries which are feminine (**die**) or plural (**die**) need the article included: **Die Schweiz ist ein Nachbarstaat Deutschlands.** Switzerland is a neighbouring country of Germany.

Key Point

To say *in* a particular country (or city), use '**in**' for neuter countries: **Ich wohne in Deutschland.** I live in Germany. **Ich wohne in Berlin.** I live in Berlin.
Use '**in**' + article for feminine and plural countries: **Ich wohne in der Schweiz** (dative feminine). I live in Switzerland. **Ich wohne in den Niederlanden** (dative plural). I live in the Netherlands.

Key Point

To say travel *to* a neuter (**das**) country, use the preposition '**nach**'. **Ich fahre nach Frankreich.** I travel to France.
Use the preposition '**in**' + '**die**' for feminine and plural countries: **Ich fahre in die Schweiz.** I travel to Switzerland.

Useful Verbs

verbringen	ich verbringe	ich habe…	ich werde…
(to spend time)		verbracht	verbringen
	wir verbringen	wir haben…	wir werden…
		verbracht	verbringen
besuchen	ich besuche	ich habe…	ich werde…
(to visit)		besucht	besuchen
	wir besuchen	wir haben…	wir werden…
		besucht	besuchen
fahren	ich fahre	ich bin…	ich werde…
(to travel)		gefahren	fahren
	wir fahren	wir sind…	wir werden…
		gefahren	fahren
bleiben	ich bleibe	ich bin…	ich werde…
(to stay)		geblieben	bleiben
	wir bleiben	wir sind…	wir werden…
		geblieben	bleiben
übernachten	ich übernachte	ich habe…	ich werde…
(to stay		übernachtet	übernachten
overnight)	wir übernachten	wir haben…	ich werde…
		übernachtet	übernachten
reisen	ich reise	ich bin…	ich werde…
(to travel)		gereist	reisen
	wir reisen	wir sind…	wir werden…
		gereist	reisen

HT Refer to yourself and others in your work so check the endings for **he** and **she** when talking about someone else's holidays and include a **wider range of tenses**. Why not compare *where you used to go in the past* with where you go now? **Früher sind wir nach Frankreich gefahren, aber jetzt fliegen wir immer nach Spanien**. We used to go to France, but now we always fly to Spain.

Transport

• **der Reisebus**	coach	**das Flugzeug**	plane
• **die Bahn / der Zug**	train	**das Motorrad**	motorbike
die Fähre	ferry	**das Schiff**	ship
• **das Auto**	car	HT **der Dampfer**	steamboat
das Boot	boat		

- **Wenn wir in den auf Urlaub fahren, fahren wir lieber mit dem Zug. Mein Vater sagt, es ist weniger ermüdend als mit dem Auto zu fahren.**
  If we go on holiday, we prefer to go by train. My dad says it's less tiring than driving.
- **Nächstes Jahr werden wir mit der Fähre nach Schottland fahren.**
  Next year, we will go to Scotland by ferry.

Key Point

Most verbs of movement use '**sein**' in the perfect tense, e.g. **fahren**, **gehen** and **laufen**. (Although **bleiben** and **sein** are not verbs of movement, they use '**sein**' as their auxiliary.) **Ich bin in die Schweiz gefahren.** I went to Switzerland. **Er ist zu Hause geblieben**. He stayed at home. **Wir sind zwei Wochen hier gewesen**. We've been here for two weeks.

Key Point

Use **mit + dative article + means of transport**, e.g. **Ich bin mit dem Auto in den Urlaub gefahren.** I went on holiday by car. **Ich bin mit der Bahn gefahren**. I went by train.

Key Vocab

in	in / to
nach	to
mit	by / with
Ich verbringe…	I spend (time)…
Ich habe… verbracht	I spent (time)…
Ich werde… verbringen	I will spend…
Ich fahre…	I travel / go…
Ich bin… gefahren	I travelled / went…
Ich werde… fahren	I will travel / go…

Travel and Tourism 2

You must be able to:

- Describe your holiday activities
- Use the perfect tense
- Use the correct word order of Time, Manner, Place.

Type of Holidays

• **am Rhein**	on the Rhine
am See	at the lake
an der Küste	on the coast
an der Ostsee	on the Baltic Sea
an der See	at the sea / ocean
am Meer	at the seaside
auf einem Campingplatz	on a campsite
auf einer Insel	on an island
auf dem Land	in the countryside
in den Bergen	in the mountains
in einem Ferienhaus	in a holiday house
in einem Ferienpark	in a holiday park
in einem Hotel	in a hotel
in einem Wohnwagen	in a caravan
in einem 4-Sterne-Hotel	in a 4-star hotel
in einer Jugendherberge	in a youth hostel
im Ausland	abroad
HT **am Bodensee**	on Lake Constance

- **Nächstes Jahr werde ich in Polen Urlaub machen und wir werden in einem 4-Sterne-Hotel übernachten.**
  Next year, I will have a holiday in Poland and we will stay in a 4-star hotel.
- **In den Ferien fahre ich gern in die Berge, weil man dort viel machen kann.**
  During the holidays I like to go to the mountains, because you can do a lot there.

Key Point

Use **in** for accommodation.

Holiday Activities

• **der Freizeitpark**	theme park
der Stadtbummel	stroll in town / window shopping
der Strand	beach
der Themenpark	theme park
• **die Führung**	guided tour
die Sehenswürdigkeit	sights
die Stadtrundfahrt	sightseeing tour
• **besichtigen**	to visit / sightsee
einen Ausflug machen	to go on an excursion
klettern	to climb
mieten	to rent / hire
schwimmen	to swim
(sich) baden	to bathe
sich sonnen	to sunbathe

skilaufen	to ski
spazieren gehen	to go for a walk
zelten	to go camping

- **Im Urlaub gehe ich wirklich gern schwimmen, und ich gehe auch gern am Strand spazieren.** On holiday I really like to go swimming and I also like to go for a walk on the beach.
- **Was ich in den Ferien am meisten mag, ist eine Stadtrundfahrt zu machen. Ich liebe alte Kirchen!** What I like the most during the holidays is to go on a guided tour. I love old churches!

Describing a Past Holiday

If you want to describe a holiday in the past, you will need to use the *perfect* tense.

- **Letztes Jahr sind wir nach Spanien gefahren und sind jeden Tag im Meer geschwommen.**
  Last year we went to Spain and we swam in the sea every day.
- **Letztes Jahr im Urlaub sind meine Schwester und ich oft am Strand spazieren gegangen.**
  Last year on holiday, my sister and I went for a walk on the beach.
- **Die Jugendherberge war sehr bequem und** es gab **drei große Schlafsäle.**
  The youth hostel was very comfortable and there were three large dormitories.
- **Während unseres Urlaubs in Griechenland gab es viel Sonnenschein, und** es war **sehr** heiß.
  During our holiday in Greece there was a lot of sunshine and it was very hot.
- **Vor zwei Jahren** haben wir **unseren Winterurlaub in der Schweiz** gemacht.
  Two years ago we had our winter holiday in Switzerland.

Word Order – Time, Manner, Place

When formulating sentences in German, you need to use the correct word order of Time, Manner, Place.

- **Ich bin letztes Jahr mit meiner Familie nach Spanien geflogen.** Last year I went to Spain with my family.
- **Letzten Sommer bin ich mit meiner Freundin mit dem Zug nach Italien gefahren.** Last summer I went to Italy by train with my friend.

 To add variety to the structures you use when describing your holiday, use the following: **Bevor** and **Nachdem**. You need to use the pluperfect tense if you use 'nachdem'.

- **Bevor** ich **ins Bett** gegangen bin, **bin ich am Strand spazieren gegangen.** Before I went to bed, I had a walk on the beach.
- **Nachdem ich schwimmen gegangen war, bin ich in die Stadt gegangen.** After I went swimming, I went to town.

Quick Test

1. What is the German for the following?
   a) I travelled by train.
   b) We were there for two weeks.
   c) On holiday I like to swim.
   d) On holiday what I like most is to walk on the beach.
   e) Three years ago I spent two weeks on an island.

Travel and Tourism 3

You must be able to:

- Organise your holiday
- Talk about problems
- Use key phrases.

Organising Accommodation

- **Unterkunft** reservieren — to book accommodation
  Ich möchte... reservieren — I would like to book…
  Haben Sie...? — Do you have…?
  Ich habe... reserviert / eine Reservierung — I have… reserved / a reservation

  Gibt es...? — Is there…?
  Kann man...? — Can we…?
  Wo kann man...? — Where can we…?
  Um wieviel Uhr...? — At what time…?
  Wo findet man...? — Where is…?
  Wo ist / sind...? — Where is / are…?
  von... bis... — from… until…

- **Guten Tag!** Haben Sie **ein Zimmer mit Meerblick für fünf Nächte?**
  Hello! Do you have a room with a sea view for five nights?
- **Guten Abend! Ich habe ein Zimmer im Namen von... reserviert.**
  Good evening! I have reserved a room in the name of….
- **Guten Tag! Wo können wir unser Auto parken?**
  Hello! Where can we park our car?

At the Hotel

der Aufzug	lift	**im ersten Stock**	on the first floor
der Koffer	suitcase		
der Meerblick	sea view	**im Hotel**	at the hotel
der Notausgang	emergency exit	**eine Nacht**	one night
die Aussicht	view	**zwei Nächte**	two nights
die Treppe	stairs	**mit Vollpension**	with full /
das Doppelzimmer	double room	**Halbpension**	half board
		parken	to park
das Einzelzimmer	single room	HT **der Empfang**	reception
das Zweibettzimmer	twin room	HT **die Klimaanlage**	air conditioning
im Erdgeschoss	on the ground floor		

At the Travel Agent

der Fahrpreis	fare	**die Vorstellung**	show / performance
der Flug	flight		
der Stadtplan	street map	**das Reisebüro**	travel agency
der Treffpunkt	meeting place	**abfahren**	to depart
die Rundfahrt	tour / round trip		

die Ermäßigung	reduction	ankommen	to arrive
die Fahrkarte	ticket	**der Fahrradverleih**	bicycle hire
die Postkarte	postcard	**die Auskunft**	information
die Linie	number (bus, tram)	**die Autovermietung**	car rental
die Öffnungszeiten	opening times	**das Verkehrsamt**	tourist information

- **Guten Tag! Um wieviel Uhr treffen wir uns für die Rundfahrt?**
  Hello! At what time / When are we meeting for the tour?
- **Guten Tag! Ich möchte zwei Karten für die Vorstellung morgen Abend um acht Uhr reservieren.**
  Hello! I would like to reserve two tickets for the performance tomorrow evening at 8pm.

Problems on Holiday

- **…ist / sind kaputt** …is / are broken
- **…ist / sind schmutzig** …is / are dirty
- **…funktioniert / funktionieren nicht** …does / do not work
- **es fehlt / es fehlen…** …is / are missing
- Ich habe… vergessen I have forgotten…
- Ich habe… verloren I have lost…
- Ich habe… zurückgelassen I have left… behind
- **Ich habe kein / keinen / keine…** I have no…
- **jemand hat… gestohlen** someone has stolen…
- **Wir haben eine Panne** We have broken down
- **der Ausweis** identity card

der Badeanzug	swimsuit	**die Sonnencreme**	sun lotion
der Geldbeutel	wallet	**das Fundbüro**	lost property office
der Sonnenbrand	sunburn		
der Wasserhahn	tap	**das Gepäck**	luggage
die Badewanne	bath tub	**das Handtuch**	towel
der Schlüssel	the key	**die Verspätung**	delay
die Seife	soap	**seekrank**	seasick
die Sonnenbrille	sunglasses		

- **Ach nein! Ich habe meine Sonnencreme zu Hause zurückgelassen.**
  Oh no! I have left my sun lotion at home.
- **Entschuldigen Sie, in meinem Zimmer funktioniert der Fernseher nicht, die Dusche ist schmutzig und es gibt keine Handtücher.**
  Excuse me… in my room, the TV does not work, the shower is dirty and there aren't any towels.
- **Was für eine Katastrophe! Meine Tasche wurde gestohlen.**
  What a catastrophe! My bag was stolen.

Key Point

If you want to describe what went wrong during your last holiday, you can use some verbs in the imperfect tense:
- **Der Fernseher funkionierte nicht.** The television didn't work.
- **Die Dusche war schmutzig.** The shower was dirty.
- **Es gab keine Handtücher.** There were no towels.

Key Vocab

reservieren	to book / reserve
Ich möchte…	I would like…
Haben Sie…?	Do you have…?
Gibt es…?	Is there…?
Kann man…?	Can we…?
Ich habe… vergessen	I have forgotten…
Ich habe… verloren	I have lost…
Ich habe… zurückgelassen	I have left … behind

Quick Test

1. Translate into German:
   a) Hello. I would like to book a room for two people for three nights please.
   b) I have left my suitcase at the airport.
2. Translate into English:
   a) Guten Tag! Ich habe ein Doppelzimmer für vier Nächte reserviert.
   b) Ich habe meinen Schlüssel verloren.
   c) Haben Sie einen Stadtplan bitte?

Review Questions

My Family and Friends & Marriage and Partnerships

1 **Wähle Wörter aus dem Kasten unten, die zu diesen Definitionen passen.**
Choose words from the box below to fit these definitions.

Onkel	Neffe	Großeltern	Oma	Schwägerin	Stiefbruder

a) Sie ist die Mutter von meiner Mutter.

b) Mein Opa und meine Oma.

c) Er ist der Sohn von meiner Schwester.

d) Sie ist die Schwester von meiner Frau.

e) Er ist der Sohn von der neuen Frau von meinem Vater.

f) Er ist der Bruder von meinem Vater.   [6 marks]

HT **2** **Lies den Text und beantworte die Fragen mit JA oder NEIN.**
Read the text and answer the questions with a YES or NO.

Mein Bruder Claas hat sich am letzten Wochenende verlobt. Er lebt seit drei Jahren mit seiner Freundin Ute zusammen und er hat immer gesagt, dass er nicht heiraten wollte. Unsere Eltern sind geschieden und das war ein Problem für Claas, aber Ute möchte Kinder haben und sie glaubt, dass es besser ist, verheiratet zu sein. Die Hochzeit ist am 6. September. Ich freue mich, weil Claas und Ute sich sehr gut verstehen.

a) Ist Claas verheiratet?

b) Ist Ute verheiratet?

c) Haben Claas und Ute Kinder?

d) Leben sie seit 3 Jahren zusammen?

e) Verstehen sie sich gut?

f) Möchte Ute Kinder haben?   [6 marks]

3 **Lies diese Magazinumfrage, die jemand ausgefüllt hat. Dann schreib, ob die folgenden Sätze richtig (R), Falsch (F) oder Nicht im Text (NT) sind.** Read this magazine survey that someone has filled in. Then say if the sentences below are true (R), false (F) or not in text (NT).

<u>Hast du eine starke Freundschaft?</u>

Wir gehen oft zusammen ins Kino.   Ja   Nein√

Wir mögen die gleichen Sportarten.   Ja√   Nein

Wir haben den gleichen Humor.   Ja   Nein√

Mein Friend ist immer treu.   Ja   Nein√

Wir treffen uns oft.   Ja√   Nein

Wir haben viel gemeinsam.   Ja√   Nein

a) They laugh at the same things.   R F NT

b) They agree about sports.   R F NT

c) They like the same food.   R F NT

d) They don't meet up very often.   R F NT

e) They enjoy the same TV shows.   R F NT

f) They don't have much in common.   R F NT

[6 marks]

Social Media & Mobile Technology

1 **Übersetze diese Sätze ins Deutsche.** Translate these sentences into German.

a) I visit websites.

b) I chat with my friends.

c) We send SMS.

d) You have to be careful.

e) You mustn't give away the password.

f) Cyberbullying is dangerous. [6 marks]

2 **Füll die Lücken mit deutschen Wörtern.** Fill the gaps with German words.

Ich chatte mit meinen Freunden, weil sie _____ (amusing) **sind. Viele Webseiten**
sind _____ (stupid) **aber das Internet ist** _____ (fast) **und**
_____ (practical). **Mein Handy finde ich** _____ (useful), **aber es**
kann _____ (expensive) **sein.**

[6 marks]

HT **3** **Lies den Text und beantworte die Fragen.** Read the text and answer the questions.

Heutzutage sind fast alle Leute täglich online, entweder mit Computer, Tablet oder Handy.
Man kann sich schnell informieren, im Notfall Hilfe rufen und mit anderen in Kontakt bleiben.
Auf der anderen Seite gibt es einige Leute, die stundenlang auf ihrem Handy sind. Sie sind fast
süchtig*! Außerdem muss man die Geräte immer wieder aufladen und die Technologie ändert
sich schnell, also ist es teuer, immer die aktuelle Version zu haben.

*süchtig = addicted

a) What ways of being online are mentioned? [3 marks]

b) Write down three advantages of technology mentioned in the article. [3 marks]

c) What can happen when people use their phones too much? [1 mark]

d) Three disadvantages are mentioned. What are they? [3 marks]

[Total: 10 marks]

Music & Cinema and TV

1 **Wie sagt man das auf Deutsch?** How do you say these things in German?

a) hit song: **der** _____

b) group: **die** _____

c) piano: **das** _____

d) artist (male): **der** _____

e) lyrics: **der** _____

f) voice: **die** _____

g) song: **das** _____

h) crime thriller: **der** _____

i) programme: **die** _____

j) adverts: **die** _____

[10 marks]

HT **2** **Übersetze diese Sätze ins Deutsche.** Translate these sentences into German.

a) I download music.

b) I most like listening to classical music.

c) I find the melody relaxing.

d) The music makes me happy.

e) I have always liked classical music even though my friends think it's stupid.

[10 marks: 2 marks per sentence]

3 **Lies diese Rezension eines Films und beantworte die Fragen.**
Read this review of a film and answer the questions.

Der Film handelt von drei Freunden, die zusammen Karten spielen und Kaffee trinken. Plötzlich geht das Licht aus. Alle haben Angst. Die Tür geht auf und ein Monster tritt ein. Was passiert dann? Dann müssen Sie den Film sehen! Aber eine Warnung: Das ist kein lustiger Zeichentrickfilm und auch keine sentimentale Liebesgeschichte. Dieser Horrorfilm ist furchtbar, weil die Spezialeffekte so schlecht sind. Man soll lieber zu Hause bleiben und fernsehen!

a) What are the actors doing? [2 marks]

b) What happens? [2 marks]

c) How can you find out what happens next? [1 mark]

d) What is this film NOT? [2 marks]

e) Why is the film so bad? [1 mark]

f) What does the reviewer recommend? [2 marks]

[Total: 10 marks]

Food and Eating Out, Sport & Customs and Festivals

1 **Wie sagt man das auf Deutsch?** How do you say these things in German?

a) packet: **die** _____

b) tin: **die** _____

c) slice: **die** _____

d) breakfast: **das** _____

e) delicious: _____

f) menu: **die** _____

g) dessert: **der** _____

h) knife: **das** _____

i) stadium: **das** _____

j) wedding: **die** _____

[10 marks]

2 **Übersetze diese Sätze ins Deutsche.** Translate these sentences into German.

a) How much is that?

b) I'd like five slices of cheese.

c) That tastes bad.

d) It's too sweet.

e) I don't eat ham.

f) I've never eaten pork.

g) Can I have the bill?

h) We'd like to order.

i) What kinds of vegetables do you have?

j) I used to play football.

[10 marks]

HT **3** **Übersetze diese Passage ins Englische.** Translate this passage into English.

Zu Weihnachten haben wir meine Schwiegereltern besucht. An Heiligabend haben wir zusammen gegessen: zuerst Tomatensuppe, dann Pute mit Kartoffeln und Gemüse. Dann haben wir die Geschenke aufgemacht. Ich habe einen schrecklichen Pullover von meiner Mutter bekommen, der mir nicht gefallen hat! Am ersten Weihnachtstag sind wir alle in die Kirche gegangen. Das habe ich sehr beruhigend gefunden, obwohl ich nicht religiös bin. Am Nachmittag sind wir im Park spazieren gegangen. Das war gut, weil wir zu viel gegessen hatten.

[16 marks: 2 marks per sentence]

At Home, Where I Live & Town or Country?

1 **Wähle das richtige Wort aus dem Kästchen, um die Beschreibung von Sebastians Haus zu vervollständigen.** Choose the missing words to complete the description of Sebastian's home.

Zimmer	das	Wohnzimmer	Stadt
Einfamilienhaus	der	neben	die

Ich wohne in einem _____. Es gibt sechs _____. Im Erdgeschoss

findet man das _____ und _____ Küche. Das Esszimmer ist

_____ dem Eingang. Es gibt viel zu tun in meiner _____.

[6 marks]

2 **Schreib deine eigene Beschreibung mit Hilfe vom Beispiel in Aufgabe 1.**
Write your own description based on the example given in exercise 1.   [8 marks]

3 **Bilde mit folgenden Wörtern Sätze. Pass auf! Es gibt ein Wort in jedem Satz, das nicht gebraucht wird.** Make sentences with the following words. Watch out! There is one word in each sentence that is not needed.

a) man / kaufen / laut / Schmuck / Kann / hier ?

b) diese / Hose / Ich / anprobieren / gestern / möchte

c) öffentliche / Wir / Verkehrsmittel / der / Wohnblock / brauchen / Stadt / in

d) auf / Land / schmutziger / zu / ruhig / ist / dem / Es

e) Ich / am / Geldbeutel / meinen / verloren / Bahnhof / habe / morgen

f) besser / wohnen / in / Stadtmitte / als / zu / Wohnzimmer / ist / der / in / einem / Dorf / Es

[6 marks]

Charity and Voluntary Work & Healthy and Unhealthy Living

1 **Lies die Aussagen und wähle die richtige Person.** Read the statements and choose the correct person.

> Ich möchte in der Zukunft Ärztin werden.

Abigail, 16 Jahre

> Ich bringe älteren Menschen Medikamente.

Max, 18 Jahre

> Ich verteile heiße Mahlzeiten in einem Obdachlosenheim.

Julia, 17 Jahre

> Ich sammle Geld für Wohltätigkeitsveranstaltungen.

Beate, 16 Jahre

> Ich würde gern für das Rote Kreuz arbeiten.

Boris, 17 Jahre

> Ich möchte Krankenschwester werden.

Carla, 16 Jahre

a) Who wants to be a nurse?

b) Who helps elderly people?

c) Who works with the homeless?

d) Who collects money for charity?

e) Who wants to work with a voluntary organisation?

[5 marks]

2 **Schreib die folgenden Sätze in der Zukunftsform.** Put the following sentences into the future tense.

a) **Ich esse gesund.**

b) **Ich treibe dreimal in der Woche Sport.**

c) **Mein Vater vermeidet Zigaretten.**

d) **Meine Schwester macht eine Diät.**

[4 marks]

3 **Ordne die Wörter, um die folgenden Sätze zu bilden, wenn sie übersetzt werden.**
Rearrange the words to make the following sentences when translated.

a) **soll / Produkte / man / vermeiden / fetthaltige** – You should avoid fatty products.

b) **bin / ziemlich / gesund / ich** – I am fairly healthy.

c) **Stress / man / sich /um / vermeiden / soll / entspannen / zu** – You should relax to avoid stress.

d) **rauchen / mein / hat / zu / Vater / aufgehört** – My dad has stopped smoking.

e) **versuchen / Diät / ich/ machen / zu / werde** – I am going to try to go on a diet.

f) **zu / bleiben / man / Wasser / Sport / treiben / trinken / um / soll / viel / mehr / fit / und** –
To stay fit, you should do more sport and drink plenty of water.

[6 marks]

The Environment & Poverty and Homelessness

1 **Wie sagt man das auf Deutsch?** How do you say these in German?

a) to waste   b) you should   c) the ozone layer   d) rubbish   e) you could

f) over-populated   g) to recycle   h) to protect   i) the greenhouse effect   j) to damage

[10 marks]

2 **Wähle die richtigen Wörter, um die Lücken zu ergänzen.** Choose the correct words to fill in the gaps.

wenig	wenige	viel	viele	genug	immer	sehr

Ich denke, dass es heutzutage zu _____ Verschmutzung gibt, und meiner

Meinung nach recyceln wir nicht _____. Leute werfen _____

mehr Müll auf die Straßen und sie benutzen zu _____ die Mülleimer, die überall

zu finden sind. Ich bin der Meinung, dass _____ Tiere und Pflanzen auch

bedroht sind.

[5 marks]

3 **Ordne die Wörter, um Sätze zu bilden. Übersetze die Sätze ins Englische.**
Rearrange the words to make sentences. Translate the sentences into English.

a) sollte / mehr / recyceln / um / die / zu / schützen / man / Umwelt.

b) Meinung / weniger / nach / wir / verschwenden / meiner / sollten.

c) müssen / alternative / entwickeln / wir / Energiequellen.

d) gibt / immer / Armut / in / es / finde / traurig / ich / dass/ mehr / es.

e) mache / die / ich / Städten / mir / Sorgen / um / in / Obdachlosen / unseren / Zahl / der.

[10 marks: 5 marks for correct ordering and 5 marks for translation]

4 **Wie sagt man das auf Deutsch?** How do you say these in German?

a) to steal   b) poor   c) unemployment   d) violence   e) refugee

f) crime   g) immigrant   h) to worry about   i) war   j) victim

[10 marks]

Travel and Tourism

1 **Wähle für jeden Satz die richtige Präposition und erkläre warum. Dann übersetze die Sätze ins Englische.** Choose the right preposition for each sentence and explain why. Then translate the sentences into English.

a) Nächstes Jahr werde ich <u>nach / in</u> die Schweiz fahren.

b) Letztes Jahre bin ich <u>nach / in</u> Österreich gefahren.

c) Ich möchte in der Zukunft <u>nach / in</u> die Niederlande fahren.

d) Vor zwei Jahren sind wir <u>nach / in</u> Spanien geflogen.

[8 marks: 4 marks for correct choice and explanation and 4 marks for translations]

2 **Wähle das richtige Wort für jeden Satz.** Choose the correct word for each sentence.

bin gegangen	verbringen	verbracht	sind gefahren	fahren

a) Jedes Jahr _____ wir unsere Ferien auf einer Insel in der Karibik.

b) Letztes Jahr _____ ich jeden Tag zum Strand _____, um mich zu sonnen.

c) Vor drei Jahren haben meine Familie und ich zwei Wochen in einem 4-Sterne-Hotel in Portugal _____.

d) Ich glaube, ich werde nächstes Jahr in die Schweiz _____, um dort mein Deutsch zu üben.

e) Als ich jünger war, _____ meine Familie und ich immer mit dem Auto nach Österreich _____. [5 marks]

3 **Schau dir die folgenden Situationen an. Was würdest du der Person an der Rezeption deines Hotels sagen?**
Look at the following situations. What would you say to the person at the reception of your hotel?

a) The shower in your room is dirty.

b) You have been given a single room instead of a double.

c) You would like to know what time they serve breakfast.

d) There are no towels in your room.

e) The television isn't working. [5 marks]

My Studies

You must be able to:

- Name your school subjects
- Say when and how often you study different subjects
- Say what you like and dislike studying and explain why.

School

- **der Direktor** — male headteacher
  der Lehrer — male teacher
  der Schüler — male pupil
  der Schulleiter — male headteacher
  der Unterricht — lesson
- **die Direktorin** — female headteacher
  die Lehrerin — female teacher
- **die Schülerin** — female pupil
  die Schulleiterin — female headteacher
  die Stunde — lesson
- **lehren** — to teach
  lernen — to learn
  unterrichten — to teach

HT **der Fremdsprachenassistent** — male language assistant
HT **die Fremdsprachenassistentin** — female language assistant

Key Point

To say which subjects you study, you must use the verb 'lernen'.
'Studieren' is only used to talk about university studies.
Ich lerne Mathe. – I study maths (at school).
Ich studiere Mathe. – I study maths (at university).

Subjects

- **der Sport** — PE
- **die Biologie** — biology
  die Chemie — chemistry
  die Erdkunde — geography
  die Fremdsprache — foreign language
  die Geschichte — history
  die Informatik — ICT
  die Kunst — art
  die Mathematik — maths
  die Physik — physics
- **die Naturwissenschaften** (pl) — science
- **die Religion** — RE
- **das Deutsch** — German
  das Englisch — English
  das Fach — lesson
  das Französisch — French
  das Latein — Latin
  das Schulfach — school subject
  das Spanisch — Spanish
  das Theater — drama
  das Werken — DT

HT **die Hauswirtschaftslehre** — home economics
HT **die Sozialkunde** — PSHE / citizenship
HT **das Pflichtfach** — compulsory subject
HT **das Wahlfach** — optional subject
HT **wählen** — to choose (as an optional subject)

- **Ich lerne zwei Fremdsprachen – Latein und Spanisch.**
  I study two foreign languages – Latin and Spanish.
- **Meine Pflichtfächer sind Mathe und Englisch.**
  My compulsory subjects are maths and English.
- HT **Letztes Jahr habe ich Religion gewählt.**
  Last year I chose RE as an option.

Key Point

All German nouns have genders, but you don't need to use the article when talking about school subjects.
(die) Erdkunde – geography
Ich mag Erdkunde. – I like geography.

Time Expressions

- **montags** — on Mondays
  dienstags — on Tuesdays
  mittwochs — on Wednesdays
  donnerstags — on Thursdays
  freitags — on Fridays

Key Point

Days of the week in German do not need a capital letter here because you are discussing something you do generally.

einmal in der Woche	once a week
zweimal in der Woche	twice a week
dreimal in der Woche	three times a week
• Ich lerne Kunst dienstags.	I study art on Tuesdays.
• Ich lerne Informatik einmal pro Woche.	I study ICT once a week.

Likes and Dislikes

• ich mag	I like	ich liebe	I love
ich mag... nicht	I don't like...	**ich bevorzuge**	I prefer
ich hasse	I hate		

HT am liebsten lerne ich...	most of all I like to learn...
• mein Lieblingsfach ist	my favourite subject is
mein(e) Lieblingslehrer(in) ist	my favourite teacher is
ich finde	I find
ich kann... nicht leiden	I can't stand...
... gefällt mir	I like...
... gefällt mir nicht	I don't like...
HT ... fällt / fallen mir schwer	...is / are difficult for me
HT ... fällt / fallen mir leicht	...is / are easy for me

• ausgezeichnet	excellent	nützlich	useful
einfach	simple / easy	nutzlos	useless
furchtbar	dreadful / awful	praktisch	practical
gerecht	fair	schwer	difficult / hard
hilfsbereit	helpful	schwierig	difficult / hard
interessant	interesting	streng	strict
klug	clever / intelligent	ungerecht	unfair
kompliziert	complicated	wichtig	important
langweilig	boring	begabt	talented
logisch	logical		

> **Key Point**
>
> Always justify your opinions using 'weil' or 'denn'. Remember that 'weil' sends the verb to the end of the sentence.

- **Religion fällt mir einfach, denn der Lehrer ist interessant und gerecht.**
  RE is easy for me because the teacher is interesting and fair.
- **Sport gefällt mir nicht, weil er schwierig ist.**
  I don't like PE because it is difficult.

Quantifiers

• ein bisschen	a bit	ziemlich	quite
nicht	not	zu	too
sehr	very	äußerst	extremely

- **Ich finde Latein zu einfach.**
  I find Latin too easy.
- **Werken ist sehr praktsich.**
  DT is very practical.

> **Key Point**
>
> Quantifiers are an easy way to add more detail to your opinions. They always come directly before the adjective they are describing.

Quick Test

1. Write five sentences in German. In each one, name a subject, say when or how often you study it, and give your opinion using a quantifier.
2. Write the opposite of each of these adjectives in German.
   langweilig, nützlich, kompliziert, gerecht, furchtbar
3. Translate the text into English.
   Der Schulleiter in meiner Schule ist ein bisschen streng, aber ich finde das ausgezeichnet. Mein Lieblingsfach ist Geschichte, weil es sehr interessant und äußerst nützlich ist. Freitags lerne ich ein Wahlfach, Theater, jedoch finde ich die Lehrerin zu langweilig.

> **Key Vocab**
>
> | Ich lerne | I study |
> |---|---|
> | Lieblingsfach | favourite subject |
> | Ich liebe | I love |
> | Ich mag | I like |
> | Ich mag nicht | I don't like |
> | Ich finde | I find |
> | sehr | very |
> | nicht | not |
> | zu | too |

Life at School 1

You must be able to:

- Describe school in Germany
- Say what facilities and classrooms there are in your school
- Use key separable and reflexive verbs to describe a typical school day.

School

• **der Kindergarten**	nursery
• **die Ganztagsschule**	school that lasts all day
die Gesamtschule	comprehensive school
die Grundschule	primary school
die Hauptschule	secondary school
die Klasse	class / form / year group
die Realschule	secondary school
die Schule	school
• **das Gymnasium**	grammar school
das Internat	boarding school
das Schulsystem	school system
ungefähr	about, approximately
HT **der Jahrgang**	school year
HT **die Sekondarstufe**	secondary education
• Ich besuche **eine Gesamtschule.**	I go to a comprehensive school.
• Es gibt **1200 Schüler und Schülerinnen.**	There are 1200 pupils.
• **Ich bin in der zehnten Klasse.**	I am in Year 11.
HT **Ich bin im zehnten Jahrgang.**	I am in Year 11.

Facilities and Classrooms

• **der Raum**	room
der Schulhof	school yard / playground
der Speisesaal	dining hall / canteen
der Umkleideraum	changing room
• **die Aula**	assembly hall
die Bibliothek	library
die Halle	hall
die Tafel	(white / black) board
die Turnhalle	sports hall
• das Klassenzimmer	classroom
das Labor	laboratory
das Lehrerzimmer	staffroom
das Sekretariat	school office / reception
das Sprachlabor	language lab
HT **der Beamer**	projector
HT **der Gang**	corridor
HT **die Mensa**	dining hall / canteen
• **Es gibt...**	There is / there are...
Wir haben...	We have...
HT **... haben wir nicht**	We don't have a... / any...

- **Wir haben kein Sprachlabor.**   We don't have a language lab.
- **Es gibt ungefähr**   There are approximately
  50 Klassenzimmer.   50 classrooms.
- **Man kann in der Bibliothek lesen.**   You can read in the library.
- HT **Ich kaufe eine Kleinigkeit**   I buy a snack in the dining hall.
  in der Mensa.

The School Day

anfangen	to start / to begin	**enden**	to end
beginnen	to begin	**verlassen**	to leave
dauern	to last		

der Schultag	school day
der Stundenplan	timetable

die Gruppe	group
die Hausaufgaben	homework
die Klassenarbeit	classwork / class test
die Pause	break
die Versammlung	assembly

- HT **die AG (Arbeitsgemeinschaft)**   after-school club
- **Ich verlasse das Haus um**   I leave the house at seven o'clock.
  sieben Uhr.
- **Die erste Stunde beginnt**   The first lesson begins at eight
  um acht Uhr.   o'clock.
- **Wir bekommen viele Hausaufgaben.**   We get a lot of homework.
- **Die Schule endet um halb vier.**   School ends at half past three.
- **Ich besuche eine Theatergruppe.**   I attend a drama group.
- **Die Pause dauert fünfzehn Minuten.**   Break lasts fifteen minutes.
- HT **Ich bin Mitglied der Musik AG.**   I am a member of the music club.

- **der Tagesablauf** daily routine

aufstehen	to get up	**sich schminken**	to put on make-up
aufwachen	to wake up	**sich umziehen**	to get changed
sich anziehen	to get dressed	**sich waschen**	to have a wash
sich ausziehen	to get undressed	**mit dem Auto /**	by car / bike /
sich die Zähne	to brush your	**Fahrrad /**	school bus
putzen	teeth	**Schulbus**	
sich rasieren	to shave	**zu Fuß gehen**	to go by/on foot, to walk

- Ich stehe **jeden Tag** um **sechs Uhr** auf.   I get up at six o'clock every day.
- **Ich schminke mich oft.**   I often put on make-up.
- Ich fahre **immer mit dem Schulbus.**   I always travel by school bus.
- **Ich gehe nie zu Fuß.**   I never walk.

Quick Test

1. Give a 30-second description of your school. Include the type of school and what facilities and/or classrooms you do and don't have.
2. Write five sentences to describe your daily routine, including each of these infinitives: **aufwachen, aufstehen, sich anziehen, verlassen, fahren**
3. Translate these sentences into German:
   a) I go to a grammar school.
   b) There are approximately 850 pupils.
   c) We have 30 classrooms but no dining hall.
   d) The school day begins at half past 8 and ends at 3 o'clock.

Key Point

For separable verbs, you need to conjugate the verb and move the prefix to the end of the sentence in the present and imperfect.
Ich stehe auf – I get up.
Ich wache um 7 Uhr auf – I wake up at 7 o'clock.
For reflexive verbs, you need to conjugate the verb and use the correct reflexive pronoun.
Ich rasiere mich – I shave.
Some verbs are both separable and reflexive, so you need to conjugate the verb, use the correct reflexive pronoun and move the prefix to the end of the sentence.
Ich ziehe mich um – I get changed.

Key Vocab

Ich besuche	I go to
Es gibt	There is / there are
Wir haben	We have
das Klassenzimmer	classroom
die Schule	school
beginnen	to begin
enden	to end
Ich stehe um... auf	I get up at…
Ich fahre	I travel
Ich verlasse	I leave

Life at School 2

You must be able to:

- Use **müssen** and **dürfen** to describe school rules
- Describe your school uniform
- Discuss exams and grades.

School Rules

• die Schulregeln (pl)	school rules	fehlen	to be absent
		fragen	to ask
• ich / man muss	I / you must / have to	mobben	to bully
		nachsitzen	to get / have a detention
wir müssen	we must / have to	plaudern	to chat
• ich / man darf	I / you may	rauchen	to smoke
wir dürfen	we may	schwatzen / schwätzen	to chat
• ich / man darf nicht	I / you must not	sich setzen	to sit down
wir dürfen nicht	we must not	tragen	to wear
• erlauben	to allow	zuhören	to listen
verbieten	to forbid / ban	HT abschreiben	to copy
		HT beantworten	to answer
• antworten	to answer	HT schwänzen	to skip school, to play truant
aufpassen	to pay attention		
blau machen	to skip school, to play truant	HT die Strafarbeit	punishment work / lines

- **Mobbing ist streng verboten.** Bullying is strictly forbidden.
- **Kaugummi ist nicht erlaubt.** Chewing gum is not allowed.
- **Man darf Handys im Klassenzimmer nicht benutzen.**
  You must not use mobile phones in the classroom.
- HT **Wenn man frech oder böse ist, bekommt man Strafarbeit.**
  If you are naughty or cheeky, you get punishment work.
- HT **Wenn man schwänzt, muss man mit dem Schulleiter nachsitzen.**
  If you skip school, you have to do a detention with the headteacher.

School Uniform

		die Schuluniform	school uniform
• der Anzug	suit	die Strumpfhose	tights
der Blazer	blazer	• das Hemd	shirt
der Rock	skirt	das Kleid	dress
der Schal	scarf	• die Jungen (pl)	boys
der Schmuck	make-up	die Mädchen (pl)	girls
• die Bluse	blouse	die Schuhe (pl)	shoes
die Hose	trousers	• tragen	to wear
die Krawatte	tie		

- **Die Mädchen und Jungen tragen eine Hose.** — Girls and boys wear trousers.
- **Wir müssen schwarze Schuhe tragen.** — We must wear black shoes.
- **Ich finde den Blazer unbequem.** — I find the blazer uncomfortable.

Grades and Exams

- der Druck — pressure
  der Erfolg — success
  der Notendruck — pressure to achieve good grades
- die Note — grade
  die Prüfung — exam
- **das Abschlusszeugnis** — school leaving certificate
  das Zeugnis — school report
- **die Hausaufgaben** (pl) — homework
- bekommen — to get / to receive
  bestehen — to pass (an exam or test)
  sitzenbleiben — to repeat a school year
  üben — to practise
  verstehen — to understand
  wissen — to know
  wiederholen — to revise
- mündlich — verbal / oral
  schriftlich — written
- HT **der Leistungsdruck** — pressure to achieve
- HT **die Leistung** — achievement
- HT **das Ergebnis** — result
- HT **durchfallen** — to fail (an exam or test)
- HT **versetzt werden** — to be moved up to the next year group

- **Ich habe Angst vor den mündlichen Prüfungen.** — I am scared of the oral exams.
- **Ich mache mir Sorgen über meine Noten.** — I am worried about my grades.
- **Mein Zeugnis ist ungenügend.** — My report is extremely poor.
- HT **Wir stehen unter Leistungsdruck.** — We are under pressure to achieve.

> **Key Point**

In Germany, grades range from 1 (the best) to 6 (the worst). German students may have to repeat a school year if their grades are not good enough.

> **Key Vocab**

Wir tragen	We wear
Wir müssen	We must / have to
Wir dürfen	We may
die Schulregeln (pl)	school rules
die Schuluniform	school uniform
verboten	forbidden
erlaubt	allowed
bekommen	to get / to receive
bestehen	to pass
der Druck	pressure
die Note	grade
die Prüfung	exam
das Zeugnis	report

> **Quick Test**

1. Make a list of ten rules or expectations in your school, using the verbs **dürfen** and **müssen**. Then write 2–3 sentences in German explaining what the punishments are for breaking school rules.
2. Write 2–3 short sentences in English explaining the grade system in Germany and the concept of **sitzenbleiben**.
3. Translate these sentences into English.
   a) Ich trage einen blauen Blazer mit einem weißen Hemd.
   b) Meine Schuluniform ist sehr bequem aber nicht sehr modisch.
   c) Wenn es kalt ist, dürfen die Mädchen eine Strumpfhose tragen.
   d) Man darf einen Schal tragen, aber nur im Winter.

Education Post-16

You must be able to:

- Describe your future plans related to education
- Discuss alternative future plans to education
- Use a range of constructions to describe your future plans.

College and University

- **der Abiturient** — male person doing the *Abitur*
  der Berufsberater — male careers adviser
  der Rat — advice
  der Studienplatz — university place
- **die Abiturientin** — female person doing the *Abitur*
  die Berufsberaterin — female careers adviser
  die Berufsschule — vocational training school
  die Oberstufe — sixth form college
- **das Abitur** — A-level(s) equivalent
  das Semester — term
  das Studium — studies
- **abwählen** — to drop a subject
  fertig — ready / done / finished
  nach der Schule — after school
  sich entscheiden — to decide
  studieren — to study (at university)
- HT **der Universitätsabschluss** — university degree
- HT **die Fachschule** — technical college
- HT **die Studiengebühren** — tuition fees
- **Der Berufsberater hat mir einen guten Rat gegeben.** — The careers adviser gave me good advice.
- **Ich will dieses Jahr Informatik abwählen.** — I want to drop ICT this year.
- **Nächstes Jahr werden wir das Abitur machen.** — Next year we will do our A-levels.
- HT **Ich möchte eine Fachschule besuchen.** — I would like to go to a technical college.

Future Plans

- **der Führerschein** — driving licence
- **die Idee** — idea
  die Freiheit — freedom
- **im Ausland** — abroad
  in der Zukunft — in the future
  sofort — immediately / straightaway
- **auf... sparen** — to save up for…
  beabsichtigen — to intend
  beschließen — to decide
  ein Jahr freinehmen — to take a gap year
  feste Pläne haben — to have firm plans

freiwillig arbeiten	to volunteer
Geld sammeln	to raise money
hoffen	to hope
keine Ahnung haben	to have no idea
Lust haben	to feel like
mit Kindern arbeiten	to work with children
mit Tieren arbeiten	to work with animals
planen	to plan
um die Welt reisen	to travel the world

HT	**die Absicht haben**	to intend to
HT	**die Verantwortung**	responsibility
HT	**vorhaben**	to intend to

- **Ich will sofort meinen Führerschein bekommen.**
  I want to get my driving licence straightaway.
- **In der Zukunft werde ich auf ein neues Auto sparen.**
  In the future I will save for a new car.
- **Ich habe keine Ahnung, was ich machen will!**
  I have no idea what I want to do!
- **Meiner Meinung nach ist Freiheit wichtiger als Geld.**
  In my opinion freedom is more important than money.
- HT **Meine Freundin und ich haben vor, freiwillig mit Kindern zu arbeiten.**
  My friend and I plan to do volunteer work with children.

Work Experience

der Ausbildungsplatz	vacancy / place for a trainee	**die Chefin**	female boss
der / die Auszubildende (Azubi)	apprentice / trainee	**die Erfahrung**	experience
		die Gelegenheit	opportunity
		die Kollegin	female colleague
der Brief	letter	**die Kundin**	female customer
der Chef	male boss		
der Kollege	colleague	die Lehre	apprenticeship
der Kunde	male customer	**die Möglichkeit**	possibility
der Kurs	course	**das Arbeitspraktikum**	work experience
der Lebenslauf	CV		
der Lohn	wage	**arbeiten**	to work
der Mindestlohn	minimum wage	**sich um… bewerben**	to apply for…
der Nebenjob	part-time job		
der Teilzeitjob	part-time job	**verdienen**	to earn
die Ausbildung	(job) training, education	**theoretisch**	theoretical
		HT **einstellen**	to employ
die Bewerbung	application		

Key Vocab	
Ich werde	I will
Ich will	I want to
Ich möchte	I would like to
das Abitur	A-levels
in der Zukunft	in future
die Lehre	apprentice-ship
nach der Schule	after school
nächstes Jahr	next year
in [fünf] Jahren	in [five] years
die Universität	university

- **Ich arbeite seit sechs Monaten in einem Schuhgeschäft.**
  I have been working in a shoe shop for six months.
- **Als Azubi hat man die Möglichkeit, Geld zu verdienen.**
  As an apprentice you have the opportunity to earn money.
- **Ich habe mich um eine Lehre beworben.**
  I have applied for an apprenticeship.

Quick Test

1. Write six sentences describing your future plans. Use each of these phrases twice: **ich werde, ich hoffe, ich will.**
2. Unjumble the following sentences and translate them:
   a) **reisen / Deutschland / plane / Jahr / nach / nächstes / ich / zu**
   b) **ich / will / mache / verdienen / denn / eine / Geld / Lehre / ich**
   c) **Erdkunde / möchte / der / in / Oberstufe / ich / abwählen**
3. Translate these sentences into German: a) I hope to do my A-levels and I want to study maths.
   b) In my opinion, the careers adviser was very helpful. c) Next year I will apply for a part-time job.
   d) In future I would like to earn a lot of money and save up for a house.

Career Choices and Ambitions

You must be able to:

- Describe which job(s) you would like to do in future
- Describe the requirements and advantages and disadvantages of different jobs
- Describe how your working life will be.

Jobs

der Arzt	doctor	**der Lehrer**	teacher
der Apotheker	pharmacist	**der LKW-Fahrer**	lorry driver
der Bäcker	baker	**der Innenausstatter**	(interior) decorator
der Bauarbeiter	building / construction worker	**der Mechaniker**	mechanic
		der Metzger	butcher
der Bauer	farmer	**der Polizist**	police officer
der Beamte	civil servant	**der Schauspieler**	actor
der Besitzer	owner	**der Sekretär**	secretary
der Briefträger	postman	**der Tierarzt**	vet
der Feuerwehrmann	male firefighter	**der Tischler**	carpenter
		der Verkäufer	sales assistant
der Fleischer	butcher	**die Arbeit**	work / job
der Friseur	hairdresser	**die Feuerwehrfrau**	female firefighter
der Gärtner	gardener		
der Geschäftsmann	business man	**die Geschäftsfrau**	business woman
der Hausmann	househusband		
der Informatiker	IT technician	**die Hausfrau**	housewife
der Ingenieur	engineer	**die Krankenschwester**	female nurse
der Kassierer	cashier		
der Klempner	plumber	**die Polizei**	police
der Koch	cook	**arbeiten**	to work
der Kosmetiker	beautician	HT **der Buchhalter**	accountant
der Krankenpfleger	male nurse	HT **der Rechtsanwalt**	lawyer

- **In der Zukunft möchte ich Gärtnerin werden.** — In future I would like to become a gardener.
- **Ich werde als Friseur arbeiten.** — I am going to work as a hairdresser.
- **Ich will bei der Polizei arbeiten.** — I want to work in the police.
- HT **Ich würde gern Kosmetiker werden.** — I would like to become a beautician.

Describing Jobs

der Alptraum	nightmare	**die Schichtarbeit**	shift work
der Nachteil	disadvantage	**das Gehalt**	salary
der Traum	dream	**fleißig**	hard-working
der Vorteil	advantage	**geduldig**	patient
der Wunsch	wish	**gut bezahlt**	well paid
die Arbeitszeit	work hours	**hoch**	high
der Urlaub	holiday	**interessant**	interesting

> ### Key Point
> To make a job feminine, you usually add 'in' to the end.
> **der Lehrer** – male teacher
> **die Lehrerin** – female teacher
> **der Krankenpfleger** – male nurse
> **die Krankenschwester** / **die Krankenpflegerin** – female nurse
> In the feminine form for jobs, an Umlaut is used in one-syllable words:
> **der Koch / die Köchin** – cook
> **der Arzt / die Ärztin** – doctor

> ### Key Point
> When giving people's occupations, you do not need to use the article.
> **Meine Mutter ist Mechanikerin.**
> My mum is a mechanic.
> **Mein Vater ist Tischler.**
> My dad is a carpenter.

stressig	stressful	**reisen**	to travel
• **erfüllen**	to fulfil	**verdienen**	to earn
HT **die Aufstiegsmöglichkeiten** (pl)		possibilities of promotion	
HT **die Berufsaussichten** (pl)		job prospects	
HT **niedrig**		low	

- **Mein Traumjob ist Arzt.** — My dream job is a doctor.
- **Ein Lehrer bekommt viele Ferien.** — A teacher gets lots of holidays.
- **Ein Polizist muss Schichtarbeit machen.** — A police officer has to do shift work.
- **Ein Krankenpfleger ist immer geduldig.** — A nurse is always patient.
- HT **Ich hätte gern ein hohes Gehalt.** — I would like a high salary.
- HT **Ein fleißiger Rechtsanwalt hat hohe Aufstiegsmöglichkeiten.**
  A hard-working lawyer has high possibilities of promotion.

The World of Work

• **der / die Angestellte**	employee	**ganztags**	all day
der Beruf	job	**im Freien**	outside / outdoors
der Teilzeitjob	part-time job		
der Termin	appointment	**Pfund**	pounds (£)
• **die Fabrik**	factory	• **besitzen**	to own
die Halbtagsarbeit	part-time employment	**bezahlen**	to pay
		gründen	to found / to start
die Karriere	career		
die Vollzeitarbeit	full-time employment	**suchen**	to look for
		HT **der Arbeitgeber**	employer
die Werkstatt	workshop / garage	HT **der Arbeitnehmer**	employee
		HT **die Besprechung**	meeting
• **das Büro**	office	HT **die Firma**	company / firm
das Geschäft	shop	HT **die Konkurrenz**	competition
das Vorstellungsgespräch	job interview	HT **selbstständig**	self-employed
• **berufstätig**	employed		

- **Ich werde ein Kleidergeschäft besitzen.** — I am going to own a clothes shop.
- **Ich möchte praktische Arbeit im Freien.** — I would like practical, outdoors work.
- HT **Ich will meine eigene Firma gründen.** — I want to start my own company.
- HT **Es gibt so viel Konkurrenz zwischen den Angestellten.**
  There is so much competition between employees.

Key Vocab

Ich werde	I will
Ich will	I want to
Ich möchte	I would like to
arbeiten	to work
werden	to become
in der Zukunft	in future
die Arbeit	work
der Beruf	job
die Karriere	career
der Traum	dream
verdienen	to earn

Review Questions

At Home, Where I Live & Town or Country?

1 **Ergänze die Beschreibung von Birgits Haus mit dem richtigen Artikel.**

Complete the description of Birgit's house using the correct article.

Ich wohne in _____ Einfamilienhaus in Augsburg. Es gibt insgesamt neun Zimmer, einschließlich vier Schlafzimmer.

Im Erdgeschoss findet man die Küche neben _____ Wohnzimmer. Wir haben auch eine Essecke gegenüber von _____ Küche.

Oben im ersten Stock gibt es vier Schlafzimmer. Mein Schlafzimmer ist zwischen _____ Badezimmer und _____ Schlafzimmer meines Bruders. [5 marks]

2 **Ergänze die Lücken mit dem richtigen Verb aus dem Kästchen.**

Complete the gaps with the correct verb from the box.

ist	putze	kann	finden	habe	gibt	befindet	möchten	gehe	wohne

a) Ich _____ in einem kleinen Reihenhaus in der Stadtmitte.

b) Mein Zimmer _____ immer ordentlich.

c) Ich _____ mein Zimmer jede Woche.

d) In meinem Zimmer _____ es eine Kommode.

e) Wir _____ am Stadtrand wohnen.

f) Man _____ mit dem Hund im Wald spazieren gehen.

g) Das Hallenbad _____ sich neben dem Bahnhof. [7 marks]

3 **Wähle vier Sätze, die deiner Meinung nach darauf hinweisen, dass das Leben auf dem Land besser als das Leben in der Stadt ist, und übersetze sie ins Deutsche.**

Choose four sentences that you think suggest that living in the countryside is better than living in the town and translate them into English.

a) Es gibt viele Möglichkeiten auszugehen. ☐

b) Es ist nicht so laut wie in einer Stadt. ☐

c) Wir haben viele schöne Geschäfte. ☐

d) Die Mieten sind teuer. ☐

e) Man kann täglich Vögel sehen und hören. ☐

f) Die Ruhe gefällt mir sehr. ☐

g) Die öffentlichen Verkehrsmittel fahren häufig. ☐

h) Man kann am Wochenende mit Freunden spazieren gehen. ☐ [4 marks]

Charity and Voluntary Work & Healthy and Unhealthy Living

1 **Wähle das richtige Wort, um die Lücke in jedem Satz zu ergänzen.**
Choose the correct word to fill the gap in each sentence.

a) **Mir geht's viel** _____ [*gut / besser / übel*].

b) **Es fehlt mir die Zeit, Freiwilligenarbeit zu** _____ [*sein / machen / sollen*].

c) **Um gesund** _____ [*auf / in / zu*] **bleiben, soll man Wasser trinken.**

d) **Zigaretten können** _____ [*vermeiden / töten / treiben*].

e) **Meine Mutter** _____ [*ist / geht / hat*] **aufgehört zu rauchen.**   [5 marks]

2 **Du bekommst eine E-Mail von einem Freund in Deutschland. Beantworte die folgenden Multiple-Choice-Fragen.** You receive an email from a friend in Germany. Answer the following multiple choice questions.

Hallo Frank,

Du hast mich gefragt, ob ich gesund bin. Bestimmt ja. Meine Eltern und ich essen ziemlich gesund – viel Obst und Gemüse und nicht zu viel Fett. Statt süßen Getränken trinkt die ganze Familie viel Wasser. Meine Eltern rauchen nicht. Mein Vater hat vor zehn Jahren aufgehört zu rauchen. Ich schlafe gut und ich spiele dreimal pro Woche Fußball.

Meine Schwester aber isst zu viele fettige Produkte wie Pizza und Pommes und sie bewegt sich wenig. Sie sagt, dass sie nächsten Monat eine Diät machen wird und auch regelmäßig schwimmen gehen wird.

Bis bald,

Max

a) Which of these health issues does Max *not* mention in his email? *smoking / exercising / relaxing*

b) What does Max's family tend to drink? *soft drinks / tea and coffee / water*

c) How often does Max play football? *once a week / three times a week / every day*

d) What did Max's father do ten years ago? *gave up drinking / gave up smoking / started going to the gym*

e) What is Max's sister going to do next month? *give up eating pizza / stop smoking / go on a diet*

[5 marks]

Review Questions

The Environment & Poverty and Homelessness

1 **Wie sagt man das auf Deutsch?** How do you say these in German?

a) flood   **b)** endangered species   **c)** acid rain   **d)** hole in the ozone layer   **e)** noise

f) aerosol   **g)** cardboard box   **h)** packaging   **i)** coal   **j)** power station

[10 marks]

2 **Wie sagt man auf Deutsch?** How do you say in German?

a) in order to protect the environment

b) in order to avoid an increase in the number of unemployed people

c) in order not to waste too much energy

d) instead of destroying the environment

e) without thinking about the consequences

[5 marks]

3 **Wähle das richtige Wort und ergänze die Lücken.** Choose the right word and complete the gaps.

a) **Wir** _____ **nicht so viel mit dem Auto fahren.**	**könntest / könnte / sollten**
b) **Man** _____ **Papier und Flaschen recyceln.**	**könnte / wollten / kannst**
c) **Was** _____ **du für die Umwelt tun?**	**machst / kannst / darf**
d) **Ich** _____ **mehr für die Umwelt tun.**	**könnten / solltest / könnte**
e) **Man** _____ **weniger Energie verschwenden.**	**müssen / sollte / sollen**

[5 marks]

4 **Bilde Sätze, indem du eine Meinung hinzufügst. Übersetze diese Sätze ins Englische.**
Make sentences by adding an opinion. Translate these sentences into English.

Beispiel: Müll auf den Straßen   <u>Ich denke, dass</u> es <u>zu viel</u> Müll auf den Straßen gibt.

Example: Rubbish on the streets   <u>I think that</u> there is <u>too much</u> rubbish on the streets.

a) Obdachlose

b) Arbeitslosigkeit

c) Armut

d) Luftverschmutzung

e) Gewalt

[10 marks: 5 marks for the sentence and 5 marks for the translation]

Travel and Tourism

1 **Wie sagt man das auf Deutsch?** How do you say it in German?

a) here   b) in a youth hostel   c) Greece   d) abroad   e) broken

f) by train   g) a lift   h) there   i) on the ground floor   j) the key   [10 marks]

2 **Ergänze die Lücken mit dem richtigen Wort und übersetze die Sätze ins Englische.**
Complete the gaps with the right word and translate the sentences into English.

möchte   sind   haben   wollten   hatten   möchten   waren

a) **Als wir in Frankreich** _____ , _____ **wir eine Panne.**

b) **Letztes Jahr** _____ **wir ins Ausland gefahren, weil wir jeden Tag schwimmen**

   _____ .

c) **Nächstes Jahr** _____ **wir bei Freunden in der Schweiz wohnen, weil wir da**

   nicht viel Geld ausgeben werden.

[8 marks: 5 marks for the correct words and 3 marks for the translated sentences]

3 **Schreib die folgenden Sätze in der Zukunft.** Write the following sentences in the future tense.

a) **Ich war in Frankreich.**

b) **Ich bin dorthin geflogen.**

c) **Er hat in einer Jugendherge übernachtet.**

d) **Meine Familie und ich haben viel Spaß dort gehabt.**   [4 marks]

4 **Sprich für ungefähr 45 Sekunden zu folgenden Themen.**
Speak for about 45 seconds on the following themes. Give as much detail as you can.

a) Your last holiday

b) What you like doing on holiday

c) Your future holiday   [3 marks]

My Studies & Life at School

1 **Lies den Text über Emmas Schule. Wähle das richtige Wort.** Read the text about Emma's school. Choose the correct word.

Fast alle meine Lehrer sind toll, denn die Stunden sind sehr interessant. Wir lernen Spanisch und Französisch und das gefällt mir, weil ich diese Fächer ziemlich einfach finde, aber es ist schade, dass wir Latein nicht lernen. Mein Lieblingsfach ist Theater, denn ich bin begabt, aber ich hasse Naturwissenschaften. Besonders Physik fällt mir schwer, weil der Lehrer nicht sehr hilfsbereit ist.

a) **Die Lehrer in Emmas Schule sind** _____ [*gut / langweilig / ausgezeichnet*].

b) **Emma lernt** _____ [*zwei / drei / keine*] **Fremdsprachen**.

c) **Emma kann** _____ [*Theater / Latein / Physik*] **nicht leiden**.

d) **Emma findet den Physiklehrer** _____ [*streng / ungerecht / nutzlos*]. [4 marks]

2 **Lies dieses Blog, wo ein junger Schweizer Leben in der Schule diskutiert. Beantworte die Fragen auf Englisch.** Read this blog post where a young Swiss boy discusses life at school. Answer the questions in English.

Es kommt mir komisch vor dass so viele Schüler sich über die Schulregeln beklagen. Ja, manche in meiner Schule sind übertrieben (warum ist es wichtig, welche Kleidung man im Unterricht trägt?), aber im Großen und Ganzen helfen uns diese Regeln. Zum Beispiel dürfen wir keine Handys benutzen. Obwohl mein bester Freund dagegen ist, ist es meiner Meinung nach toll, weil es jetzt weniger Mobbing gibt. Auch sind die Schüler freundlicher und wir plaudern mehr miteinander. Jetzt möchte ich eine Schule, wo Kaugummi verboten ist – die Klassenzimmer sind immer schmutzig und ich mag das nicht.

a) Which school rule does Timo not understand? _____

b) Which rule does he agree with? _____

c) Name **one** advantage of this rule. _____

d) Which rule would he like to see introduced? _____ [4 marks]

Education Post-16 & Career Choices and Ambitions

HT **1** **Lies den Text. Schreib R, wenn die Aussage richtig ist, F, wenn die Aussage falsch ist, NT, wenn die Aussage nicht im Text ist.** Read the text. Write R if the statement is correct, F if the statement is false and NT if the statement is not mentioned.

- **In Deutschland gibt es heute mehr Studenten als Azubis – und achtzig Prozent der Abiturienten wollen an die Universität gehen. Die Studenten kommen aus vielen verschiedenen Hintergründen und viele von ihnen sind Bürger aus der ganzen Welt, die ein Semester an einer deutschen Universität verbringen möchten.**

- **Als Alternative zum Studentenleben entscheiden sich einige junge Leute, ein Jahr freizunehmen. Es ist nicht immer nötig, im Ausland zu arbeiten – es gibt auch das freiwillige soziale Jahr, das man in Deutschland machen kann.**

- **Ein Fünftel der Abiturienten beginnen eine Berufsausbildung, und diese Entscheidung ist beliebter bei Frauen als bei Männern. Viele sagen, dass der Vorteil ist, dass man gleichzeitig arbeiten, lernen und Geld verdienen kann.**

a) In the past, apprenticeships were always more popular than university. ....

b) 90% of A-level students want to go to university. ....

c) Many international students come to German universities. ....

d) You need to go abroad if you are taking a year out. ....

e) Apprenticeships are more popular with women than men. ....

f) Most apprenticeships pay above the minimum wage. .... [6 marks]

2 **Lies Svetlanas E-Mail und kreuze die drei richtige Sätze an.**
Read Svetlana's email and tick the three correct sentences.

Was ich nach der Schule machen will? Na ja, ich muss zugeben, dass ich eigentlich keine festen Pläne habe. Meine Schwester hat eine Berufsschule besucht und sie verdient jetzt viel Geld, aber ich denke, ich würde lieber an der Universität studieren, obwohl es ganz teuer ist und es sehr schwierig ist, einen Studienplatz zu bekommen. In der Zukunft möchte ich ins Ausland reisen und vielleicht dort einen gut bezahlten Job finden. Ich habe mein Arbeitspraktikum in einer Grundschule gemacht und es war nicht für mich, deshalb habe ich keine Lust, mit Kindern zu arbeiten.

A Svetlana has firm plans for her future. ☐

B Svetlana's sister attended a vocational training school. ☐

C Svetlana would like to follow in her sister's footsteps. ☐

D Svetlana thinks university would be an easy option. ☐

E Svetlana would like to travel. ☐

F Svetlana has worked in a primary school. ☐ [6 marks]

Gender, Plurals and Articles

You must be able to:

- Use the correct genders of nouns
- Make nouns plural
- Use definite and indefinite articles.

Gender

- All nouns in German have a gender. There are three genders: masculine, feminine and neuter.
- **Masculine:**
  - Most nouns ending in **–er, –ist, –ling, –ent** (e.g. **Lehrer** – male teacher)
  - Most nouns ending in **–ig** or **–ismus** (e.g. **König** – king)
  - Names of seasons, months and days (e.g. **Frühling** – spring)
- **Feminine:**
  - Most nouns of two or more syllables that end in **–e** (e.g. **Lampe** – lamp)
  - Words for females ending in **–in** (e.g. **Lehrerin** – female teacher)
  - Nouns ending in **–ie, –ei, –heit, –keit, –schaft, –ung, –ion, –tät, –ade, –ik, –ur, –unft, –enz** (e.g. **Prüfung** – exam)
- **Neuter:**
  - Words ending in **–lein** or **–chen** (e.g. **Mädchen** – girl)
  - Most words ending in **–um** (e.g. **Museum** – museum)

Plurals

- Words that form their plural by adding **–er** to the end and an Umlaut to the vowel:

Buch	book
Bücher	books

  Other examples: **Wort** – word, **Haus** – house, **Glas** – glass, **Mann** – man, **Rad** – bike, **Land** – country, **Dorf** – village

- Words whose plural is the same as the singular:

Wagen	car
Wagen	cars

  Other examples: **Zimmer** – room, **Fenster** – window, **Computer** – computer, **Schüler** – male pupil, **Pullover** – pullover, **Messer** – knife

- Words that simply add **–e** to the end:

Tisch	table
Tische	tables

  Other examples: **Papier** – paper, **Berg** – mountain, **Hund** – dog, **Tag** – day

- Words that add **–e** to the end and an Umlaut to the vowel:

Stuhl	chair
Stühle	chairs

  Other examples: **Gast** – guest, **Hand** – hand, **Baum** – tree, **Stadt** – town, **Arzt** – doctor

- Words that add **–n**, **–en** or **–nen** to the end:

Lampe   lamp
Lampen   lamps

Other examples: **Uhr** – clock, **Frau** – woman, **Student** – student, **Toilette** – toilet, **Freundin** – female friend

- Most words which end in **–e** add **–n** to form their plural.

- Words that just add an Umlaut:

Vater   father
Väter   fathers

Other examples: **Mutter** – mother, **Bruder** – brother, **Garten** – garden

- Words that just add **–s**:

Auto   car
Autos   cars

Other examples: **Radio** – radio, **Laptop** – laptop, **Handy** – mobile phone, **Restaurant** – restaurant, **Party** – party

- Most of these are words taken from English or other languages.

The Definite Article

- The definite article is the equivalent of 'the' in English. In German, there are four definite articles for the three genders and plural:
  - Masculine: **der Film** – the film
  - Feminine: **die Marmelade** – the jam
  - Neuter: **das Rad** – the bike
  - Plural (used with all genders): **die Hunde** – the dogs

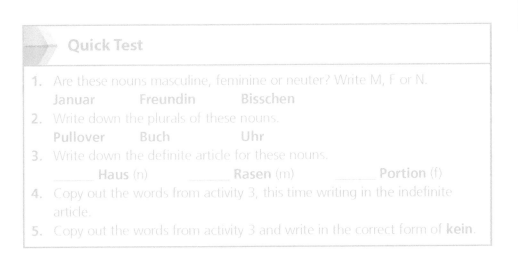

The Indefinite Article

- The indefinite article is the equivalent of the English 'a' or 'an'. There are three indefinite articles in German, two of which are the same:
  - Masculine: **ein Hamburger** – a hamburger
  - Feminine: **eine Tasche** – a bag
  - Neuter: **ein Flugzeug** – an aeroplane

> **Key Point**
>
> The examples here are in the nominative case. Details of the other cases are on the next spread.

> **Key Point**
>
> **kein** (indicating 'not a') follows the same pattern as the indefinite article:
> M: **kein Platz** – no room
> F: **keine Zeit** – no time
> N: **kein Geld** – no money
> Pl: **keine Autos** – no cars

> **Quick Test**
>
> 1. Are these nouns masculine, feminine or neuter? Write M, F or N.
>   Januar   Freundin   Bisschen
> 2. Write down the plurals of these nouns.
>   Pullover   Buch   Uhr
> 3. Write down the definite article for these nouns.
>   _____ Haus (n)   _____ Rasen (m)   _____ Portion (f)
> 4. Copy out the words from activity 3, this time writing in the indefinite article.
> 5. Copy out the words from activity 3 and write in the correct form of **kein**.

Cases

You must be able to:

- Understand subjects, objects and indirect objects
- Understand nominative, accusative, dative and genitive
- Know and use the correct forms for those cases.

Cases

- Cases are a way of showing the function of nouns in a sentence (whether they are the subject or object or have some other function). There are four cases in German: nominative, accusative, dative and genitive.

> **Key Point**
>
> Remember, the subject is the person or thing doing the action. The object is the person or thing having the action done to it.

The Nominative Case

- The subject of the sentence is in the nominative case. These articles accompany a noun when it is the subject:

	Masculine	Feminine	Neuter		Masculine	Feminine	Neuter
the	der	die	das	her / its / their	ihr	ihre	ihr
a / an	ein	eine	ein	our	unser	unsere	unser
this	dieser	diese	dieses	your (familiar pl.)	euer	eure	euer
my	mein	meine	mein	your (polite)	Ihr	Ihre	Ihr
your (familiar sing.)	dein	deine	dein	not a	kein	keine	kein
his / its	sein	seine	sein				

- **Meine Katze**   My cat
- **Unser Haus**   Our house

> **Key Point**
>
> Note that only masculine articles are different in the nominative and accusative.

The Accusative Case

- The object of the sentence is always in the accusative case. Here are the forms of the articles that accompany a noun in the accusative:

	Masculine	Feminine	Neuter		Masculine	Feminine	Neuter
the	den	die	das	her / its / their	ihren	ihre	ihr
a / an	einen	eine	ein	our	unseren	unsere	unser
this	diesen	diese	dieses	your (familiar pl.)	euren	eure	euer
my	meinen	meine	mein	your (polite)	Ihren	Ihre	Ihr
your (familiar sing.)	deinen	deine	dein	not a	keinen	keine	kein
his / its	seinen	seine	sein				

- **Ich mag meinen Bruder.**   I like my brother.
- **Der Mann isst einen Apfel.**   The man eats an apple.

The Dative Case

- The dative case denotes the indirect object. The indirect object is something or someone 'to whom' something is being given, done, said etc.

Subject	Indirect Object	Object
Der Lehrer gibt	**dem Schüler**	**ein Buch.**
The teacher gives	(to) the pupil	a book.

	Masculine	Feminine	Neuter		Masculine	Feminine	Neuter
the	**dem**	**der**	**dem**	her / its / their	**ihrem**	**ihrer**	**ihrem**
a / an	**einem**	**einer**	**einem**	our	**unserem**	**unserer**	**unserem**
this	**diesem**	**dieser**	**diesem**	your (familiar pl.)	**eurem**	**eurer**	**eurem**
my	**meinem**	**meiner**	**meinem**	your (polite)	**Ihrem**	**Ihrer**	**Ihrem**
your (familiar sing.)	**deinem**	**deiner**	**deinem**	not a	**keinem**	**keiner**	**keinem**
his / its	**seinem**	**seiner**	**seinem**				

The Genitive Case

- The genitive case indicates 'possession' of something ('of...').

	Masculine	Feminine	Neuter		Masculine	Feminine	Neuter
the	**des**	**der**	**des**	her / its / their	**ihres**	**ihrer**	**ihres**
a / an	**eines**	**einer**	**eines**	our	**unseres**	**unserer**	**unseres**

- **Das Auto der Lehrerin**.   The car of the teacher / The teacher's car.
- In the masculine and neuter genitive forms, you need to add **–s** or **–es** to the noun.
- **Die Seiten des Buch<u>es</u>**.   The pages of the book / The book's pages.

Quick Test

1. Write down the definite article in the nominative case.
   a) _____ Stadt (f) ist schön.   b) _____ Schnee (m) ist kalt.
   c) _____ Haus (n) ist alt.
2. Write down the indefinite article in the nominative case.
   a) _____ Arzt (m) verdient viel Geld.
   b) _____ Motorrad (n) fährt schnell.
   c) _____ Katze (f) ist niedlich.
3. Write down the definite article in the accusative case.
   a) Hast du _____ Film (m) gesehen?   b) Ich sehe _____ Haus (n).
   c) Ich möchte _____ Schokolade (f).
4. Write down the indefinite article in the accusative case.
   a) Ich habe _____ Katze (f).   b) Ich möchte _____ Hamburger (m).
   c) Papa hat _____ Auto (n).
5. Write in the correct endings to the articles accompanying the indirect object.
   a) Er schenkt sein_____ Lehrer einen Apfel.
   b) Sie schenkt ihr_____ Lehrerin eine Apfelsine.
6. Rewrite three sentences from activities 1–3, using these articles:
   mein–   dies–   dein–   unser–   –ihr

Key Point

You are more likely to need to recognise the genitive than to use it.

Adjectives and Adverbs

You must be able to:

- Understand and use adjectives
- Understand and use comparative and superlative adjectives
- Understand and use adverbs.

Adjectives

Adjectives after the Verb

- When an adjective is placed after a verb, no ending is added:
- **Der Hund ist schwarz.** The dog is black.
- **Die Stadt ist groß.** The town is big.
- **Das Messer ist scharf.** The knife is sharp.

Adjectives before Nouns

- Adjectives before nouns must have endings. The ending depends on:
  - whether the noun is singular or plural
  - what gender the noun is
  - what case the noun is in
  - whether the article is definite or indefinite

Key Point

The genitive is rarely used, so hasn't been included in the adjective endings table.

Key Point

If it is plural, it doesn't matter what gender the noun is.

Key Point

These endings are also used after **dieser** (this), **jener** (that) and **welcher** (which).

Adjective Endings after the Definite Article

	Masculine	Feminine	Neuter	Plural
Nominative	**der schwarze Hund**	**die große Stadt**	**das scharfe Messer**	**die tollen Konzerte**
Accusative	**den schwarzen Hund**	**die große Stadt**	**das scharfe Messer**	**die tollen Konzerte**
Dative	**dem schwarzen Hund**	**der großen Stadt**	**dem scharfen Messer**	**den tollen Konzerten**

Adjective Endings after the Indefinite Article

	Masculine	Feminine	Neuter	Plural
Nominative	**ein schwarzer Hund**	**eine große Stadt**	**ein scharfes Messer**	**tolle Konzerte**
Accusative	**einen schwarzen Hund**	**eine große Stadt**	**ein scharfes Messer**	**tolle Konzerte**
Dative	**einem schwarzen Hund**	**einer großen Stadt**	**einem scharfen Messer**	**tollen Konzerten**

Comparative Adjectives

- Comparative adjectives are used when comparing people and things. In English, you normally add '–er' to the adjective, or say 'more'. In German, simply add **–er** to the adjective to make a comparative adjective:

interessant	interesting	**interessanter**	more interesting
langweilig	boring	**langweiliger**	more boring
modern	modern	**moderner**	more modern

- Many (but not all) short, one-syllable adjectives also add an Umlaut:

alt	old	**älter**	older

- No ending is added when a comparative adjective comes after a verb: **Meine Beine sind länger als meine Ärme.** My legs are longer than my arms.
- When the comparative adjective comes before a noun, the same endings apply as for adjectives with definite and indefinite articles:
  - Masculine: **Der größere Wagen ist ein Mercedes.** The bigger car is a Mercedes.
  - Feminine: **Wir nehmen die breitere Straße.** We take the wider street.
  - Neuter: **Jens hat ein kleineres Haus als Kamil.** Jens has a smaller house than Kamil.

Superlative Adjectives

- In English, you normally just add '–est' to the end of the adjective or say 'most'. In German, you add **–st** or **–est**:

klein	small	**kleinst**	smallest
neu	new	**neuest**	newest

- Superlative adjectives normally come before nouns and have the same endings as adjectives using the definite article:
  - Masculine: **Ich habe den teuersten Pullover.**
    I have the most expensive pullover.
  - Feminine: **Foo Fighters spielen die lauteste Musik.**
    Foo Fighters play the loudest music.
  - Neuter: **Das höchste Gebäude ist der Fernsehturm.**
    The highest building is the TV tower.

Adverbs

- Adverbs are used to describe or explain verbs. In English, we normally add '–ly'. In German, no ending is added: **Er läuft langsam.** He runs slowly.

Comparative Adverbs

- These are the same as comparative adjectives but add no endings:
- **Ich bin früher nach Hause gekommen als meine Schwester.**
  I came home earlier than my sister.

Superlative Adverbs

- These come after the verb and use **am** followed by the adverb with **–sten** on the end:
  Sebastian Vettel fährt am schnellsten. Sebastian Vettel drives fastest.
- Short adverbs with one syllable also add an Umlaut.

Key Point

Use adjective endings listed after these articles:
kein, mein, dein, sein, ihr, unser, euer, Ihr

Key Point

Use the word **als** (than) in a sentence when making a comparison.

Key Point

Comparative exceptions:
gut (good) – **besser** (better), **hoch** (high) – **höher** (higher), **nah** (near) – **näher** (nearer)

Key Point

Superlative exceptions: **gut** (good) – **best** (best), **hoch** (high) – **höchst** (highest) **nah** (near) – **nächst** (nearest)

Quick Test

1. Write down the correct adjective endings when using a definite article.
   a) Nominative: **die schön__ Landschaft** (f)   b) Accusative: **den klein__ Hund** (m)
   c) Dative: **dem alt__ Auto** (n)
2. Write down the correct adjective endings when using an indefinite article.
   a) Nominative: **ein nett__ Mädchen** (n) b) Accusative: **eine lang__ Reise** (f) c) Dative: **einem gut__ Freund** (m)
3. Write down the comparative forms of these adjectives:
   groß   alt   glücklich   gut
4. Write down the superlative forms (no endings required) of these adjectives: **schön   klein   reich   billig**
5. Write down the correct adverb.
   a) **Olli geht _____** (fast).   b) **Priti geht _____** (faster).   c) **Udo geht _____** (fastest).

Prepositions

You must be able to:

- Identify and use prepositions
- Use prepositions with the dative, accusative and genitive
- Know when to use the dative or accusative with dual case prepositions.

Prepositions Followed by the Dative

- The prepositions **aus** – out of, **bei** – at the home of, **nach** – after, **seit** – since, **von** – from, **mit** – with and **zu** – to, are always followed by an article in the dative case.

	the	a	my	her	our	this
Masculine	dem	einem	meinem	ihrem	unserem	diesem
Feminine	der	einer	meiner	ihrer	unserer	dieser
Neuter	dem	einem	meinem	ihrem	unserem	diesem
Plural	den	–	meinen	ihren	unseren	diesen

- **aus dem Haus** — out of the house
- **zur Schule** — to school

Prepositions Followed by the Accusative

- The prepositions **für** – for, **ohne** – without, **gegen** – against, **durch** – through, and **um** – round (also **entlang** – along), are always followed by an article in the accusative case.

	the	a	my	her	our	this
Masculine	den	einen	meinen	ihren	unseren	diesen
Feminine	die	eine	meine	ihre	unsere	diese
Neuter	das	ein	mein	ihr	unser	dieses
Plural	die	–	meine	ihre	unsere	diese

- **um die Ecke** — round the corner
- **durch den Wald** — through the wood

Dual Case Prepositions

- There are prepositions that can be used either with the accusative or the dative. They are **in** – in, **auf** – on, **an** – at, **hinter** – behind, **vor** – in front of, **unter** – under, **über** – over, **zwischen** – between and **neben** – next to.

- They are followed by the accusative when there is movement:
  Die Katze springt auf den Tisch. The cat jumps onto the table.

- They are followed by the dative when there is no movement:
  Die Lampe hängt über dem Tisch. The lamp is hanging over the table.

Key Point

zu dem and zu der are often shortened to **zum** and **zur.** bei dem is usually shortened to **beim.**

Key Point

entlang (along) also takes the accusative but it comes after the noun.

Key Point

in dem (in which) is normally shortened to **im** and **in das** (in that) is normally shortened to **ins.** **an dem** (where) is normally shortened to **am** and **an das** (to the) is normally shortened to **ans.**

Prepositions Followed by the Genitive

- A small number of prepositions are followed by an article in the genitive case. The most common ones are **wegen** (because), **während** (during), **statt** (instead of) and **trotz** (despite).

	the	a	my	her	our	this
Masculine	des	eines	meines	ihres	unseres	dieses
Feminine	der	einer	meiner	ihrer	unserer	dieser
Neuter	des	eines	meines	ihres	unseres	dieses
Plural	den	–	meiner	ihrer	unserer	dieser

- **während der Woche** — during the week
- **trotz des Wetters** — despite the weather

 Key Point

Be extra careful to use the correct case with dual case prepositions, otherwise misunderstandings can occur.

 Key Point

You are more likely to need to recognise genitive prepositions than to use them.

Key Point

Genders need to be learnt. If you don't know the gender, you can't use the prepositions correctly.

Quick Test

1. Choose the correct article in the dative case.
   a) Ich fahre zu dem / das / den Supermarkt (m).
   b) Wir fahren mit diesem / dieser / dieses Schiff (n).
   c) Wir essen bei meinem / meiner / mein Tante (f).
2. Write in the correct endings for these articles in the accusative case.
   a) ohne mein___ Auto (n)
   b) um d___ Kurve (f)
   c) für unser___ Onkel (m)
3. Are these articles in the accusative or dative? Write A (accusative) or D (dative).
   a) in der Stadt
   b) in die Stadt
4. Write in the correct endings for these articles.
   a) Mein Garten ist vor mein___ Haus (n).
   b) Gehst du in d___ Schule (f)?
5. Write in the correct genitive definite articles.
   a) wegen _____ Wetters (n)
   b) während _____ Stunde (f)

Review Questions

My Studies & Life at School

1 **Lies die Meinungen über die Schulfächer. Schreib den Namen ins Kästchen.**
Read the opinions about school subjects. Write the name of the correct person in the table.

Ulrike: Latein fällt mir schwer, aber ich mag dieses Fach, denn es ist nützlich.

Lea: Obwohl der Lehrer sehr nett und hilfsbereit ist, mag ich Geschichte überhaupt nicht.

Simone: Mein Lieblingslehrer ist sehr streng aber auch immer gerecht.

Ava: Ich mag die Schule, deshalb finde ich alle meine Fächer gut. Die Lehrer sind auch nicht schlecht, wenn sie gute Laune haben!

Thomas: Ich hasse Religion, die Lehrerin ist streng und die Stunden sind langweilig.

Katja: Warum muss ich Kunst lernen? Ich bin nicht begabt und es ist zu kompliziert.

Max: Ich liebe Naturwissenschaften, obwohl der Lehrer äußerst langweilig ist!

a) I like the subject but not the teacher. _____
b) I like the teacher but not the subject. _____
c) I don't like having a strict teacher. _____
d) I like having a strict teacher. _____
e) I like the subject even though it's hard. _____
f) I don't like the subject because it's hard. _____ [6 marks]

2 **Lies das Online-Gespräch über Prüfungen. Schreib R, wenn die Aussage richtig ist, F, wenn die Aussage falsch ist, NT, wenn die Aussage nicht im Text ist.** Read the online chat about exams. Write **R** if the statement is correct, **F** if the statement is false and **NT** if the statement is not mentioned.

Franziska: Abdul, hast du dein Zeugnis bekommen? Wie war das? Ich habe mein Zeugnis noch nicht gesehen, aber ich hoffe, dass ich nicht sitzenbleiben muss. Letztes Jahr hatte ich eine Drei in Mathe, was nicht total furchtbar ist, aber meine Eltern waren sehr enttäuscht. Es ist so ein schwieriges Fach!

Abdul: Ja, mein Zeugnis ist gestern gekommen. Glücklicherweise habe ich tolle Noten gekriegt, sogar in der schriftlichen Prüfung in Deutsch! Zum Glück hatte ich keine englische Prüfung! Es gibt so viel Druck heutzutage, alle Prüfungen zu bestehen. Ich verstehe, dass es wichtig ist, aber viele junge Leute werden krank, denn sie sind so gestresst.

a) Franziska hat ihr Zeugnis schon bekommen. _____
b) Franziskas Lehrer sind nicht sehr gut. _____
c) Franziska findet Mathe schwierig. _____
d) Abdul hat keine gute Noten bekommen. _____
e) Abdul hatte eine schriftliche Prüfung in Englisch. _____
f) Abdul findet, dass der Notendruck zu hoch ist. _____ [6 marks]

Education Post-16 & Career Choices and Ambitions

1 **Ergänze die Lücken mit dem richtigen Verb.** Fill in the gaps with the correct verb.

abwählen	reisen	finden	freinehmen	machen
entscheiden	arbeiten	bewerben	studieren	sparen

a) **Nächstes Jahr werde ich das Abitur** _____.

b) **In der Zukunft möchte ich im Ausland** _____.

c) **Ich habe vor, um die Welt zu** _____.

d) **Ich hasse Geschichte, deshalb werde ich dieses Fach** _____.

e) **Nächste Woche will ich mich um einen Teilzeitjob** _____.

f) **Ich plane, auf ein neues Auto zu** _____.

g) **An der Universität habe ich Lust, Deutsch zu** _____.

h) **Bevor ich an die Uni gehe, will ich ein Jahr** _____. [8 marks]

2 **Wähl das richtige Wort.** Choose the correct word.

a) **Ein Vorteil ist, dass der Beruf** _____ [*reisen / stressig / gut bezahlt*] **ist**.

b) **Das Gehalt muss sehr** _____ [*hoch / niedrig / verdienen*] **sein**.

c) **Ich will meine eigene Firma** _____ [*finden / gründen / arbeiten*].

d) **Es ist mir super wichtig, viel** _____ [*Besitzer / Arbeitszeit / Urlaub*] **zu bekommen**.

e) **Ein guter Polizist ist immer** _____ [*berufstätig / geduldig / selbstständig*] **und fleißig**.

f) **Mit einer Arbeit als Kosmetiker würde ich meinen Traum** _____ [*erfüllen / bezahlen / werden*].

g) **Mein Vater ist Hausmann, aber er hat** _____ [*einen Wunsch / einen Termin / eine Halbtagsarbeit*].

h) **Ich liebe meinen Beruf, aber ich mag** _____ [*den Nachteil / die Schichtarbeit / die Werkstatt*] **nicht**. [8 marks]

Gender, Plurals and Articles & Cases

1 **Sind diese Substantive Maskulin, Feminin oder Neutrum? Schreib M, F oder N.**
Are these nouns masculine, feminine or neuter? Write M, F or N.

a) Montag _____   e) Lehrerin _____   i) Polizist _____   m) Freundschaft _____

b) Küche _____   f) Praktikum _____   j) Sängerin _____   n) Fräulein _____

c) Sommer _____   g) Gymnasium _____   k) Zukunft _____   o) Kapitalismus _____

d) Limonade _____   h) Sportler _____   l) Freiheit _____   [15 marks]

2 **Schreib den bestimmten Artikel.** Write in the definite article.

a) _____ Mountainbike (n)   e) _____ Arm (m)   h) _____ Fest (n)

b) _____ Bratwurst (f)   f) _____ Party (f)   i) _____ Leinwand (f)

c) _____ Garten (m)   g) _____ Haus (n)   j) _____ Computer (m)

d) _____ Banane (f)   [10 marks]

3 **Kopiere die Wörter aus Übung 2 und schreib diesmal den unbestimmten Artikel.**
Copy out the words from activity 2, this time writing in the indefinite article.

[10 marks]

4 **Wähle fünf Wörter aus Übung 2 und schreib die richtige Form von kein.**
Choose five words from activity 2 and write in the correct form of **kein**.

[5 marks]

5 **Schreib den richtigen unbestimmten Artikel im Nominativ.**
Write the correct indefinite article in the nominative case.

a) _____ Baby (n) ist klein.

b) _____ Kirsche (f) ist rot.

c) _____ Einzelzimmer (n) ist klein.

d) _____ Katze (f) ist niedlich.

e) _____ Betriebspraktikum (n) dauert 6 Wochen.

f) _____ Horrorfilm (m) macht mir Angst.

g) _____ Erdbeertorte (f) schmeckt gut.

h) _____ Motorrad (n) kostet viel Geld.

i) _____ Scheibe Wurst (f) ist auf dem Teller.

j) _____ Zahnarzt (m) verdient viel Geld.   [10 marks]

Adjectives and Adverbs & Prepositions

1 **Schreib die richtigen Adjektiv-Endungen (bestimmter Artikel).**
Write in the correct adjective endings (definite article).

a) Nominative: **die schmutzig__ Umwelt** (f)   f) Dative: **dem scharf__ Messer** (n)

b) Accusative: **den nett__ Jungen** (m)   g) Nominative: **das lecker__ Eis** (n)

c) Dative: **dem alt__ Auto** (n)   h) Accusative: **den unfreundlich__ Kellner** (m)

d) Nominative: **der bitter__ Apfel** (m)   i) Dative: **der intelligent__ Schülerin** (f)

e) Accusative: **die blöd__ Werbung** (f)

[9 marks]

2 **Schreib die Komparativ-Formen.** Write the comparative forms.

a) **dick**   c) **kalt**   e) **hübsch**   g) **jung**   i) **schön**

b) **stark**   d) **groß**   f) **neu**   h) **interessant**   j) **langweilig**

[10 marks]

3 **Wähle den richtigen Artikel in der Dativ-Form nach einer Präposition.**
Choose the correct article in the dative form used after a preposition.

a) **Wir treffen uns nach der / dem / das Essen** (n).   d) **Wir fahren mit dem / der / den Bus** (m).

b) **Ich stehe vor der / dem / die Schule** (f).   e) **Ich bin seit den / die / der Party** (f) **krank**.

c) **Kommst du zum / zur Jugendklub** (m)?   f) **Er kommt aus das /den / dem Haus** (n).

[6 marks]

4 **Präpositionen mit Akkusativ oder Dativ. Schreib A (Akkusativ) oder D (Dativ).**
Prepositions with the accusative or dative. Write A (accusative) or D (dative).

a) **ins Rathaus** ___   d) **unter den Tisch** ___   g) **vor das Auto** ___

b) **im Rathaus** ___   e) **auf dem Berg** ___   h) **vor dem Auto** ___

c) **unter dem Tisch** ___   f) **auf den Berg** ___

[8 marks]

5 **Schreib die richtigen Endungen für diese Possessivpronomen oder Artikel nach Präpositionen.**
Write in the correct endings for these possessive pronouns or articles after prepositions.

a) **Mein Garten ist vor mein___ Haus** (n).

b) **Deine Schuhe liegen hinter dies___ Tür** (f).

c) **Gehst du in d___ Schule** (f)?

d) **Wir gehen in ein___ Park** (m).

[4 marks]

Pronouns

You must be able to:

- Use personal pronouns in the nominative, accusative and dative
- Use appropriate forms of address
- Use reflexive, relative and indefinite pronouns.

Personal Pronouns

- A pronoun is a word used instead of a noun.

Nominative Pronouns (Subject)

- These personal pronouns replace nouns when they are the subject of a sentence:

Singular – German	Singular – English
ich	I
du	you
er	he
sie	she
es	it

Plural – German	Plural – English
wir	we
ihr	you
sie	they
Sie	you (formal)

- **Sie spielt gern Tennis.**   She likes playing tennis.
- **Kannst du gut singen?**   Can you sing well?

Accusative Pronouns (Object and after Certain Prepositions)

- These personal pronouns replace nouns when they are the object of a sentence:

Singular – German	Singular – English
mich	me
dich	you
ihn	him
sie	her
es	it

Plural – German	Plural – English
uns	us
euch	you
sie	them
Sie	you (formal)

- **Ich liebe sie.**   I love her.   •   **Liebst du mich?**   Do you love me?

Dative Pronouns (Indirect Object and after Certain Prepositions)

- These personal pronouns replace nouns when they are the indirect object of a sentence:

Singular – German	Singular – English
mir	to me
dir	to you
ihm	to him
ihr	to her
ihm	to it

Plural – German	Plural – English
uns	to us
euch	to you
ihnen	to them
Ihnen	to you (formal)

- **Lukas hat <u>mir</u> ein Geschenk gegeben.**   Lukas gave me a present.
- **Wie geht es <u>Ihnen</u>?**   How are you?

'man'

- **man** is very commonly used as a way of saying 'one' or 'you' non-specifically.
- **Man kann hier parken.**   You can park here. / One can park here.
- **Was sieht man in Berlin?**   What do you / What does one see in Berlin?

Forms of Address

- German has three ways to say 'you':
  - **du / dich / dir** is for a person you know well.
  - **ihr / euch / euch** is for two or more people you know well.
  - **Sie / Sie / Ihnen** is the formal mode of address, for people you don't know well.
- Informal: **Ich sehe dich.**   I see you.
- Informal, plural: **Wo seid ihr?**   Where are you?
- Formal: **Kommen Sie herein.**   Come in.

Reflexive Pronouns

- Reflexive pronouns form part of reflexive verbs, referring to 'oneself'. These pronouns are explained in the section on reflexive verbs (page 94).
- **Er zieht sich an.**   He gets dressed.

Indefinite Pronouns

- Indefinite pronouns are used when making generalisations rather than being specific about particular people or things.

niemand	nobody
alle	all / everybody
etwas	something
jemand	somebody
andere	others

- **Niemand ist gekommen.**   Nobody came.
- **Möchtest du etwas?**   Would you like something?

> **Key Point**
>
> Remember that there are three different meanings of the word **sie**:
> **sie** – she / her
> **sie** – they / them
> **Sie** – you (formal)

Relative Pronouns

- Relative pronouns are used to make relative clauses.
- **Der Mann, *den ich gesehen habe*, war krank.**   The man *(whom) I saw* was ill.

- **Der Filmstar, *dessen Namen ich vergessen habe*, ...** The film star, *whose name I have forgotten*, ...

> **Key Point**
>
> In English, relative pronouns are words such as who, which, whose, whom, that, etc.

Quick Test

1. Write the German nominative pronoun: we   you (one friend)   'one'
2. Choose the correct accusative pronoun.
   a) **Der Pullover ist schön. Ich kaufe ihn / er.**   b) **Ich habe dich / dir nicht gesehen.**
3. Fill in the blanks with dative pronouns.
   a) **Kommst du mit _____ (me)?**   b) **Ich gebe _____ (him) Geld.**
4. Fill in the blanks with the indefinite pronouns.
   a) **Wer ist da? _____ (nobody)**   b) **_____ (something) hat mich schockiert.**

Present Tense Verbs 1

You must be able to:

- Use regular verbs in the present tense
- Recognise and use reflexive verbs
- Recognise and use separable verbs.

Regular Verbs in the Present Tense

- To form the present tense of regular verbs, take the 'stem' from the infinitive and add these endings:

> **Key Point**
>
> In English, verbs hardly change: I play, you play, we play. In German, the endings vary and are essential.

Pronoun	Stem	Ending	Present Tense	Meaning
ich	mach–	–e	ich mache	I do
du	mach–	–st	du machst	you do
er / sie / es	mach–	–t	er macht	he does
wir	mach–	–en	wir machen	we do
ihr	mach–	–t	ihr macht	you do
sie / Sie	mach–	–en	sie / Sie machen	they / you do

- Here are some verbs that are regular in the present tense: **spielen** – to play, **gehen** – to go, **kommen** – to come, **machen** – to do, **fliegen** – to fly, **bleiben** – to stay
- **Ich mache meine Hausaufgaben.**   I do my homework.
- **Wir spielen oft Handball.**   We often play handball.

Reflexive Verbs in the Present Tense

- In German, you have to say 'I wash myself' or 'I shave myself' (rather than just 'I wash' or 'I shave'). This is called a reflexive verb. The word for 'myself', 'yourself', 'herself' etc. comes after the verb.

> **Key Point**
>
> Other important reflexive verbs: **sich freuen** – to be happy, **sich amüsieren** – to enjoy oneself, **sich entscheiden** – to decide.

English	Infinitive	Present Tense	Meaning
to wash	**sich waschen**	**ich wasche mich**	I wash
to shave	**sich rasieren**	**du rasierst dich**	you shave
to hurt oneself	**sich verletzen**	**er verletzt sich**	he hurts himself
to meet	**sich treffen**	**wir treffen uns**	we meet
to sit down	**sich hinsetzen**	**ihr setzt euch hin**	you sit down
to be happy	**sich freuen**	**sie freuen sich**	they are happy

- **Ich rasiere mich jeden Tag.**   I shave every day.
- **Er zieht sich jetzt an.**   He's getting dressed now.

Separable Verbs

- Separable verbs consist of two parts: a prefix and the verb.
- When in the infinitive, the two parts are together, but in most other forms, the prefix is separate and comes at the end of the sentence.

English	Infinitive	Present Tense	Meaning
to get up	**aufstehen**	**ich stehe …auf**	I get up …
to watch TV	**fernsehen**	**wir sehen …fern**	we watch TV …
to arrive	**ankommen**	**wann kommt er an?**	when does he arrive?
to get off (a bus / train)	**aussteigen**	**wir steigen …aus**	we get off …
to start	**anfangen**	**der Film fängt …an**	the film starts …
to put on (clothes)	**anziehen**	**sie zieht …an**	she put on …
to come with	**mitkommen**	**kommst du mit?**	are you coming?

- **Wann kommt der Zug an?**   When does the train arrive?
- **Reva steht um 7 Uhr auf.**   Reva gets up at 7 o'clock.

Present Tense of Inseparable Verbs

- Verbs can be formed by adding a prefix to an existing verb:

suchen – to look for	→	**besuchen** – to visit
fallen – to fall	→	**gefallen** – to please
stehen – to stand	→	**verstehen** – to understand

- **Ich verstehe nicht.**   I don't understand.
- **Wir besuchen unsere Freunde.**   We visit our friends.
- **Das gefällt mir nicht.**   I don't like it.

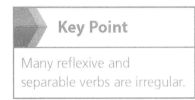

Key Point

Many reflexive and separable verbs are irregular.

Key Point

It is important to use the correct prefix:
ausgehen – to go out
hereinkommen – to come in

Quick Test

1. Write in the correct present tense endings of these regular verbs.
   a) du spiel__
   b) wir mach__
   c) er bleib__
2. Write in the correct reflexive pronoun.
   a) Wir setzen _____ hin.
   b) Mika verletzt _____ oft.
3. Choose the correct separable pronoun.
   a) Wo steigen wir _____ (out)? **(aussteigen)**
   b) Wir stehen früh _____ (up). **(aufstehen)**
4. Translate into German:
   we visit _____ it pleases me _____ I understand

Present Tense Verbs 2

You must be able to:

- Use irregular verbs in the present tense
- Use modal verbs in the present tense
- Use infinitive constructions and impersonal verbs.

Irregular Verbs in the Present Tense

- With irregular verbs in the present tense, the stem changes in the **du** and **er** forms.

Pronoun	Infinitive	Ending	Present Tense	Meaning
ich	essen	–e	ich esse	I eat
du	essen	–st	du isst	you eat
er / sie / es	essen	–t	er isst	he eats
wir	essen	–en	wir essen	we eat
ihr	essen	–t	ihr esst	you eat
sie / Sie	essen	–en	sie / Sie essen	they / you eat

- Other irregular verbs in the present tense include:

fahren (to drive)	**du fährst** (you drive)	**er fährt** (he drives)
lesen (to read)	**du liest** (you read)	**er liest** (he reads)
laufen (to run)	**du läufst** (you run)	**er läuft** (he runs)
treffen (to meet)	**du triffst** (you meet)	**er trifft** (he meets)
nehmen (to take)	**du nimmst** (you take)	**er nimmt** (he takes)

- **Sie fährt nach Köln.**   She drives to Cologne.
- **Liest du gern?**   Do you like reading?

Modal Verbs in the Present Tense

- Modal verbs are always used with the infinitive of another verb at the end of the sentence.
- Some modal verbs include:

Pronoun	können (to be able to)	wollen (to want to)	müssen (to have to / must)
ich	kann	will	muss
du	kannst	willst	musst
er / sie / es	kann	will	muss
wir	können	wollen	müssen
ihr	könnt	wollt	müsst
sie / Sie	können	wollen	müssen

Pronoun	dürfen (to be allowed to)	mögen (to like)	sollen (should)
ich	darf	mag	soll
du	darfst	magst	sollst
er / sie / es	darf	mag	soll
wir	dürfen	mögen	sollen
ihr	dürft	mögt	sollt
sie / Sie	dürfen	mögen	sollen

- **Ich muss in die Stadt gehen.** — I have to go into town.
- **Natalia kann gut zeichnen.** — Natalia can draw well.
- **Wir wollen zu Hause bleiben.** — We want to stay at home.
- **Du darfst hier nicht parken.** — You're not allowed to park here.

Infinitive Constructions

- The most common infinitive construction is **um… zu…** (in order to…). This is used to link two clauses, in this way:
- **Wir gehen ins Café, <u>um</u> Kuchen <u>zu</u> essen.**
  We're going to the café (in order) to eat cake.
  Ich lerne Deutsch, <u>um</u> mit deutschen Freunden <u>zu</u> chatten.
  I'm learning German (in order) to chat with German friends.

Impersonal Verbs in the Present Tense

- These are verbs that don't have a conventional subject:
  es regnet — it's raining
  es stinkt — it stinks
  es geht — it's okay
- By far the most important impersonal verb, used very frequently, is
  es gibt… — there is…

- **Es gibt nichts zu essen.** — There's nothing to eat.
- **Es gibt einen guten Film im Fernsehen.** — There's a good film on TV.
- **Es gibt ein schönes Schloss in Cochem.** — There's a nice castle in Cochem.

Key Point

es gibt is followed by the accusative.

Quick Test

1. Fill in the blanks with irregular verbs in the present tense.
   a) Was _____ (nehmen) du?
   b) Ahmed _____ (lesen) die Zeitung.
2. Choose the correct modal verbs.
   a) they must: **sie wollen / müssen / dürfen**
   b) do you like? **musst / darfst / magst du?**
3. Insert the appropriate words to complete these infinitive constructions.
   a) Ich gehe ins Kino, ____ einen Film ____ sehen.
   b) Wir gehen zum Supermarkt, ____ Brot ____ kaufen.
4. Translate:
   a) There is a café in town.
   b) There is a lot to do. (**viel** = a lot, **zu tun** = to do)

Perfect Tense Verbs

You must be able to:

- Recognise and use the perfect tense
- Know how to use the verb 'haben' in the perfect
- Know how to use the verb 'sein' in the perfect.

Perfect Tense

- The perfect tense is the most common way of talking about the past.
- It is formed using: the subject + auxiliary verb + past participle.
- There are two auxiliary verbs – **haben** and **sein**.

Perfect Tense with 'haben'

- To form the perfect tense with the verb 'haben' (to have), use the correct form of **haben** plus the past participle at the end.

ich habe	**wir haben**
du hast	**ihr habt**
er / sie / es hat	**sie / Sie haben**

Regular Past Participles	Meaning	Irregular Past Participles	Meaning
gefragt	asked	**getrunken**	drunk
gespielt	played	**gegessen**	eaten
gesagt	said	**gegeben**	given
gemacht	done	**gelesen**	read
gehört	heard	**geschlafen**	slept
gekauft	bought	**geschrieben**	written
gekostet	cost	**gesehen**	seen
geantwortet	answered	**gefunden**	found

- **Wir haben gut gespielt.** — We (have) played well.
- **Das Essen hat viel gekostet.** — The meal (has) cost a lot.

Perfect Tense with 'sein'

- To form the perfect tense with the verb 'sein' (to be), use the correct form of **sein** plus the past participle at the end.

ich bin	**wir sind**
du bist	**ihr seid**
er / sie / es ist	**sie / Sie sind**

Past Participles	Meaning	Past Participles	Meaning
gegangen	gone / walked	**gelaufen**	run
gefahren	driven / travelled	**geklettert**	climbed
gekommen	come	**gestorben**	died
geblieben	stayed	**geworden**	become
geflogen	flown	**gewesen**	been

> **Key Point**
>
> **haben** and **sein**, when used in the perfect tense, are known as auxiliary verbs (in German, **Hilfsverb** – helping verb).

> **Key Point**
>
> Most **sein** verbs are verbs of motion or movement. The main exceptions are **bleiben** (to remain / stay) and **sein** (to be).

- **Ich bin nicht lang geblieben.** I didn't stay long.
- **Sascha ist zum Arzt gegangen.** Sascha went to the doctor.

Reflexive Verbs in the Perfect Tense

- When using a reflexive verb in the perfect tense, put the reflexive pronoun straight after the auxiliary verb (**haben**).
- Present: **Ich wasche mich.** I wash (myself).
  Perfect: **Ich habe mich gewaschen.** I washed (myself).
- Present: **Wir treffen uns.** We meet (each other).
  Perfect: **Wir haben uns getroffen.** We met (each other).

Separable Verbs in the Perfect Tense

- To form the perfect tense of a separable verb, make the past participle by putting the separable prefix before the **ge–**.

English	Infinitive	Past Participle
to wash up	abwaschen	abgewaschen
to shop	einkaufen	eingekauft
to arrive	ankommen	angekommen
to tidy up	aufräumen	aufgeräumt

- **Ich komme um 18 Uhr zurück.** I'll come back at 6 o'clock.
- **Ich bin um 18 Uhr zurückgekommen.** I came back at 6 o'clock.
- **Wir räumen jeden Tag auf.** We tidy up every day.
- **Wir haben jeden Tag aufgeräumt.** We tidied up every day.

Separable and Reflexive Verbs in the Perfect Tense

- A small number of verbs are both separable and reflexive.
- **sich anziehen** to get dressed
  sich hinsetzen to sit down
  sich aufregen to get excited

- **Er hat sich schnell angezogen.** He got dressed quickly.
- **Die Großeltern haben sich hingesetzt.** The grandparents sat down.
- **Die Kinder haben sich aufgeregt.** The children got excited.

> **Key Point**
>
> For a list of the most common reflexive verbs, see page 94.

> **Key Point**
>
> All reflexive verbs take **haben** in the perfect tense.

> **Key Point**
>
> Some prefixes are inseparable (for example **ver-**) and do not add a **ge-** in their past participle, e.g.
> **ich verstehe** I understand
> **ich habe verstanden** I understood

Quick Test

1. Write the correct past participles of these **haben** verbs: **finden   spielen**
2. Fill in the correct part of **haben** and the past participle.
   a) _____ du dieses Buch _____? (lesen)
   b) Wer _____ meinen Geldbeutel _____? (nehmen)
3. Write the correct past participle of these **sein** verbs: **fahren   gehen**
4. Fill in the correct part of **sein** and the past participle.
   a) Ich _____ eine halbe Stunde_____. (bleiben) b) Wir _____ nie in Köln _____. (sein)
5. Write the correct reflexive pronoun and past participle.
   a) Die Kinder haben _____. (treffen) b) Ich habe _____. (waschen)
6. Write the correct past participle.
   a) Hast du _____ (abwaschen)? b) Wann seid ihr _____ (ankommen)?

Imperfect Tense Verbs (Simple Past)

You must be able to:

- Recognise and use the imperfect tense
- Know how to use regular verbs in the imperfect
- Know how to use irregular verbs in the imperfect.

The Imperfect Tense

- The imperfect tense is the simple past tense in German.
- It is most frequently used in written German (stories, newspaper articles etc).

Regular Verbs in the Imperfect Tense

- Regular verbs take the stem from the infinitive and add these endings:

Pronoun	Stem	Ending	Imperfect Tense	Meaning
ich	wohn–	–te	ich wohnte	I lived
du	wohn–	–test	du wohntest	you lived
er / sie / es	wohn–	–te	er wohnte	he lived
wir	wohn–	–ten	wir wohnten	we lived
ihr	wohn–	–tet	ihr wohntet	they lived
sie / Sie	wohn–	–ten	sie / Sie wohnten	they / you lived

- Other regular verbs: **kaufen** (to buy), **hören** (to hear), **lernen** (to learn), **kochen** (to cook), **spielen** (to play), **fragen** (to ask), **sagen** (to say), **machen** (to make)

- **Die Schüler lernten Mathe.**   The pupils learned maths.
- **Die Familie wohnte in Leipzig.**   The family lived in Leipzig.

Irregular Verbs in the Imperfect Tense

- Irregular verbs have different stems, which need to be learned.
- The endings are different from regular verbs.
- Example: **sein** (to be)

Pronoun	Stem	Ending	Imperfect Tense	Meaning
ich	war–	–	ich war	I was
du	war–	–st	du warst	you were
er / sie / es	war–	–	er war	he / she / it was
wir	war–	–en	wir waren	we were
ihr	war–	–t	ihr wart	you were
sie / Sie	war–	–en	sie / Sie waren	they / you were

> **Key Point**
>
> If the stem already ends in –t, add an extra –e after the –t: arbeiten – ich arbeitete (I worked).

- Irregular verbs:

beginnen – ich begann	to begin – I began	**finden – ich fand**	to find – I found
fahren – ich fuhr	to go – I went	**gehen – ich ging**	to go – I went
kommen – ich kam	to come – I came	**sein – ich war**	to be – I was
lesen – ich las	to read – I read	**singen – ich sang**	to sing – I sang
nehmen – ich nahm	to take – I took	**sprechen – ich sprach**	to speak – I spoke
schlafen – ich schlief	to sleep – I slept	**trinken – ich trank**	to drink – I drank
sehen – ich sah	to see – I saw		

- **Das Konzert begann um 20 Uhr.**   The concert began at 8 o'clock.
- **Die Politiker fuhren nach Washington.** The politicians drove to Washington.

'es gab'

- Remember **es gibt…**, meaning 'there is…'? It is an extremely common expression, often also used in the imperfect: **es gab ….** It is only used in the singular and is followed by the accusative.
- **Es gab viele Fische im Fluss.**   There were lots of fish in the river.
- **Es gab ein schönes Museum in**   There was a nice museum in
  Frankfurt.   Frankfurt.

Modal Verbs in the Imperfect Tense

- Here are the imperfect forms of the most common modal verbs:

Pronoun	können (to be able to)	wollen (to want to)	müssen (to have to / must)
ich	konnte	wollte	musste
du	konntest	wolltest	musstest
er / sie / es	konnte	wollte	musste
wir	konnten	wollten	mussten
ihr	konntet	wolltet	musstet
sie / Sie	konnten	wollten	mussten

Pronoun	dürfen (to be allowed to)	mögen (to like)	sollen (should)
ich	durfte	mochte	sollte
du	durftest	mochtest	solltest
er / sie / es	durfte	mochte	sollte
wir	durften	mochten	sollten
ihr	durftet	mochtet	solltet
sie / Sie	durften	mochten	sollten

Key Point

When using a modal verb in the past, always use the imperfect, not the perfect.

- **Wir durften nicht ausgehen.**   We weren't allowed to go out.
- **Ich konnte nicht atmen.**   I couldn't breathe.

Quick Test

1. Change these regular present tense verbs into the imperfect tense.
   a) **wir hören**   b) **er spielt**
2. Fill in the gaps with irregular verbs in the imperfect tense.
   a) **Er _____ (sprechen) laut.**   b) **Wir _____ (stehen) vor der Kirche.**
3. Choose the correct imperfect modal verb form.
   a) **Ich mochte / mag die Musik gern.**   b) **Wir wollen / wollten schwimmen gehen.**

Future Time Frame

You must be able to:

- Use the present tense to talk about the future
- Recognise and use the future tense
- Recognise and use the conditional tense.

Present Tense as Future

- In German, the present tense is often used to talk about the future. English often does the same.

- **Ich spiele morgen Golf.**
  I'm playing golf tomorrow.
- **Wir fahren nächste Woche nach Zürich.**
  We're travelling to Zürich next week.

The Future Tense

- The official future tense is formed by the present tense of the verb **werden**, plus the infinitive at the end of the sentence.

ich werde	I will
du wirst	you will
er / sie / es wird	he / she / it will
wir werden	we will
ihr werdet	they will
sie / Sie werden	they / you will

- **Ich werde morgen meine Oma besuchen.** — I will visit my granny tomorrow.
- **Morgen werde ich einkaufen.** — Tomorrow I will go shopping.

Key Point

A future expression of time is often used with the present to make it clear that the future is being talked about:
morgen – tomorrow
am nächsten Mittwoch – next Wednesday
bald – soon

Key Point

Remember that the verb always comes second in a sentence.

The Conditional with 'wenn'

- **wenn** means 'if' and is used with the conditional.
- It is combined with the conditional form of **haben** or **sein**, plus **würde**…

- **Wenn ich…, würde ich…**   If I…, I would…
  (+ infinitive at the end)

Pronoun	(if I) were…	(if I) had…	(I) would…
ich	wäre	hätte	würde
du	wär(e)st	hättest	würdest
er / sie / es	wäre	hätte	würde
wir	wären	hätten	würden
ihr	wär(e)t	hättet	würdet
sie / Sie	wären	hätten	würden

- **Wenn ich viel Geld hätte, würde ich ein Auto kaufen.**
  If I had a lot of money, I would buy a car.
- **Wenn es nicht so laut ware, würde ich besser hören.**
  If it wasn't so noisy, I would hear better.

Pluperfect Tense, Subjunctive Mood and Imperatives

You must be able to:

- Recognise and use the pluperfect tense
- Be aware of the subjunctive mood
- Recognise and use the imperative.

HT▸ Pluperfect Tense

- The pluperfect tense is used to describe something that <u>had</u> happened in the past, i.e. further in the past than past tense.
- It is formed by using the imperfect of **haben** or **sein**, plus the past participle at the end.
- It is often used with **nachdem** (after):
- **Nachdem wir den Film gesehen hatten, sind wir nach Hause gegangen.**
  After we had seen the film, we went home.

Key Point

You will probably need to recognise the pluperfect more often than use it.

Pronoun	Imperfect of haben	Imperfect of sein
ich	hatte	war
du	hattest	warst
er / sie / es	hatte	war
wir	hatten	waren
ihr	hattet	wart
sie / Sie	hatten	waren

- **Ich <u>hatte</u> schon meine Hausaufgaben <u>gemacht</u>, als ich Abendbrot gegessen habe.**
  I <u>had</u> already done my homework when I ate dinner.
- **Meine Freunde <u>waren</u> schon nach Berlin <u>gefahren</u>, bevor sie nach Potsdam gefahren sind.**
  My friends <u>had</u> already driven to Berlin before they drove to Potsdam.

HT Subjunctive Mood

- The subjunctive mood is an advanced piece of grammar that you need to recognise more than use. It is a form of the conditional.

• **hätte**	would have
• **wäre**	would be
• **würde**	would
• **könnte**	could (would be able)

- **Wir wären traurig gewesen**. We would have been sad.
- **Ich hätte kein Fleisch gekauft.** I wouldn't have bought any meat.
- **Er würde nicht ins Theater gehen.** He wouldn't go to the theatre.
- **Könntest du mir bitte helfen?** Could you help me please?

HT Imperative

- The imperative form is used to give orders or instructions (tell someone what to do).
- As there are three words for 'you' in German, there are three ways of forming the imperative.

- **du** form: Take the **–st** off the **du** form of the verb and drop the **du**:
  du stehst auf.
  Imperative: **Steh auf!** Stand up!

- **ihr** form: Just drop the **ihr**:
  ihr steht auf.
  Imperative: **Steht auf!** Stand up!

- **Sie** form: Swap the verb and the **Sie**:
  Sie stehen auf.
  Imperative: **Stehen Sie auf**! Stand up!

> ### Key Point
> You are already using the subjunctive mood whenever you say **Ich möchte...**
> (I would like…).

> ### Key Point
> An exception is the verb **sein** (to be):
>
> **Sei ruhig! Seid ruhig!**
> **Seien Sie ruhig!** Be quiet!

Quick Test

1. Insert the correct pluperfect form.
   a) Wir sind ins Bett gegangen, nachdem wir gegessen _____.
   b) Er _____ krank gewesen.
2. Use the imperative to tell someone to do these things:
   a) Take the first road. (to a stranger)
   b) Go straight on. (to a friend)
3. Choose the correct word to make subjunctive constructions.
   a) _____ (wären / möchtet) ihr mitkommen?
   b) Wir _____ (wären / möchtet) nicht geblieben.

> ### Key Point
> Watch out for irregular verbs: **du nimmst...**
> Imperative: **Nimm...!**

Word Order and Conjunctions

You must be able to:

- Put words in the right order in German sentences
- Ask questions correctly
- Use subordinating conjunctions.

Simple Word Order

- Simple word order in German is the same as in English:

Subject	Verb	Object
Mein Bruder	**hat**	**einen Computer.**
My brother	has	a computer.

The Verb as 'second idea'

- Verbs in German, including auxiliary and modal verbs, <u>always</u> come second in the sentence.

- **Wir <u>sind</u> letzten Sommer nach Frankreich gefahren.**
  We went to France last summer.
- **Letzten Sommer <u>sind</u> wir nach Frankreich gefahren.**
  Last summer we went to France.
- **Markus <u>besucht</u> seine Oma am Wochenende.**
  Markus visits his granny at the weekend.
- **Am Wochenende <u>besucht</u> Markus seine Oma.**
  At the weekend Markus visits his granny.

> **Key Point**
>
> Remember the letters TMP (Time, Manner, Place). Then you won't go wrong with the word order.

Time – Manner – Place

- In German, you must always put <u>when</u> you do something (Time) before <u>how</u> you do it (Manner) before <u>where</u> you do it (Place).

- **Ich fahre am Dienstag** (T) **mit dem Rad** (M) **in die Stadt** (P).
  I'm going into town by bike on Tuesday.
- **Wir haben am Wochenende** (T) **mit den Kindern** (M) **im Garten** (P) **gespielt.**
  We played with the children in the garden at the weekend.

Word Order in Questions

Questions with Question Words

- The verb comes straight after the question word.

wer?	who?	**wohin?**	where to?
wo?	where?	**woher?**	where from?
wann?	when?	**warum?**	why?
wie?	how?	**wie viel?**	how much?
was?	what?	**was für?**	what kind of?

- **Was hat sie gesagt?**   What did she say?
- **Wo ist mein Handy?**   Where is my mobile phone?

> **Key Point**
>
> Don't be deceived into thinking that **wer?** means 'where?'; it means 'who?'.

Questions with no Question Words

- When there is no question word, the verb comes first.

- **War der Film gut?** Was the film good?
- **Hat er gewonnen?** Did he win?

Word Order with Conjunctions

- Several conjunctions have no effect on the word order.
- They include **aber** (but), **oder** (or), **denn** (because) and **und** (and).
- **Marta geht in die Stadt <u>und</u> sie kauft ein Geschenk.**
  Marta goes to town <u>and</u> she buys a gift.
- **Marta geht in die Stadt, <u>aber</u> sie kauft kein Geschenk.**
  Marta goes to town <u>but</u> she doesn't buy a gift.

Conjunctions 'weil', 'wenn' and 'als'

- The most common subordinating conjunctions are **weil** (because), **wenn** (if / whenever), **als** (when - talking about the past) and **obwohl** (although). They always send the verb to the end.
- **Ich bin müde, weil ich nicht geschlafen habe.**
  I am tired because I haven't slept.
- **Wir schwimmen im Freibad, wenn das Wetter gut ist.**
  We swim in the open-air pool if the weather is good.
- **Karla geht oft einkaufen, obwohl sie kein Geld hat.**
  Karla often goes shopping although she hasn't got any money.

HT **Other Subordinating Conjunctions**

dass	that	**bevor**	before
damit	so that	**nachdem**	after
ob	whether		

- **Ich glaube, dass Lady Gaga gut singt.**
  I think that Lady Gaga sings well.
- **Ich habe einen Ball gekauft, damit ich Fußball spielen kann.**
  I have bought a ball so that I can play football.
- **Ich weiß nicht, ob ich morgen kommen kann.**
  I don't know whether I can come tomorrow.

> **Key Point**
>
> **als** and **wenn** both mean <u>when</u>, but **als** refers to the past and **wenn** refers to the present or future.

> **Key Point**
>
> Always put a comma before **weil** and **wenn** and all other subordinating and most coordinating conjunctions.

> **Key Point**
>
> Remember that **dass** (the connective) has a double 's', whereas **das** (meaning <u>the</u>) only has one 's'.

 Quick Test

1. Unjumble the words into the correct order. Start with the underlined word.
   a) <u>Wir</u> gut in Frankreich essen immer
   b) <u>Ich</u> in einem Geschäft arbeite jeden Tag
2. Put these words in the correct order to form questions.
   a) beginnt / der / Film / Wann?
   b) das / Wer / gesagt / hat?
3. Insert the right conjunction.
   a) Ich weiß, _____ (that) du hier bist.
   b) Wir essen Kuchen, _____ (but) er ist nicht gut.

Gender, Plurals and Articles & Cases

1 **Sind diese Substantive Singular oder Plural? Schreib S, wenn das Substantiv singular ist, P wenn es Plural ist oder E, wenn es Singular oder Plural sein könnte.** Are these nouns singular or plural? Write S if the noun is singular, P if it is plural or E if it could be either.

a) **Handy**   d) **Häuser**   g) **Kino**   j) **Computer**   m) **Männer**

b) **Tische**   e) **Autos**   h) **Mann**   k) **Wagen**   n) **Zimmer**

c) **Bilder**   f) **Supermarkt**   i) **Umwelt**   l) **Bücher**   o) **Schule**   [15 marks]

2 **Vervollständige diese Sätze mit <u>der</u>, <u>die</u> oder <u>das</u> (Artikel im Nominativ).**
Complete these sentences with **der**, **die** or **das** (articles in the Nominative).

a) _____ **Film ist langweilig.** (m)

b) _____ **Bank ist geschlossen.** (f)

c) _____ **Bus fährt schnell.** (m)

d) _____ **Laptop ist kaputt**. (m)

e) _____**Haus ist teuer**. (n)

f) _____ **Schülerin heißt Doris**. (f)   [6 marks]

3 **Zeichne eine gerade Linie unter dem Subjekt, eine gewellte Linie unter dem Objekt und eine gepunktete Linie unter dem indirekten Objekt in diesen Sätzen.** Put a straight line under the subject, a wiggly line under the object and a dotted line under the indirect object in these sentences.

a) **Ich schenke meiner Mutter Pralinen.**

b) **Du schreibst deinem Onkel einen Brief.**

c) **Die Tante hat ihrer Nichte ein Geschenk gegeben.**

d) **Ich habe dieser Organisation Geld gegeben.**

[12 marks: 1 mark for correct subject, 1 mark for each object and 1 mark for each indirect object]

HT **4** **Übersetze diese Sätze ins Deutsche.** Translate these sentences into German.

a) We have three chairs.   d) Have you forgotten your laptop?

b) I've lost my brother.   e) Our car is old.

c) I give my uncle a present.   f) We work in our office.   [6 marks]

Adjectives and Adverbs & Prepositions

1 **Füll die Lücken mit den Adjektiven mit den richtigen Endungen.**
Fill the gaps with the adjectives using the correct endings.

a) Der _____ Schüler bekommt eine gute Note. (m, **intelligent**)

b) Wir fahren mit dem _____ Zug nach München. (m, **nächst**)

c) Der _____ Lehrer ist streng. (m, **altmodisch**)

d) Ich kaufe dieses _____ T-Shirt. (n, **schwarz**)

e) Heute gehen wir ins _____ Einkaufszentrum. (n, **neu**)

f) Ich habe eine _____ Freundin. (f, **nett**)

g) Es gibt kein _____ Obst. (n, **frisch**)

h) Diese _____ Leute nerven mich. (pl, **blöd**)

i) Meine Tante hat einen_____ Unfall gehabt. (m, **schwer**)

j) Hamsa hat sein _____ Handy verloren. (n, **neu**)   [10 marks]

HT **2** **Übersetze diese Sätze ins Deutsche**. Translate these sentences into German.

a) I am taller than Andi.

b) English is easier than German.

c) Your marks are worse than mine.

d) Paris is nicer than London.

e) Olli runs faster than Tim.

f) Maths is more boring than art.   [6 marks]

3 **Füll die Lücken mit den superlativen Ausdrücken im Nominativ.**
Fill in the gaps with the superlative expressions in the nominative.

a) der _____ Schüler (oldest)

b) die _____ Sendung (most boring)

c) das _____ Essen (cheapest)   [3 marks]

4 **Unterstreiche den richtigen Artikel in jedem Satz.** Underline the correct article in each sentence.

a) Ich fahre in die / der Stadt.

b) Die Straßenbahn steht an die / der Haltestelle.

c) Das Essen steht auf dem / den Tisch.

d) Der Hund ist hinter dem / den Schrank.

e) Ich stelle die Milch in den / dem Kühlschrank.

f) Mein Hut ist auf meinen / meinem Kopf.

g) Ich hänge das Bild an die / der Wand.

h) Ich komme zu deine / deiner Party.

i) Wir sind seit dem / den Sommer hier.

j) Wir sprechen nicht während des / die Films.   [10 marks]

Pronouns & Present Tense Verbs 1

1 **Wähle die richtigen Akkusativpronomen.** Choose the correct accusative pronouns.

a) Der Kuli ist schön. Ich kaufe **ihn / er.**

b) Wir haben **dich / dir** nicht gesehen.

c) Ich rufe **Ihnen / Sie** an.

d) Hast du **wir / uns** gesehen?

e) Kennst du **ich / mich?**

f) Meine Schwester heißt Anna. Ich mag **sie / ihr** gern.

g) Die Kinder sind artig. Ich mag **sie / ihn** gern.

h) Wir besuchen **uns / euch.**

i) Ich habe **dich / dir** ein Geschenk gekauft.

j) Geben Sie **mir / mich** die Speisekarte bitte.   [10 marks]

2 **Schreib die richtigen Indefinitpronomen und übersetze die Sätze ins Englische.**
Insert the correct indefinite pronouns and translate the sentences into English.

a) Wen hast du gesehen? _____ (Nobody)

b) Ich habe _____ (something) **vergessen.**

c) _____ (Somebody) **war in unserem Haus.**

d) _____ (Everybody) **sind zum Konzert gekommen.**

e) Wir haben _____ (nothing) **gefunden.**

[10 marks: 1 mark for each correct indefinite pronoun, 1 mark for each translation]

3 **Füll die Lücken mit den richtigen Reflexivpronomen.**
Fill in the blanks with the correct reflexive pronouns.

a) Er setzt _____ im Wohnzimmer hin.

b) Aua! Ich habe _____ verletzt!

c) Ich rasiere _____ jeden Morgen.

d) Sie treffen _____ um 16 Uhr.

e) Wo treffen wir _____?

f) Sie wäscht _____ im Badezimmer.   [6 marks]

4 **Übersetze ins Deutsche.** Translate into German.

a) I don't understand   b) she visits   c) it pleases us   [3 marks]

Present Tense Verbs 2 & Perfect Tense Verbs

1 **Füll die Lücken mit unregelmäßigen Verben im Präsens.** Fill in the blanks with irregular verbs in the present tense.

a) Thomas _____ (nehmen) den Bus.

b) Andrea _____ (lesen) ein gutes Buch.

c) Wir _____ (treffen) unsere Freunde um 16 Uhr.

d) Karla _____ (laufen) 10 Kilometer.

e) Was _____ (essen) du?

f) Ein BMW _____ (fahren) schnell. [6 marks]

2 **Übersetze ins Deutsche.** Translate into German.

a) There is a plate on the table. (**Teller** is Masculine)

b) There's a problem. (**Problem** is Neuter)

c) There is a cathedral in Cologne. (**Dom** is Masculine, **Cologne** is **Köln.**) [3 marks]

3 **Schreib die richtigen Partizipien für diese 'haben'-Verben.** Write down the correct past participles for these **haben** verbs.

Infinitive	Past Participle		Infinitive	Past Participle
a) schreiben	→	f)	finden	→
b) geben	→	g)	spielen	→
c) lesen	→	h)	nehmen	→
d) kaufen	→	i)	sehen	→
e) sagen	→	j)	trinken	→

[10 marks]

4 **Füll die Lücken mit der richtigen Form von 'sein' und dem Partizip Perfekt.** Fill in the blanks with the correct part of **sein** and the past participle.

a) Wir _____ zwanzig Minuten _____ . (bleiben)

b) Ich _____ krank _____ . (sein)

c) Meine Eltern _____ oft in die Türkei _____ . (fliegen)

d) Du _____ zu spät _____ . (kommen)

e) Die Kinder _____ in den Park _____ . (gehen)

f) Mo Farah _____ sehr schnell _____ . (laufen) [6 marks]

Imperfect Tense Verbs & Future Time Frame

1 **Schreib diese regelmäßigen Präsens-Verben in das Imperfekt.** Write these regular present tense verbs in the imperfect tense.

a) sie arbeiten →   f) man kocht →

b) man lernt →   g) ich spiele →

c) Was sagt er? →   h) du fragst →

d) du hörst →   i) sie kauft →

e) wir spielen →   j) sie wohnen →

[10 marks]

2 **Wähle die richtige Imperfekt-Modalverbform in jedem Satz.** Choose the correct imperfect modal verb form in each sentence.

a) Wir mochten / mögen die Fernsehsendung gern.

b) Ich will / wollte tanzen gehen.

c) Lydia konnte / kann nicht schnell laufen.

d) Musstest / musst du so laut sein?

e) Wir sollen / sollten um sechs Uhr zu Hause sein.

f) Olaf durfte / darf im Restaurant nicht rauchen.   [6 marks]

3 **Füll die Lücken mit den richtigen Wörtern, um Konditionalsätze zu bilden.** Fill in the gaps with the correct words to make conditional sentences.

a) _____ der Lehrer nicht so langweilig _____ , _____ ich besser lernen.

b) _____ wir älter _____ , _____ wir allein in die Stadt gehen dürfen.

c) _____ ich Zeit _____ , _____ ich mehr Sport treiben.

d) _____ mein Vater hungrig _____ , _____ er etwas essen.

e) _____ Sonja reich _____ , _____ sie ein Pferd kaufen.

f) _____ ich mehr Geld _____ , _____ ich für Kinder in Afrika spenden.

[6 marks]

4 **Übersetze die Sätze in Übung 3 ins Englische.** Translate the sentences in activity 3 into English.

[6 marks]

Pluperfect Tense, Subjective Mood and Imperative & Word Order and Conjunctions

HT

1 **Füll die Lücken mit den richtigen Wörtern aus dem Kästchen, um Konjunktiv-Konstruktionen zu bilden.** Fill in the gaps with the correct words from the box to complete subjunctive constructions.

wären	wäre	möchtet	hätte

a) _____ ihr mitkommen?

b) Wir _____ nicht geblieben.

c) Lara _____ nicht gelacht.

d) Es _____ schön gewesen.   [4 marks]

2 **Übersetze die Sätze in Übung 1 ins Englische.** Translate the sentences in activity 1 into English.

[4 marks]

3 **Bring die Wörter in die richtige Reihenfolge, um Fragen zu bilden. Fang mit den unterstrichenen Wörtern an.** Put these words in the correct order to form questions. Start with the underlined words.

a) beginnt / das / Konzert / <u>Wann</u>?

b) du / müde / <u>Bist</u>?

c) kostet / <u>Wie viel</u> / Buch / dieses ?

d) du / <u>Wer</u> / bist ?

e) gekauft / du / <u>Was</u> / hast ?

f) alt / ist / <u>Wie</u> / sie?

g) ist / <u>Warum</u> / sie / nicht / hier ?

h) magst / du / <u>Was für</u> / Musik ?

i) mit / <u>Kommst</u> / du ?

j) Tennis / <u>Spielt</u> / gern / ihr ?   [10 marks]

HT

4 **Schreib die richtigen Konjunktionen, um die Sätze zu vervollständigen.** Write in the correct conjunctions to complete the sentences.

a) Ich weiß, _____ du unglücklich bist. (that)

b) Wir haben Kuchen gegessen, _____ er war nicht gut. (but)

c) Weißt du, _____ es draußen kalt ist? (whether)

d) Quentin war unfreundlich, _____ er krank war. (when)

e) Ich mag Grammatikübungen, _____ sie interessant sind. (because)

f) Wir lernen Französisch, _____ wir mit unseren französischen Freunden sprechen können. (so that)   [6 marks]

Review Questions

Pronouns & Present Tense Verbs 1

1 **Füll die Lücken mit den richtigen Pronomen.** Fill in the blanks with the correct pronouns.

a) **Ich komme mit** _____. (you, familiar)

b) **Wie heißt** _____? (you, familiar)

c) **Wie heißen** _____? (you, formal)

d) **Wir essen bei** _____. (me)

e) **Ist das Geschenk für** _____? (me)

f) **Mein Vater ist super. Ich mag** _____ **gern.** (him)

g) **Wo ist meine Handtasche? Ich habe** _____ **verloren.** (it, f)

h) **Ich liebe** _____. (you, familiar)

i) **Liebst du** _____? (me)

j) **Kommst du zu** _____? (us)   [10 marks]

2 **Schreib die richtige Form des Präsens–Verbs.**
Write in the correct form of the present tense verb (regular verbs).

a) **wir** _____ (swim)   e) **du** _____ (play)

b) **ich** _____ (come)   f) **ihr** _____ (sing)

c) **sie** (Plural) _____ (say)   g) **sie** (Singular) _____ (fly)

d) **es** _____ (do)   h) **meine Eltern** _____ (go) [8 marks]

3 **Füll die Lücken mit dem richtigen Reflexivpronomen.**
Fill in the blanks with the correct reflexive pronoun.

a) **Er verletzt** _____.   d) **Wir interessieren** _____.

b) **Sie freut** _____.   e) **Sie amüsieren** _____.

c) **Ich rasiere** _____.   [5 marks]

HT **4** **Übersetze ins Deutsche.** Translate into German.

a) I often go to the cinema.   e) Do you play tennis? (familiar, Singular)

b) We are interested in music.   f) What are you doing? (formal)

c) I never get up before 9 o'clock.   g) Are you coming? (familiar, Plural)

d) They swim in the sun.   h) Ella drinks coffee.   [8 marks]

Present Tense Verbs 2 & Perfect Tense Verbs

1 **Schreib die du und er / sie / es Formen dieser Verben im Präsens.**
Write in the **du** and **er / sie / es** forms of these verbs in the present tense.

a) fahren: du ....   er / sie / es ....

b) schlafen: du ....   er / sie / es ....

c) essen: du ....   er / sie / es ....

d) sprechen: du ....   er / sie / es ....

e) nehmen: du ....   er / sie / es ....

f) lesen: du ....   er / sie / es ....

[12 marks: 1 mark for each du form and 1 mark for each er / sie / es form]

2 **Füll die Lücken mit der richtigen Form des Präsens.**
Fill in the blanks with the correct form of the present tense.

a) Kevin .... (essen) nicht gern Fleisch.

b) Fatima .... (sprechen) sehr gut Deutsch.

c) Benjamin .... (fahren) nach Hause.

d) Mein Opa .... (geben) mir 10 Euro.

e) .... (nehmen) du Milch und Zucker?

f) .... (schlafen) du? [6 marks]

HT **3** **Schreib diese Präsens-Sätze im Perfekt.** Put these present tense sentences into the perfect tense.

a) Meine Mutter fährt nach Ibiza.

b) Nimmst du mein Handy?

c) Wir treffen uns um 15 Uhr.

d) Wir bleiben zu Hause.

e) Er trinkt ein Glas Wasser.

f) Der Zug fährt ab.

g) Marita spricht Spanisch.

h) Meine Oma stirbt. [8 marks]

4 **Füll die Lücken mit den Partizipien dieser trennbaren und reflexiven Verben.**
Fill in the blanks with the past participles of these separable and reflexive verbs.

a) Wir sind .... (aussteigen)

b) Ich habe ein Spiel .... (herunterladen)

c) Wann bist du .... ? (aufstehen)

d) Der Zug ist schon .... (abfahren)

e) Ich habe mich .... (freuen)

f) Wir haben uns noch nicht .... (entscheiden) [6 marks]

Imperfect Tense Verbs & Future Time Frame

1 **Sind diese Verben im Präsens oder Imperfekt? Schreib P für Präsens oder I für Imperfekt.**
Are these verbs in the present or imperfect tense? Write P for present or I for imperfect.

a) kam _____

b) ist _____

c) gibt _____

d) hatte _____

e) höre _____

f) schneit _____

g) habe _____

h) fahre _____

i) sitze _____

j) schreibe _____

k) hörte _____

l) fuhr _____

m) fand _____

n) gab _____

o) war _____

p) komme _____

q) saß _____

r) finde _____ [18 marks]

HT **2** **Übersetze die folgenden Sätze ins Deutsche mit dem Imperfekt. Benutze die Wörter im Kästchen als Hilfe.** Translate the following sentences into German using the imperfect tense. Use the vocabulary in the box to help you.

der Politiker – politician	**Kollegen** – colleagues	**produktiv** – productive	**Gespräche** – talks

The politician travelled to Berlin. He arrived on Tuesday and sat and spoke with colleagues. He found the talks very productive.

[5 marks: 1 mark for each correct verb in the imperfect tense]

HT **3** **Übersetze ins Deutsche.** Translate into German.

a) We had to go home.

b) They were able to speak English.

c) We wanted to chat online.

d) She was allowed to go to bed late. [4 marks]

4 **Füll die Lücken mit der richtigen Form von 'werden', um diese Sätze zu vervollständigen.** Fill in the blanks with the correct form of **werden** to complete these sentences.

a) Was _____ du machen?

b) Wir _____ fernsehen.

c) Man _____ mit Mobbing ein Problem haben.

d) Ich _____ immer recyceln.

e) Wir _____ Ramadan feiern. [5 marks]

Pluperfect Tense, Subjunctive Mood and Imperative & Word Order and Conjunctions

1 **Setz diese Perfekt-Sätze ins Plusquamperfekt um. Um das zu machen, schreib die Formen von 'haben' und 'sein' im Imperfekt.** Make these perfect tense sentences pluperfect. In order to do that, write down the forms of **haben** and **sein** in the imperfect tense.

a) **Ich bin mit dem Rad zur Schule gefahren.** ....

b) **Bist du früh angekommen?** ....

c) **Mein Vater ist einkaufen gegangen.** ....

d) **Wir sind nach Amerika geflogen.** ....

e) **Seid ihr lange geblieben?** ....

f) **Meine Eltern sind krank gewesen.** ....

g) **Ich habe zu viel gegessen.** ....

h) **Du hast dein Handy vergessen.** ....

i) **Elise hat zu laut gesungen.** ....

j) **Wir haben Tennis gespielt.** ....

k) **Habt ihr diesen Film gesehen?** ....

l) **Sie haben hart gearbeitet.** ....

[12 marks]

2 **Welche Konjunktionen ändern die Wortstellung? Schreib die Wörter ins richtige Kästchen.**
Which of these conjunctions change the word order? Write them in the correct box.

so dass   weil   als   ob   aber   wenn   und   dass   obwohl

Change	No change

[9 marks]

Reading

1 You are going to stay with your German friend to practise your German. His parents send you some information about where they live. Translate this description into English for your parents.

Wir wohnen auf dem Land. Es ist ruhiger hier als in der Stadt und man kann viel spazieren gehen. Der Bauernhof hat vier Schlafzimmer, zwei Badezimmer und eine große Küche. Jeden Samstag gibt es einen Markt im Dorf.

[9 marks]

2 Read the sentences below about what some people think about the environment and match the names to the statements.

Agatha	Wir sollten weniger fossile Brennstoffe verwenden.
Ansel	Ich denke, wir sollten duschen statt baden.
Fritz	Wir sollten versuchen, mit den öffentlichen Verkehrsmitteln zu fahren.
Gabi	Ohne Tiere und Pflanzen können wir nicht überleben.
Manuela	Wir sollten weniger Plastiktüten benutzen.
Petra	Pfandflaschen sind die Zukunft.

a) We need to avoid using cars.

b) We need to use more renewable energy.

c) We need to save water.

d) We need to recycle.

e) We need to protect endangered species.

[5 marks]

3 Read this article and tick the correct sentences.

Viele junge Leute finden, dass traditionelle Feste langweilig und altmodisch sind. Auf der einen Seite feiern viele Leute in Süddeutschland Fasching, aber auf der anderen Seite interessieren sich die Norddeutschen nicht so sehr dafür. Weihnachten feiert man überall in Deutschland, in Österreich und in der Schweiz. Es ist ein wichtiges Fest, wo Familien sich treffen und zusammen essen.

a) All young people are bored by traditional festivals. ☐

b) Many young people think traditional festivals are old-fashioned. ☐

c) Everybody in South Germany celebrates carnival. ☐

d) Everybody in North Germany celebrates carnival. ☐

e) Christmas is popular in all the German-speaking countries. ☐

f) Christmas is an important festival. ☐

g) People get together at Christmas. ☐

h) Only North Germans enjoy Christmas. ☐

[4 marks]

Mixed Exam-Style Questions

4 Read what these German teenagers say about where they live. Write the name of the correct person for each statement in English.

Wohnst du gern in deiner Gegend?

Ich liebe meine Wohnung, aber es gibt zu viel Verkehr in der Stadtmitte.   **Bernd, 15 Jahre**

Die Straßen sind schmutzig in der Stadt.   **Ivonne, 16 Jahre**

Wenn ich am Wochenende mit Freunden einkaufen gehen will, muss ich
mit dem Bus fahren.   **Sabrine, 14 Jahre**

Es ist sauberer hier als in der Stadt und das gefällt mir.   **Hans, 15 Jahre**

Aus dem Fenster kann ich Hügel und Bäume sehen, aber leider haben wir
keine Nachbarn.   **Anja, 14 Jahre**

Ich wohne gern hier in der Stadtmitte, weil es so viel zu tun gibt.   **Angela, 15 Jahre**

Die Stadtmitte ist zu laut für mich und die Mieten sind teurer als auf dem Lande.   **Jens, 18 Jahre**

a) Who has to use public transport to meet their friends at the weekend?

b) Who loves where they live but is worried about the amount of traffic?

c) Who complains about how noisy it is in the town centre?

d) Who likes the cleanliness of where they live?

e) Who likes the view from their window, but complains about having no neighbours?

f) Who likes the fact that there's lots to do where they live?   [6 marks]

5 Your Austrian exchange partner has sent you this email about your upcoming visit next week. Your sister does not speak German and wants you to translate it for her.

Die erste Stunde fängt jeden Tag um halb acht an. Wir treffen uns in der Aula, wo du die Schulleiterin sehen wirst. Du darfst kein Handy mitbringen, denn sie sind verboten – letzte Woche hat mein Mathelehrer mein Handy gesehen und ich muss diese Woche nachsitzen. Das ist nicht gut!   [9 marks]

6 Read what these people are saying about where they live. Write the name of the correct person for each question in English.

> Was ich nicht mag, ist die Anzahl von Obdachlosen auf den Straßen, die immer um Geld bitten.

Birgit

> Was mich stört, ist, wieviel Verkehr in der Stadtmitte erlaubt ist. Die Luftverschmutzung wird immer schlimmer.

Frank

> Leider ist die Gewalt in der Gegend gestiegen. Besonders an Wochenenden ist die Gewalt ein großes Problem.

Ahmed

> Ich denke, wir sollten den Obdachlose helfen, Arbeit zu finden.

Kirstin

> Für mich ist es klar, dass die Arbeitslosigkeit ein Problem ist, und es macht mir traurig, dass ich so viele Leute sehe, die auf der Straße wohnen und um Geld bitten.

Sebastian

a) Who feels that crime is increasing?

b) Who thinks that homeless people should be helped to look for jobs?

c) Who thinks that pollution is an issue?

d) Who is worried about unemployment?

e) Who doesn't like to see homeless people begging for money?

[5 marks]

7 Read this article about nutrition. Fill in the gaps in the sentences below with English words.

Das traditionelle deutsche Essen ist nicht besonders gesund. Manche Familien essen täglich Fleisch und Wurst. Das kann fettig sein und viel zu salzig. Eine Scheibe Wurst hat fünfzig Kalorien – das ist gefährlich. Die aktuelle Mode für junge Leute ist, vegetarisch oder sogar vegan zu essen. Veganer essen nur Speisen, die nichts mit Tieren zu tun haben.

a) .... German food is not ....

b) Many .... eat .... and sausages.

c) They are full of .... and ....

d) There are 50 calories in one .... of ....

e) Now it's cool to be .... or ....

f) Vegans only eat food that ....   [12 marks: 2 marks per sentence]

8 Draw a line to link these German and English sentences.

Mein Vater ist intelligent aber sehr streng.
Wir verstehen uns gut.
Ich streite mich nie mit meiner Schwester.
Meine Schwester ist ruhig und artig.
Ich streite mich manchmal mit meiner Schwester.
Mein Vater ist stur aber oft großzügig.

We get on well.
I sometimes argue with my sister.
My father is stubborn but often generous.
I never argue with my sister.
My sister is quiet and well-behaved.
My father is intelligent but very strict.

[6 marks]

9 Read what these people are saying about holidays. Write the name of the correct person for each question in English.

> **Die Sonne finde ich entspannend und ich gehe so viel wie möglich zum Strand, wo ich in der Sonne liegen kann.**

Hans

> **Ich bin der Meinung, dass Urlaub überbewertet ist, und bleibe lieber zu Hause.**

Beate

> **Wenn wir in Urlaub fahren, fahren wir lieber mit dem Zug.**

Fred

> **Ich mag das kalte Wetter und würde gern im Winter in Urlaub gehen.**

Bernadette

> **In einer Jugendherberge kann man viel besser andere Leuten kennenlernen.**

Michael

> **Für mich sind Ferien mit Freunden viel besser als mit den Eltern, weil man mehr Freiheit hat.**

Sebastian

a) Who prefers holidays where they can do winter sports?

b) Who likes the sun and wants to go on a beach holiday?

c) Who thinks youth hostelling is better than staying in a hotel?

d) Who thinks it's better to stay at home during the school holidays?

e) Who would prefer to go on holiday with their friends?

[5 marks]

10 These people are describing their friends. Answer the questions below, using the names of the people described.

Mein bester Freund heißt Damien. Wir verstehen uns sehr gut, weil wir den gleichen Humor haben.

Meine beste Freundin heißt Bettina. Sie hat hellbraune Haare und grüne Augen.

Meine Freundin Aisa ist größer als ich und trägt eine Brille.

Ich habe mit Kevin viel gemeinsam, weil er immer gut gelaunt ist. Er ist absolut nicht schüchtern.

Cara ist sehr nervig und ich verstehe mich nicht gut mit ihr.

Mohammed ist ein guter Freund. Manchmal ist er ein bisschen egoistisch, aber wir streiten uns nie.

Laura und ich sind gute Freunde. Wir kennen uns seit fünf Jahren und wir gehen oft zusammen ins Kino.

Rosa ist sehr ruhig und fleißig und wir verstehen uns gut.

a) Who is a bit selfish?

b) Who has the same sense of humour?

c) Who likes to go to the cinema?

d) Who has light brown hair and blue eyes?

e) Who is very hard-working?

f) Who is short-sighted?

g) Who is irritating?

h) Who is always in a good mood?

[8 marks]

11 Read the text about school and fill in the gaps using the words in the box.

schwer	Geschichte	nutzlos	hilfsbereit	langweiliges
Unterricht	furchtbar	Kunst	Lehrerin	wichtiges
	klug	leicht	Direktor	

Ich mag meine Schule. Ich finde die Schulleiterin sehr nett und _____,
obwohl sie manchmal streng sein kann. Meine Lieblingsfächer sind praktische Fächer wie
_____ **, und meine Lieblings** _____ **lehrt Deutsch, was ein sehr**
_____ **Fach ist. Ich denke, ich bin sehr** _____ **und fleißig, und die**
meisten Fächer fallen mir ziemlich _____ **.**   [6 marks]

12 Detlev describes his musical taste. Tick the four true statements below.

Meine Lieblingskünstlerin ist Emma Meyer. Emma ist Sängerin und spielt auch Klavier und
Schlagzeug. Ich lade Emmas Musik herunter, weil ich ihre Stimme mag und die Musik mich
glücklich macht. Klassische Musik höre ich nie.

a) Emma Meyer is a drummer.

b) Detlev doesn't like Emma's voice.

c) Detlev is a lover of classical music.

d) Emma is a multi-instrumentalist.

e) Emma doesn't sing.

f) Emma is Detlev's favourite artist.

g) Her music makes Detlev happy.

h) Detlev doesn't believe in downloading music.   [4 marks]

HT **13** Manuela is describing her relationship with her family. Translate what she says into English.

Ich bin seit 21 Jahren mit meinem Mann verheiratet. Wir haben zwei Kinder, einen Sohn und eine
Tochter. Viele Ehen enden mit Scheidung aber wir lieben uns sehr. Die Ehe ist ein Zeichen der Liebe.

[8 marks: 2 marks per sentence]

Mixed Exam-Style Questions

Writing

1 Translate the following sentences into German.

a) I get up at half past six.

b) My sister goes to a primary school.

c) We have a playground but it is small.

d) Tomorrow I will eat in the dining hall.

e) Yesterday I went to school by car.

[10 marks: 5 marks for communication, 5 marks for application of grammar]

2 Write down the German words for these technological terms. Find the words in the box below.

suchen	herunterladen	Startseite	Tastatur	drucken
Nachrichten	hochladen	Bildschirm	WLAN	Webseite

a) keyboard

b) home page

c) Wi-Fi

d) screen

e) to download

f) website

g) to search

h) to print

i) messages

j) to upload

[10 marks]

3 Translate the following passage into German.

Last year my mum and I went to Greece during the school holidays. We walked on the beach every day and we read a lot. We had a lot of fun together. It was better than I thought it would be. In December, we will be going skiing in Switzerland.

[12 marks: 6 marks for communication, 6 marks for grammar]

4 Translate the following sentences into German.

a) The pharmacy is in front of the train station.

b) I like living in the countryside.

c) I lost my wallet in the street.

d) You can buy some nice presents.

e) There is a large bookshop.

[10 marks: 5 marks for communication, 5 marks for grammar]

HT 5 Translate the following passage into German.

In the past, I was not very healthy. I was a slave to the computer and I watched too much television. Now I eat at least five portions of fruit and vegetables per day and I avoid fatty products. In the future, I shall definitely not smoke and I will get regular exercise.

[12 marks: 6 marks for communication, 6 marks for grammar]

6 **Schreib fünf Sätze mit einer Auswahl aus jeder Spalte.** Write five sentences using a choice from each column.

Ich möchte	älteren Menschen	arbeiten
Ich würde gern	Geld	helfen
	Medikamente	sammeln
	Mahlzeiten	fahren
	Kinder	liefern
	als Krankenschwester	verteilen

[5 marks]

7 **Übersetze jeden Satz aus Übung sechs ins Englische.** Translate each sentence from activity 6 into English.

[5 marks]

8 Dein Freund Matthias hat dich über deinen Teilzeitjob gefragt. Du schreibst ihm eine E-Mail.

Schreib:

- etwas über deinen Teilzeitjob

- warum du deinen Teilzeitjob magst oder nicht magst

- was du letzte Woche bei der Arbeit gemacht hast

- etwas über deine Berufspläne in der Zukunft

Du muss ungefähr 90 Wörter auf Deutsch schreiben. Schreib etwas über alle Punkte der Aufgabe.

[16 marks: 10 marks for content and 6 marks for quality of language]

9 Übersetze ins Englische.

a) Das bringt mich zum Weinen.

b) Es macht mir Angst.

c) Wovon handelt es?

d) Wir laden lieber Filme herunter.

e) Man soll lieber zu Hause bleiben.

f) Die Plätze sind bequemer.

[6 marks]

10 Deine Freundin Silke aus Österreich hat dich über deine Stadt gefragt. Du schreibst Silke eine E-Mail über deine Stadt.

Schreib:

- etwas über deine Stadt

- warum du deine Stadt gern oder nicht gern magst

- was du letztes Wochenende in deiner Stadt gemacht hast

- was man machen sollte, um deine Stadt zu verbessern

Du musst ungefähr 90 Wörter auf Deutsch schreiben. Schreib etwas über alle Punkte der Aufgabe.

[16 marks: 10 marks for content and 6 marks for quality of language]

11 **Übersetze ins Deutsche.**

I chat with my friends online but I never buy online. In my opinion, you have to be careful. The internet helps with my homework and I chat with my friends too.

[6 marks: 2 marks per sentence]

12 **Übersetze ins Englische.**

Meine Freundin Ella ist mit ihrer Familie essen gegangen. Es war in einem teuren Restaurant in der Stadtmitte. Als Vorspeise hat Ella Thunfischsalat gewählt, aber er hat nicht geschmeckt. Als Hauptspeise hat sie Hähnchen bestellt, aber es war kalt! Sie hat keinen Nachtisch genommen und sie hat auch nicht bezahlt.

[10 marks: 2 marks per sentence]

13 **Übersetze ins Deutsche.**

When I was young, I often went swimming but nowadays I'd rather go fishing. I'd like to try winter sports but they are often dangerous.

[8 marks: 2 marks per sentence]

14 **Du schreibst einen Artikel über einen Urlaub.**

Schreib:

- **etwas über den Urlaub – deine Eindrücke und deine Meinungen.**

- **vergleich diesen Urlaub mit einem Urlaub, den du in der Zunkunft haben möchtest**

Du musst ungefähr 150 Wörter auf Deutsch schreiben und etwas über beide Punkte der Aufgabe schreiben.

[32 marks: 15 marks for content, 12 marks for range of language, 5 marks for accuracy]

Die deutsche Aussprache

Knowing key sounds will help you improve your speaking and listening skills. Here is a summary of key German sounds.

Letters	Sounds like...	Examples
b/d/f/h/k/lm/n/p/t	The same as in English	Bonn/Deutsch/falsch/Haus/kein/ lachen/Mutter/nein/Polen/Tisch
j	Like the English **y**	**J**a!
s	Sometimes like the English **z** Sometimes like the English **sh** Sometimes like the English **s**	**s**ieben **s**pielen lu**s**tig
ß or ss	Like the English **s**	Fu**ß**ball
v	Like the English **f**	**v**iel
w	Like the English **v**	**W**asser
z	Like the English **ts**	**Z**eit
ch	Like the Scottish **och**	a**ch**t
g at the end of the word	Like the German **ch**	lusti**g**
sch	Like the English **sh**	**sch**lecht
zw	Like the Engish **ts** and **v**	**zw**ei
a	Sometimes like the English **cat** Sometimes like the English **ah**	b**a**cken V**a**ter
e	Sometimes like the English **get** Sometimes like the English **eh**	T**e**nnis L**e**ben
i	Always like the English **in**	K**i**nd
o	Sometimes like the English **off** Sometimes like the English **oh**	Schl**o**ss gr**o**ß
u	Sometimes like the English **took** Sometimes like the English **ooh**	l**u**stig B**u**ch
ie	Like the English **keep**	v**ie**r
ei	Like the English **eye**	m**ei**n
au	Like the English **cow**	H**au**s
ä	Sometimes like the English **air**	V**ä**ter h**ä**tte
ö	Like the English **fur**	h**ö**ren
ü	Like the French **sur**	T**ü**r

Answers

Pages 6–7 Review Questions

1. a) der Sommer [1], b) der Winter [1],
   c) März [1], d) Mai [1], e) Juli [1],
   f) Oktober [1], g) Dezember [1],
   h) Dienstag [1], i) Mittwoch [1],
   j) Donnerstag [1]
2. a) der vierzehnte Februar   [1]
   b) der einunddreißigste Oktober   [1]
   c) der fünfundzwanzigste Dezember [1]
   d) der fünfte November   [1]
   e) der erste April   [1]
   f) der erste Januar   [1]
3. Answers will vary. Example answers:
   a) Ich heiße Chloe.   [1]
   b) Ich bin sechzehn Jahre alt.   [1]
   c) Ich habe am neunzehnten Februar
      Geburtstag.   [1]
   d) Ich wohne in Birmingham.   [1]
   e) Ja, ich habe einen Bruder und
      eine Schwester.   [1]
   f) Ja, ich habe einen Hund.   [1]
4. a) 4 [1]   14 [1]   40 [1]   44 [1]
   b) 82 [1] 28 [1] 18 [1]   8 [1]
   c) 30 [1] 13 [1] 33 [1]   3 [1]
   d) 17 [1] 77 [1]   7 [1] 70 [1]
5. a) sechsundsechzig   [1]
   b) vierundsiebzig   [1]
   c) dreiundzwanzig   [1]
   d) zwölf   [1]
   e) einundfünfzig   [1]
   f) elf   [1]
   g) vierundachtzig   [1]
   h) neunzehn   [1]
   i) siebenundvierzig   [1]
6. a) halb sieben – 6.30   [1]
   b) Viertel vor acht – 7.45   [1]
   c) fünf nach halb zwölf – 11.35 [1]
   d) Viertel nach zwei – 2.15   [1]
   e) fünf nach halb eins – 12.35   [1]
   f) halb sechs – 5.30   [1]
   g) zwanzig vor zehn – 9.40   [1]
7. a) Viertel vor sieben   [1]
   b) halb vier   [1]
   c) halb fünf   [1]
   d) fünf nach halb elf   [1]
   e) fünf vor halb zehn   [1]

Pages 8–29 Revise Questions

Page 9 Quick Test
1. I get on very well with my sister. She is very young but she is very nice and generous.
2. Ich verstehe mich nicht sehr gut mit meinem Vater. Er ist ziemlich alt und sehr streng. Wir streiten uns oft.

Page 11 Quick Test
1. Mein bester Freund hat blaue Augen und lange glatte braune Haare. Er ist sehr ehrlich und wir mögen die gleichen Sportarten.
2. Suzanne ist oft neidisch.
3. Wir mögen die gleiche Musik und wir gehen oft ins Kino.
4. Answers will vary. Example answer: Er / sie hat braune Haare und ist sehr nett. Wir verstehen uns gut.

Page 13 Quick Test
1. to get engaged   to marry   to die
2. ledig   geschieden   die Ehe
3. I would like to stay single. I wouldn't like to get married.
4. Meine Tante ist seit 12 Jahren verheiratet.
5. Answers will vary. Example answer: Ich möchte (nicht) heiraten, weil ich Zusammenleben besser finde.

Page 15 Quick Test
1. Possible answers are Tastatur, Bildschirm, Drucker, WLAN, hochladen, herunterladen
2. Answers will vary. Example answers:
   a) Man muss vorsichtig sein.
   b) Man darf nicht das Passwort verraten.
3. Answers will vary. Example answer: Ich schicke und empfange E-Mails. Ich besuche Webseiten.

Page 17 Quick Test
1. cheap   useful   boring
2. sich informieren because it is reflexive.
3. My friend is on her mobile phone for hours. I think that's stupid.
4. Meiner Meinung nach ist die Mobiltechnologie praktisch. Man kann schnell einkaufen.

Page 19 Quick Test
1. 'ich höre gern' – I like listening, 'ich höre lieber' – I prefer listening
2. Lieblingssängerin is feminine, therefore Ed Sheeran can't be the right answer. The singer must be female. Mein Lieblingssänger must be used for a male singer.
3. I'm interested in rap music even though it's often too loud. Classical music makes me sad.
4. Ich war noch nie auf dem Lorelei-Festival.

Page 21 Quick Test
1. Wovon handelt es?
2. You should rather download films. / It's better to download films.
3. a) Die Plätze sind nicht sehr bequem.
   b) Man will die Werbung nicht sehen.

Page 23 Quick Test
1. fünf Scheiben Käse, ein Stück Fleisch, eine Dose Limonade
2. I rarely eat potatoes and I've never tried ham.
3. Ich esse nie Ketchup, weil es zu süß ist.
4. manchmal   ab und zu   jeden Tag

Page 25 Quick Test
1. Answers will vary. Example answers:
   a) Forelle, Lachs
   b) Rindfleisch, Schweinefleisch
   c) Bratwurst, Currywurst
   d) Erdbeer, Ananas
2. a) What kinds of ice cream do you have?
   b) I'd like strawberry tart for dessert.
3. Wir haben in einem türkischen Restaurant gegessen. Es hat ziemlich gut geschmeckt, aber die Suppe war scharf.

Page 27 Quick Test
1. Ich spiele Hockey.
2. Ich laufe Ski is present tense and ich bin Ski gelaufen is perfect tense.
3. We used to go skateboarding.
4. Vor fünf Jahren bin ich zum Jugendklub gegangen.
5. Ich möchte Extremsport probieren.

Page 29 Quick Test
1. a) Weihnachten
   b) Heiligabend
   c) der erste Weihnachtstag
   d) der zweite Weihnachtstag
2. a) Good luck!
   b) Congratulations!
   c) Happy Easter!
   d) All the best!
3. We ate, sang and danced.
4. Einige Leute finden, dass Feste sehr faszinierend sind.

Page 30–33 Practice Questions

Page 30
1. a) Meine Schwester **nervt [1]** mich und wir **streiten [1]** uns oft aber ich **verstehe mich [1]** sehr gut mit meinem kleinen Bruder. Er ist **artig [1]** und **ruhig [1]**.
   b) Meine Oma hat **lockige [1] Haare [1]** und **graue [1] Augen [1]**.
   c) Ich möchte lieber **ledig [1]** bleiben und nicht **heiraten [1]**, weil meine Eltern **geschieden [1]** sind.
2. a) Wir treffen uns immer am Wochenende und **wir spielen zusammen Videospiele [1]**. We always meet at weekends and we play video games together [1].
   b) Wir haben viel gemeinsam, weil **wir den gleichen Humor haben [1]**. We have a lot in common because we have the same sense of humour [1].
   c) Wir streiten uns nie, **weil wir uns seit fünf Jahren kennen [1]**. We never argue, because we have known each other for five years [1].
   d) Auf der einen Seite möchte ich Kinder haben, aber **auf der anderen Seite bin ich zu jung [1]**. On the one hand I would like to have children, but on the other hand I'm too young [1].
3. Meine Eltern sind **seit [1]** über zwanzig Jahren **verheiratet [1]** und sind sehr **glücklich [1]**. Sie **streiten [1]** sich nie, aber die Eltern von meiner Freundin Melissa sind **geschieden [1]**, weil sie sich nicht gut **verstehen [1]**. Die Situation ist ziemlich **traurig [1],** aber der Mann ist zu **egoistisch [1]**.

Page 31
1. a) Laptop – laptop   [1]
   b) Maus – mouse   [1]
   c) chatten – to chat   [1]
   d) klicken – to click   [1]
   e) Mobbing – bullying   [1]
   f) Passwort – password   [1]

Answers

g) surfen – to surf [1]
h) herunterladen – to download [1]
i) Webseite – website [1]
j) WLAN – Wi-Fi [1]
2. a) Man kann mit Freunden in Kontakt bleiben. V [1]
b) Cybermobbing ist gefährlich. N [1]
c) Man kann sich mit Freunden unterhalten. V [1]
d) Man muss regelmäßig das Passwort ändern. N [1]
e) Man muss vorsichtig sein. N [1]
f) Man kann online einkaufen. V [1]
g) Manchmal gibt es keinen Empfang. N [1]
h) Man kann im Notfall Hilfe rufen. V [1]
3. a) Man muss das Gerät immer wieder aufladen. [1]
b) Viele Leute sind stundenlang an ihrem Handy. [1]
c) Das Internet hilft bei meinen Hausaufgaben. [1]
d) Ich chatte mit meinen Freunden. [1]
e) Ich besuche oft meine Lieblingswebseiten. [1]

Page 32

1. a) i) Schlager [1], ii) Techno [1], iii) klassische [1] Musik [1]
b) i) Schlagzeug [1], ii) Gitarre [1], iii) Klavier [1]
c) i) Sänger [1], ii) Sängerin [1]
2. ich mag es gern – I like it [1] es bringt mich zum Weinen – it makes me cry [1] es nervt mich – it irritates me [1] ich finde es beruhigend – I find it relaxing [1] es macht mich glücklich – it makes me happy [1] es gefällt mir – it pleases me [1] es bringt mich zum Lachen – it makes me laugh [1] es macht mich traurig – it makes me sad [1]
3. a) cartoon film [1]
b) adverts [1]
c) news [1]
d) soap opera [1]
e) programme [1]
f) game show [1]
g) crime drama [1]
h) war film [1]
i) sound [1]
j) story [1]
4. a) Der Ton ist besser. [1]
b) Die Karten sind teurer. [1]
c) Ich höre am liebsten Popmusik. [1]
d) Ich sehe lieber Filme im Kino. [1]
e) Man soll lieber zu Hause bleiben. [1]

Page 33

1. a) Ich möchte sechs Scheiben Schinken. [1]
b) Wir essen jeden Tag Kuchen. [1]
c) Mein Onkel isst nie Fleisch. [1]
d) Was für Suppen haben Sie? [1]
e) Das Essen hat lecker geschmeckt. [1]
2. a) I'd like six slices of ham. [1]
b) We eat cake every day. [1]
c) My uncle never eats meat. [1]
d) What kinds of soup do you have? [1]
e) The food tasted delicious. [1]

3. a) Ich habe keinen Löffel. [1]
b) Die Suppe war kalt. [1]
c) Was ist Döner eigentlich? [1]
d) Wir möchten bestellen. [1]
e) Haben Sie einen Tisch für sechs Personen? [1]
f) Als Nachtisch möchte ich Erdbeertorte. [1]
4. a) Wir sind zur Eishalle **gegangen**. [1]
b) Ich bin im kalten Meer **geschwommen**. [1]
c) Papa hat früher Tennis **gespielt**. [1]
d) Wir sind sechs Kilometer **gewandert**. [1]
e) Ich habe keine Nachspeise **bestellt**. [1]
f) Meine Schwester hat nie Bier **getrunken**. [1]
5. a) Muttertag [1]
b) Silvester [1]
c) Fasching / Karneval [1]
d) Weihnachten [1]
e) Heiligabend [1]
f) Ostern [1]
g) Aprilstreich [1]
h) Ramadan [1]
i) Pfingsten [1]
j) Kostüm [1]

Pages 34–55 **Revise Questions**

Page 35 Quick Test

1. Ich wohne in einem Doppelhaus. Oben gibt es drei Schlafzimmer. Mein Schlafzimmer ist ordentlich und ich habe einen Schrank neben meinem Bett. Ich habe einige Bilder an der Wand. Ich putze mein Zimmer jede Woche. Andererseits ist das Schlafzimmer meiner Schwester immer unordentlich.
2. I live in a small terraced house. There are six rooms. On the ground floor there is the living room and the kitchen. On the first floor are two bedrooms and the bathroom.
3. Answers will vary. Example answer: Mein Schlafzimmer ist ziemlich groß. In meinem Zimmer gibt es ein Bett, einen Schrank und ich habe einen Nachttisch neben meinem Bett. Ich habe viele Poster an der Wand. Mein Zimmer ist immer sauber und ordentlich. Ich putze mein Zimmer jeden Samstag.

Page 37 Quick Test

1. Answers will vary. Example answer: Meine Stadt ist ganz klein. Wir haben ein schönes Kino aber keinen Bahnhof.
2. a) In my town there are many nice shops where you can buy pretty clothes.
b) Can I try on these trousers?
c) My dad paid with his credit card.
3. Answers will vary. Example answer: Meine Lieblingskleider sind meine Jeanshose und mein gelber Pullover. Ich trage auch gern meine weißen Turnschuhe.

Page 39 Quick Test

1. a) Häuser in der Stadt sind kleiner als auf dem Land.
b) Es gibt weniger Geschäfte auf dem Land.

2. I like living in the town centre, because I can walk to school. My friend lives on the outskirts of town and she has to get the bus.
3. Answers will vary. Example answer: Ich wohne auf dem Land. Das Leben hier ist sehr ruhig. Aus dem Fenster kann ich viele Blumen und Hügel sehen.

Page 41 Quick Test

1. I do voluntary work. I deliver medicines to elderly people in the village where I live.
2. Ich verteile Mahlzeiten und Trinkwasser an Obdachlose auf der Straße. In der Zukunft möchte ich Arzt / Ärztin werden. Ich möchte benachteiligten Menschen helfen.
3. Answers will vary. Example answer: Ich mache freiwillige Arbeit. Ich sammle Geld für eine Wohltätigkeitsorganisation, die älteren Menschen hilft. Ich möchte in der Zukunft Krankenschwester werden.

Page 43 Quick Test

1. Answers will vary. Example answer: Ich bin ganz gesund, weil ich viel Gemüse esse und genug Wasser trinke. Ich werde versuchen, weniger Süßigkeiten zu essen.
2. Answers will vary. Example answer: Man soll mindestens acht Stunden pro Nacht schlafen. Man soll gesunde Mahlzeiten essen. Man soll zu viel Fett vermeiden.
3. Ich esse ziemlich gesund, aber ich treibe nicht genug Sport. Um fit zu bleiben, werde ich Tennis spielen und zu viel Fett vermeiden.

Page 45 Quick Test

1. a) I think that there is too much pollution worldwide.
b) We're doing as much as we can but it's not nearly enough.
2. a) Soweit es mich betrifft, verbrauchen wir alle zu viel Energie.
b) Ich denke, dass ich zu viel verschwende und nicht genug recycle.

Page 47 Quick Test

1. a) Ich denke, dass man mehr recyceln könnte. I think that we could recycle more.
b) Meiner Meinung nach sollten wir weniger Plastiktüten benutzen. In my opinion, we should use less plastic bags.
c) Um die Umwelt zu schützen, müssen wir mehr öffentliche Verkehrsmittel benutzen. In order to protect the environment, we need to use more public transport.
2. a) Um… zu sparen; um… zu verbessern; um… zu schützen; um… nicht mehr zu verschmutzen.
b) statt… zu recyceln; ohne an die Tier- und Pflanzenwelt zu denken.

Page 49 Quick Test

1. a) There's a lot of unemployment.
b) The most important problem is the number of homeless people on the streets.
c) Nowadays there is too much crime.
d) In the news we hear about more and more violence.
e) I worry about the increase in poverty in the world.

Page 51 Quick Test
1. a) mit; in, b) mit; nach
2. a) haben; übernachtet, b) werde; verbringen

Page 53 Quick Test
1. a) Ich bin mit dem Zug gefahren.
   b) Wir waren zwei Wochen dort.
   c) Im Urlaub gehe ich gern schwimmen.
   d) Im Urlaub gehe ich am liebsten am Strand spazieren.
   e) Vor drei Jahren habe ich zwei Wochen auf einer Insel verbracht.

Page 55 Quick Test
1. a) Guten Tag! Ich möchte bitte ein Zimmer für zwei Personen für drei Nächte reservieren.
   b) Ich habe meinen Koffer am Flughafen vergessen.
2. a) Hello! I have booked a double room for four nights.
   b) I have lost my key.
   c) Do you have a map of the town please?

Pages 56–59 Review Questions
1. a) Oma **[1]**
   b) Großeltern **[1]**
   c) Neffe **[1]**
   d) Schwägerin **[1]**
   e) Stiefbruder **[1]**
   f) Onkel **[1]**
2. a) Nein **[1]**
   b) Nein **[1]**
   c) Nein **[1]**
   d) Ja **[1]**
   e) Ja **[1]**
   f) Ja **[1]**
3. a) F **[1]**
   b) R **[1]**
   c) NT **[1]**
   d) R **[1]**
   e) NT **[1]**
   f) F **[1]**

Page 57
1. a) Ich besuche Webseiten. **[1]**
   b) Ich chatte mit meinen Freunden. **[1]**
   c) Wir schicken uns SMS. **[1]**
   d) Man muss vorsichtig sein. **[1]**
   e) Man darf das Passwort nicht verraten. **[1]**
   f) Online-Mobbing ist gefährlich. **[1]**
2. Ich chatte mit meinen Freunden, weil sie **lustig [1]** sind. Viele Webseiten sind **doof [1]** aber das Internet ist **schnell [1]** und **praktisch [1]**. Mein Handy finde ich **nützlich [1]**, aber es kann **teuer [1]** sein.
3. a) computer **[1]**; tablet **[1]**; mobile phone **[1]**.
   b) You can get information fast **[1]**; you can call for help in an emergency **[1]**; you can stay in touch with other people **[1]**.
   c) They can become addicted to them. **[1]**
   d) You have to keep charging your devices **[1]**; the technology changes quickly **[1]**; it's expensive to have the latest version **[1]**.

Page 58
1. a) der Schlager **[1]**
   b) die Gruppe / die Band **[1]**
   c) das Klavier **[1]**
   d) der Künstler **[1]**
   e) der Text **[1]**
   f) die Stimme **[1]**
   g) das Lied **[1]**
   h) der Krimi **[1]**
   i) die Sendung **[1]**
   j) die Werbung **[1]**
2. a) Ich lade Musik herunter. **[2]**
   b) Ich höre am liebsten klassische Musik. **[2]**
   c) Ich finde die Melodie entspannend. **[2]**
   d) Die Musik macht mich glücklich. **[2]**
   e) Ich habe immer gern klassische Musik gehört, obwohl meine Freunde sie doof finden. **[2]**
3. a) Playing cards and drinking coffee. **[2]**
   b) The light goes out, the door opens and a monster comes in. **[2]**
   c) You'll have to see the film! **[1]**
   d) It's not a funny cartoon or a sentimental love story. **[2]**
   e) Because the special effects are so bad. **[1]**
   f) To stay at home and watch TV. **[2]**

Page 59
1. a) die Packung **[1]**
   b) die Dose **[1]**
   c) die Scheibe **[1]**
   d) das Frühstück **[1]**
   e) lecker **[1]**
   f) die Speisekarte **[1]**
   g) der Nachtisch **[1]**
   h) das Messer **[1]**
   i) das Stadion **[1]**
   j) die Hochzeit **[1]**
2. a) Was macht das? **[1]**
   b) Ich möchte fünf Scheiben Käse. **[1]**
   c) Das schmeckt nicht. **[1]**
   d) Es ist zu süß. **[1]**
   e) Ich esse keinen Schinken. **[1]**
   f) Ich habe nie Schweinefleisch gegessen. **[1]**
   g) Zahlen bitte. **[1]**
   h) Wir möchten bestellen. **[1]**
   i) Was für Gemüse haben Sie? **[1]**
   j) Früher habe ich Fußball gespielt. **[1]**
3. We visited my parents-in-law for Christmas. **[2]** On Christmas Eve we ate together: first tomato soup, then turkey with potatoes and vegetables. **[2]** Then we opened the presents. **[2]** I got a terrible pullover from my mother, which I didn't like at all! **[2]** On Christmas Day we all went to church. **[2]** I found that very calming although I am not religious. **[2]** In the afternoon we went for a walk in the park. **[2]** That was good because we had eaten too much. **[2]**

Page 60–63 Practice Questions

Page 60
1. Answers in order: Einfamilienhaus **[1]**, Zimmer **[1]**, Wohnzimmer **[1]**, die **[1]**, neben **[1]**, Stadt **[1]**
2. Answer will vary. **[8]**

3. a) Kann man hier Schmuck kaufen? **[1]**
   b) Ich möchte diese Hose anprobieren. **[1]**
   c) Wir brauchen öffentliche Verkehrsmittel in der Stadt. **[1]**
   d) Es ist zu ruhig auf dem Lande. **[1]**
   e) Ich habe meine Geldbeutel am Bahnhof verloren. **[1]**
   f) Es ist besser, in einem Dorf als in der Stadtmitte zu wohnen. **or** Es ist besser, in der Stadtmitte als in einem Dorf zu wohnen. **[1]**

Page 61
1. a) Carla **[1]**, b) Max **[1]**, c) Julia **[1]**, d) Beate **[1]**, e) Boris **[1]**
2. a) Ich werde gesund essen. **[1]**
   b) Ich werde dreimal in der Woche Sport treiben. **[1]**
   c) Mein Vater wird Zigaretten vermeiden. **[1]**
   d) Meine Schwester wird eine Diät machen. **[1]**
3. a) Man soll fetthaltige Produkte vermeiden. **[1]**
   b) Ich bin ziemlich gesund. **[1]**
   c) Man soll sich entspannen, um Stress zu vermeiden. **[1]**
   d) Mein Vater hat aufgehört zu rauchen. **[1]**
   e) Ich werde versuchen, Diät zu machen. **[1]**
   f) Um fit zu bleiben, soll man mehr Sport treiben und viel Wasser trinken. **[1]**

Page 62
1. a) verschwenden **[1]**
   b) man sollte / du solltest / Sie sollten **[1]**
   c) die Ozonschicht **[1]**
   d) der Abfall / der Müll **[1]**
   e) man könnte / du könntest / Sie könnten **[1]**
   f) überbevölkert **[1]**
   g) recyceln **[1]**
   h) schützen **[1]**
   i) der Treibhauseffekt **[1]**
   j) schaden **[1]**
2. Answers in this order: viel **[1]**, genug **[1]**, immer **[1]**, wenig **[1]**, viele **[1]**
3. a) Man sollte mehr recyceln, um die Umwelt zu schützen. **[1]** We must recycle more to protect the environment. **[1]**,
   b) Meiner Meinung nach sollten wir weniger verschwenden. **[1]** In my opinion, we should waste less. **[1]**,
   c) Wir müssen alternative Energiequellen entwickeln. **[1]** We should develop alternative energy sources. **[1]**,
   d) Ich finde es traurig, dass es immer mehr Armut gibt. **[1]** I think it's sad that there is more and more poverty. **[1]**,
   e) Ich mache mir Sorgen um die Zahl der Obdachlosen in unseren Städten. **[1]** I'm worried about the number of homeless people in our towns. **[1]**
4. a) stehlen **[1]**
   b) arm **[1]**
   c) die Arbeitslosigkeit **[1]**
   d) die Gewalt **[1]**
   e) der Flüchtling **[1]**
   f) das Verbrechen **[1]**

Answers

g) der Einwanderer [1]
h) sich Sorgen machen um [1]
i) der Krieg [1]
j) das Opfer [1]

Page 63

1. **a)** in (die – f) [1] Next year I will go to Switzerland. [1]
   b) nach (das – n) [1] Last year I went to Austria. [1]
   c) in (die – pl) [1] I would like to go to the Netherlands in the future. [1]
   d) nach (das – n) [1] Two years ago, we flew to Spain. [1]
2. **a)** verbringen [1]
   b) bin gegangen [1]
   c) verbracht [1]
   d) fahren [1]
   e) sind gefahren [1]
3. **a)** Die Dusche in meinem Zimmer ist schmutzig. [1]
   b) Ich habe ein Doppelzimmer reserviert. [1]
   c) Um wieviel Uhr ist das Frühstück? [1]
   d) Es gibt keine Handtücher in meinem Zimmer. [1]
   e) Der Fernseher funktioniert nicht. [1]

Pages 64–73 **Revise Questions**

Page 65 Quick Test

1. Answers will vary. Example answer:
   Ich lerne Mathe fünfmal pro Woche. Ich liebe Mathe, weil es äußerst logisch ist. Wir haben Latein montags und dienstags. Latein gefällt mir, denn es ist ziemlich nützlich. Ich lerne Erdkunde zweimal pro Woche. Ich kann Erdkunde nicht leiden, denn es ist ziemlich kompliziert. Wir lernen Kunst einmal pro Woche. Kunst gefällt mir nicht, denn ich bin nicht sehr kreativ. Ich lerne Physik mittwochs und freitags. Ich liebe Physik, aber der Lehrer ist zu streng.
2. interessant, nutzlos, einfach, ungerecht, ausgezeichnet
3. The head(teacher) in my school is a bit strict but I find that excellent. My favourite subject is history because it is very interesting and extremely useful. On Fridays I study an option subject, drama, however I find the teacher too boring.

Page 67 Quick Test

1. Answers will vary. Example answer:
   Ich besuche eine große Gesamtschule und ich bin in der zehnten Klasse. Es gibt eintausend Schüler und Schülerinnen und ungefähr achtzig Lehrer. Wir haben eine große Bibliothek und die Klassenzimmer sind hell und modern. Wir haben einen Schulhof, aber er ist klein und nicht so schön. Ich esse immer im Speisesaal und in der Pause spiele ich Fußball.
2. Answers will vary. Example answer:
   Ich wache um sechs Uhr auf.
   Ich stehe immer um Viertel nach sechs auf.
   Ich ziehe mich nach dem Frühstück an.
   Ich verlasse das Haus um halb acht.
   Ich fahre immer mit dem Rad zur Schule.

3. **a)** Ich besuche ein Gymnasium.
   b) Es gibt ungefähr 850 / achthundertfünfzig Schüler.
   c) Wir haben 30 Klassenzimmer aber keinen Speisesaal / keine Mensa.
   d) Der Schultag beginnt um halb neun / acht Uhr dreißig und endet um drei / fünfzehn Uhr.

Page 69 Quick Test

1. Answers will vary. Example answers:
   Man darf keine Handys benutzen.
   Man darf kein Kaugummi kauen.
   Man muss eine Schuluniform tragen.
   Man darf nicht blau machen.
   Man darf nicht rauchen.
   Man muss die Hausaufgaben machen.
   Man darf im Unterricht nicht plaudern.
   Man muss im Unterricht gut aufpassen.
   Man muss gute Noten bekommen.
   Man darf nicht mobben.
   Wenn man ein Handy im Unterricht benutzt, muss man nachsitzen. Wenn man die Hausaufgaben nicht macht, muss man eine Strafarbeit machen.
2. Answers will vary. Example answer:
   In Germany, grades range from 1-6, where 1 is the best. If your grades aren't good enough, you may have to repeat a school year, which is called sitzenbleiben.
3. **a)** I wear a blue blazer with a white shirt.
   b) My school uniform is very comfortable but not very trendy.
   c) When/if it is cold, the girls are allowed to wear tights.
   d) You are allowed to wear a scarf, but only in winter.

Page 71 Quick Test

1. Answers will vary. Example answer:
   Ich werde auf die Uni gehen.
   Ich werde Mathe oder Naturwissenschaften studieren.
   Ich hoffe, ein Jahr freizunehmen.
   Ich hoffe, mit Kindern zu arbeiten.
   Ich will mich um eine Lehre bewerben.
   Ich will einen Ausbildungsplatz finden.
2. **a)** Nächstes Jahr plane ich, nach Deutschland zu reisen.
   b) Ich mache eine Lehre, denn ich will Geld verdienen.
   c) In der Oberstufe möchte ich Erdkunde abwählen.
3. **a)** Ich hoffe, das Abitur zu machen, und will ich Mathe studieren.
   b) Meiner Meinung nach war der Berufsberater sehr hilfsbereit.
   c) Nächstes Jahr werde ich mich um einen Nebenjob / Teilzeitjob bewerben.
   d) In der Zukunft möchte ich viel Geld verdienen und auf ein Haus sparen.

Page 73 Quick Test

1. Answers will vary.
2. Answers will vary. Example answer:
   Ich möchte nicht LKW-Fahrer werden, denn die Arbeitszeit ist zu lang.
   Ich will Rechtsanwalt werden, weil es interessant ist.

Ich möchte Lehrer werden, da ich gern mit Kindern arbeite.
Ich will nicht als Koch arbeiten, denn es ist stressig.
Ich möchte Schauspieler sein, weil man viel reisen kann.

3. **a)** Ich werde vierzigtausend Pfund verdienen und als Innenausstatter arbeiten.
   b) Mein Bruder ist Fleischer / Metzger und er besitzt ein Geschäft und eine Fabrik.
   c) Ich will nicht im Freien arbeiten, aber ich will für meine Arbeit reisen.
   d) Mein Traumjob ist gut bezahlt und interessant und ich möchte viel Urlaub.

Pages 74–77 **Review Questions**

Page 74

1. einem [1], dem [1], der [1], dem [1], dem [1]
2. **a)** wohne [1]
   b) ist [1]
   c) putze [1]
   d) gibt [1]
   e) möchten [1]
   f) kann [1]
   g) befindet [1]
3. Students may give any 4 sentences and the marks are for the correct translation of each up to a maximum of 4 marks.
   a) Es gibt viele Möglichkeiten auszugehen. There are lots of possibilities for going out.
   b) Es ist nicht so laut wie in einer Stadt. It is not as loud as in a town.
   c) Wir haben viele schöne Geschäfte. We have a lot of nice shops.
   d) Die Mieten sind teuer. Rents are expensive.
   e) Man kann täglich Vögel sehen und hören. You can see and hear birds every day.
   f) Die Ruhe gefällt mir sehr. I really like the peace.
   g) Die öffentlichen Verkehrsmittel fahren häufig. Public transport is frequent.
   h) Man kann am Wochenende mit Freunden spazieren gehen. You can go walking with friends at the weekend.

Page 75

1. **a)** besser [1]
   b) machen [1]
   c) zu [1]
   d) töten [1]
   e) hat [1]
2. **a)** relaxing [1]
   b) water [1]
   c) three times a week [1]
   d) gave up smoking [1]
   e) go on a diet [1]

Page 76

1. **a)** die Überschwemmung [1]
   b) gefährdete/bedrohte Arten [1]
   c) der saure Regen [1]
   d) das Ozonloch [1]
   e) der Lärm [1]
   f) die Spraydose [1]
   g) der Karton [1]
   h) die Verpackung [1]
   i) die Kohle [1]
   j) das Kraftwerk [1]

2. **a)** um die Umwelt zu schützen [1]
   b) um eine Zunahme der
      Arbeitslosen zu vermeiden [1]
   c) um nicht zu viel Energie zu
      verschwenden [1]
   d) statt die Umwelt zu zerstören [1]
   e) ohne über die Folgen nachzudenken [1]
3. **a)** sollten [1]
   b) könnte [1]
   c) kannst [1]
   d) könnte [1]
   e) sollte [1]
4. Answers will vary. Example answers:
   a) Ich finde, dass es immer mehr
      Obdachlose in meiner Stadt gibt. [1]
      I think that there are more and more
      homeless people in my town. [1]
   b) Meiner Meinung nach ist die
      Arbeitslosigkeit das wichtigste Problem
      heutzutage. [1] In my opinion,
      unemployment is the most important
      problem nowadays. [1]
   c) Ich denke, dass wir etwas gegen
      Armut in der Welt machen sollten. [1]
      I think we should do something about
      poverty in the world. [1]
   d) Ich bin der Meinung, dass wir
      Luftverschmutzung verhindern sollten.
      [1] I'm of the opinion that we should
      prevent air pollution. [1]
   e) Ich denke, dass die Gewalt in unseren
      Städten immer schlimmer wird. [1]
      I think that the violence in our towns is
      getting worse and worse. [1]

Page 77
1. **a)** hier [1]
   b) in einer Jugendherberge [1]
   c) Griechenland [1]
   d) ins/im Ausland [1]
   e) kaputt [1]
   f) mit dem Zug [1]
   g) ein Aufzug [1]
   h) da [1]
   i) im Erdgeschoss [1]
   j) der Schlüssel [1]
2. **a)** waren [1], hatten [1] When we were
      in France, our car broke down. [1]
   b) sind [1], wollten [1] Last year we
      went abroad, because we wanted to
      swim every day. [1]
   c) möchten [1] Next year, we'd like to
      stay with friends in Switzerland,
      because we won't spend much
      money there. [1]
3. **a)** Ich werde nach Frankreich fahren. [1]
   b) Ich werde dorthin fliegen. [1]
   c) Er wird in einer Jugendherberge
      übernachten. [1]
   d) Meine Familie und ich werden dort
      viel Spaß haben. [1]
4. Answers will vary. For example: Letztes Jahr
   sind meine Familie und ich für zwei Wochen
   nach Spanien geflogen. Wir sind viel im
   Meer geschwommen und wir sind viel am
   Strand spazieren gegangen. Ich gehe sehr
   gern schwimmen. Wir haben auch oft Eis
   gegessen – lecker! Nächstes Jahr möchte

ich einen Winterurlaub in Österreich
machen, weil ich Skifahren lernen will.

Pages 78–79 **Practice Questions**
Page 78
1. ausgezeichnet [1], zwei [1], Physik [1],
   nutzlos [1]
2. **a)** School uniform [1]
   b) No mobile phones / banning
      mobile phones [1]
   c) Any one from: less bullying / students
      are friendlier / students talk to each
      other more [1]
   d) A ban on chewing (gum) / no
      chewing (gum) allowed [1]

Page 79
1. **a)** NT [1]
   b) F [1]
   c) R [1]
   d) F [1]
   e) R [1]
   f) NT [1]
2. B [1] E [1] F [1]

Pages 80–87 **Revise Questions**
Page 81 Quick Test
1. Januar M; Freundin F; Bisschen N
2. Pullover; Bücher; Uhren
3. das Haus; der Rasen; die Portion
4. ein Haus; ein Rasen; eine Portion
5. kein Haus; kein Rasen; keine Portion

Page 83 Quick Test
1. **a)** Die Stadt ist schön.
   b) Der Schnee ist kalt.
   c) Das Haus ist alt.
2. **a)** Ein Arzt verdient viel Geld.
   b) Ein Motorrad fährt schnell.
   c) Eine Katze ist niedlich.
3. **a)** Hast du den Film gesehen?
   b) Ich sehe das Haus.
   c) Ich möchte die Schokolade.
4. **a)** Ich habe eine Katze.
   b) Ich möchte einen Hamburger.
   c) Papa hat ein Auto.
5. **a)** Er schenkt seinem Lehrer einen Apfel.
   a) Sie schenkt ihrer Lehrerin eine Apfelsine.
6. Answers will vary. Example answers:
   Unsere Stadt ist schön.
   Ihr Haus ist alt.
   Dieser Arzt verdient viel Geld.
   Mein Motorrad fährt schnell.
   Ich sehe dein Haus.

Page 85 Quick Test
1. **a)** die schöne Landschaft
   b) den kleinen Hund
   c) dem alten Auto
2. **a)** ein nettes Mädchen
   b) eine lange Reise
   c) einem guten Freund
3. größer; älter; glücklicher; besser
4. schönst–; kleinst–; reichst–; billigst–
5. **a)** Olli geht schnell.
   b) Priti geht schneller.
   c) Udo geht am schnellsten.

Page 87 Quick Test
1. **a)** Ich fahre zu dem / zum Supermarkt.
   b) Wir fahren mit diesem Schiff.
   c) Wir essen bei meiner Tante.
2. **a)** ohne mein Auto
   b) um die Kurve
   c) für unseren Onkel
3. **a)** D, **b)** A
4. **a)** Mein Garten ist vor meinem Haus.
   b) Gehst du in die Schule?
5. **a)** wegen des Wetters
   b) während der Stunde

Pages 88–89 **Review Questions**
Page 88
1. **a)** Max [1]
   b) Lea [1]
   c) Thomas [1]
   d) Simone [1]
   e) Ulrike [1]
   f) Katja [1]
2. **a)** F [1]
   b) NT [1]
   c) R [1]
   d) F [1]
   e) F [1]
   f) R [1]

Page 89
1. **a)** machen [1]
   b) arbeiten [1]
   c) reisen [1]
   d) abwählen [1]
   e) bewerben [1]
   f) sparen [1]
   g) studieren [1]
   h) freinehmen [1]
2. **a)** gut bezahlt [1]
   b) hoch [1]
   c) gründen [1]
   d) Urlaub [1]
   e) geduldig [1]
   f) erfüllen [1]
   g) eine Halbtagsarbeit [1]
   h) die Schichtarbeit [1]

Page 90–91 **Practice Questions**
Page 90
1. **a)** M [1], **b)** F [1], **c)** M [1], **d)** F [1],
   e) F [1], **f)** N [1], **g)** N [1], **h)** M [1],
   i) M [1], **j)** F [1], **k)** F [1], **l)** F [1],
   m) F [1], **n)** N [1], **o)** M [1]
2. **a)** das Mountainbike [1]
   b) die Bratwurst [1]
   c) der Garten [1]
   d) die Banane [1]
   e) der Arm [1]
   f) die Party [1]
   g) das Haus [1]
   h) das Fest [1]
   i) die Leinwand [1]
   j) der Computer [1]
3. **a)** ein Mountainbike [1]
   b) eine Bratwurst [1]
   c) ein Garten [1]
   d) eine Banane [1]

Answers

e) ein Arm **[1]**
f) eine Party **[1]**
g) ein Haus **[1]**
h) ein Fest **[1]**
i) eine Leinwand **[1]**
j) ein Computer **[1]**
4. Answers will vary. Example answers:
kein Mountainbike; keine Bratwurst; kein Garten; keine Banane; kein Arm; keine Party; kein Haus; kein Fest; keine Leinwand; kein Computer **[10]**
5. a) Ein Baby ist klein. **[1]**
b) Eine Kirsche ist rot. **[1]**
c) Ein Einzelzimmer ist klein. **[1]**
d) Eine Katze ist niedlich. **[1]**
e) Ein Betriebspraktikum dauert 6 Wochen. **[1]**
f) Ein Horrorfilm macht mir Angst. **[1]**
g) Eine Erdbeertorte schmeckt gut. **[1]**
h) Ein Motorrad kostet viel Geld. **[1]**
i) Eine Scheibe Wurst ist auf dem Teller. **[1]**
j) Ein Zahnarzt verdient viel Geld. **[1]**

Page 91
1. a) Nominative: die schmutzige Umwelt **[1]**
b) Accusative: den netten Jungen **[1]**
c) Dative: dem alten Auto **[1]**
d) Nominative: der bittere Apfel **[1]**
e) Accusative: die blöde Werbung **[1]**
f) Dative: dem scharfen Messer **[1]**
g) Nominative: das leckere Eis **[1]**
h) Accusative: den unfreundlichen Kellner **[1]**
i) Dative: der intelligenten Schülerin **[1]**
2. a) dicker **[1]**
b) stärker **[1]**
c) kälter **[1]**
d) größer **[1]**
e) hübscher **[1]**
f) neuer **[1]**
g) jünger **[1]**
h) interessanter **[1]**
i) schöner **[1]**
j) langweiliger **[1]**
3. a) Wir treffen uns nach dem Essen. **[1]**
b) Ich stehe vor der Schule. **[1]**
c) Kommst du zum Jugendklub? **[1]**
d) Wir fahren mit dem Bus. **[1]**
e) Ich bin seit der Party krank. **[1]**
f) Er kommt aus dem Haus. **[1]**
4. a) A **[1]**
b) D **[1]**
c) D **[1]**
d) A **[1]**
e) D **[1]**
f) A **[1]**
g) A **[1]**
h) D **[1]**
5. a) Mein Garten ist vor meinem Haus. **[1]**
b) Deine Schuhe liegen hinter dieser Tür. **[1]**
c) Gehst du in die Schule? **[1]**
d) Wir gehen in einen Park. **[1]**

Pages 92–107 **Revise Questions**

Page 93 Quick Test
1. wir; du; man

---

2. a) Der Pullover ist schön. Ich kaufe ihn.
b) Ich habe dich nicht gesehen.
3. a) Kommst du mit mir?
b) Ich gebe ihm Geld.
4. a) Wer ist da? Niemand.
b) Etwas hat mich schockiert.

Page 95 Quick Test
1. a) du spielst **b)** wir machen **c)** Er bleibt
2. a) Wir setzen uns hin.
b) Mika verletzt sich oft.
3. a) Wo steigen wir aus?
b) Wir stehen früh auf.
4. Wir besuchen; Es gefällt mir; Ich verstehe

Page 97 Quick Test
1. a) Was nimmst du?
b) Ahmed liest die Zeitung.
2. a) sie müssen
b) magst du?
3. a) Ich gehe ins Kino, um einen Film zu sehen.
b) Wir gehen zum Supermarkt, um Brot zu kaufen.
4. a) Es gibt ein Café in der Stadt.
b) Es gibt viel zu tun.

Page 99 Quick Test
1. gefunden
gespielt
2. a) Hast du dieses Buch gelesen?
b) Wer hat meinen Geldbeutel genommen?
3. gefahren
gegangen
4. a) Ich bin eine halbe Stunde geblieben.
b) Wir sind nie in Köln gewesen.
5. a) Die Kinder haben sich getroffen.
b) Ich habe mich gewaschen.
6. a) Hast du abgewaschen?
b) Wann seid ihr angekommen?

Page 101 Quick Test
1. a) wir hörten
b) er spielte
2. a) Er sprach laut.
b) Wir standen vor der Kirche.
3. a) Ich mochte die Musik gern.
b) Wir wollten schwimmen gehen.

Page 103 Quick Test
1. a) I'm going home soon.
b) We are going to the cinema on Friday.
2. a) Ich werde bald nach Hause gehen.
b) Wir werden am Freitag ins Kino gehen.
3. a) Wenn die Lehrerin besser wäre, würde ich mehr arbeiten.
b) Wenn wir alter wären, würden wir allein in die Stadt gehen.
4. a) If the teacher was better I would work more.
b) If we were older we would go into town on our own.

Page 105 Quick Test
1. a) Wir sind ins Bett gegangen, nachdem wir gegessen hatten.
b) Er war krank gewesen.
2. a) Nehmen Sie die erste Straße!
b) Fahr / Geh geradeaus!
3. a) Möchtet ihr mitkommen?
b) Wir wären nicht geblieben.

Page 107 Quick Test
1. a) Wir essen immer gut in Frankreich.
b) Ich arbeite jeden Tag in einem Geschäft.
2. a) Wann beginnt der Film?
b) Wer hat das gesagt?
3. a) Ich weiß, dass du hier bist.
b) Wir essen Kuchen, aber er ist nicht gut.

Pages 108–109 **Review Questions**

Page 108
1. a) S **[1]**, **b)** P **[1]**, **c)** P **[1]**, **d)** P **[1]**,
e) P **[1]**, **f)** S **[1]**, **g)** S **[1]**, **h)** S **[1]**,
i) S **[1]**, **j)** E **[1]**, **k)** E **[1]**, **l)** P **[1]**,
m) P **[1]**, **n)** E **[1]**, **o)** S **[1]**
2. a) Der Film ist langweilig. **[1]**
b) Die Bank ist geschlossen. **[1]**
c) Der Bus fährt schnell. **[1]**
d) Der Laptop ist kaputt. **[1]**
e) Das Haus ist teuer. **[1]**
f) Die Schülerin heißt Doris. **[1]**
3. a) Ich **[1]** schenke meiner Mutter **[1]** Pralinen. **[1]**
b) Du **[1]** schreibst deinem Onkel **[1]** einen Brief. **[1]**
c) Die Tante **[1]** hat ihrer Nichte **[1]** ein Geschenk **[1]** gegeben.
d) Ich **[1]** habe dieser Organisation **[1]** Geld **[1]** gegeben.
4. a) Wir haben drei Stühle. **[1]**
b) Ich habe meinen Bruder verloren. **[1]**
c) Ich gebe meinem Onkel ein Geschenk. **[1]**
d) Hast du deinen Laptop vergessen? **[1]**
e) Unser Auto ist alt. **[1]**
f) Wir arbeiten in unserem Büro. **[1]**

Page 109
1. a) Der intelligente **[1]** Schüler bekommt eine gute Note.
b) Wir fahren mit dem nächsten **[1]** Zug nach München.
c) Der altmodische **[1]** Lehrer ist streng.
d) Ich kaufe dieses schwarze **[1]** T-Shirt.
e) Heute gehen wir ins neue **[1]** Einkaufszentrum.
f) Ich habe eine nette **[1]** Freundin.
g) Es gibt kein frisches **[1]** Obst.
h) Diese blöden **[1]** Leute nerven mich.
i) Meine Tante hat einen schweren **[1]** Unfall gehabt.
j) Hamsa hat sein neues **[1]** Handy verloren.
2. a) Ich bin größer als Andi. **[1]**
b) Englisch ist einfacher als Deutsch. **[1]**
c) Deine Noten sind schlechter als meine. **[1]**
d) Paris ist schöner als London. **[1]**
e) Olli läuft schneller als Tim. **[1]**
f) Mathe ist langweiliger als Kunst. **[1]**
3. a) der älteste **[1]** Schüler
b) die langweiligste **[1]** Sendung
c) das billigste **[1]** Essen
4. a) Ich fahre in die **[1]** Stadt.
b) Die Straßenbahn steht an der **[1]** Haltestelle.
c) Das Essen steht auf dem **[1]** Tisch.
d) Der Hund ist hinter dem **[1]** Schrank.

e) Ich stelle die Milch in den **[1]** Kühlschrank.

f) Mein Hut ist auf meinem **[1]** Kopf.

g) Ich hänge das Bild an die **[1]** Wand.

h) Ich komme zu deiner **[1]** Party.

i) Wir sind seit dem **[1]** Sommer hier.

j) Wir sprechen nicht während des **[1]** Films.

Page 110–113 Practice Questions

Page 110

1. a) Der Kuli ist schön. Ich kaufe ihn **[1]**.

b) Wir haben dich **[1]** nicht gesehen.

c) Ich rufe Sie **[1]** an.

d) Hast du uns **[1]** gesehen?

e) Kennst du mich **[1]**?

f) Meine Schwester heißt Anna. Ich mag sie **[1]** gern.

g) Die Kinder sind artig. Ich mag sie **[1]** gern.

h) Wir besuchen euch **[1]**.

i) Ich habe dir **[1]** ein Geschenk gekauft.

j) Geben Sie mir **[1]** die Speisekarte bitte.

2. a) Wen hast du gesehen? Niemand. **[1]**; Who did you see? Nobody **[1]**

b) Ich habe etwas vergessen. **[1]**; I forgot something. **[1]**

c) Jemand war in unserem Haus. **[1]**; Somebody was in our House. **[1]**

d) Alle sind zum Konzert gekommen. **[1]**; Everyone came to the concert. **[1]**

e) Wir haben nichts gefunden. **[1]**; We have found nothing. **[1]**

3. a) Er setzt sich **[1]** im Wohnzimmer hin.

b) Aua! Ich habe mich **[1]** verletzt!

c) Ich rasiere mich **[1]** jeden Morgen.

d) Sie treffen sich **[1]** um 16 Uhr.

e) Wo treffen wir uns **[1]**?

f) Sie wäscht sich **[1]** im Badezimmer.

4. a) ich verstehe nicht **[1]**

b) sie besucht **[1]**

c) es gefällt uns **[1]**

Page 111

1. a) Thomas nimmt **[1]** den Bus.

b) Andrea liest **[1]** ein gutes Buch.

c) Wir treffen **[1]** unsere Freunde um 4 Uhr.

d) Karla läuft **[1]** 10 Kilometer.

e) Was isst **[1]** du?

f) Ein BMW fährt **[1]** schnell.

2. a) Es gibt einen Teller auf dem Tisch. **[1]**

b) Es gibt ein Problem. **[1]**

c) Es gibt einen Dom in Köln. **[1]**

3. a) geschrieben **[1]**

b) gegeben **[1]**

c) gelesen **[1]**

d) gekauft **[1]**

e) gesagt **[1]**

f) gefunden **[1]**

g) gespielt **[1]**

h) genommen **[1]**

i) gesehen **[1]**

j) getrunken **[1]**

4. a) Wir sind zwanzig Minuten geblieben. **[1]**

b) Ich bin krank gewesen. **[1]**

c) Meine Eltern sind oft in die Türkei geflogen. **[1]**

d) Du bist zu spät gekommen. **[1]**

e) Die Kinder sind in den Park gegangen. **[1]**

f) Mo Farah ist sehr schnell gelaufen. **[1]**

Page 112

1. a) sie arbeiteten **[1]**

b) man lernte **[1]**

c) Was sagte er? **[1]**

d) du hörtest **[1]**

e) wir spielten **[1]**

f) man kochte **[1]**

g) ich spielte **[1]**

h) du fragtest **[1]**

i) sie kaufte **[1]**

j) sie wohnten **[1]**

2. a) Wir mochten **[1]** die Fernsehsendung gern.

b) Ich wollte **[1]** tanzen gehen.

c) Lydia konnte **[1]** nicht schnell laufen.

d) Musstest **[1]** du so laut sein?

e) Wir sollten **[1]** um sechs Uhr zu Hause sein.

f) Olaf durfte **[1]** im Restaurant nicht rauchen.

3. a) Wenn der Lehrer nicht so langweilig wäre, würde ich besser lernen. **[1]**

b) Wenn wir älter wären, würden wir allein in die Stadt gehen dürfen. **[1]**

c) Wenn ich Zeit hätte, würde ich mehr Sport treiben. **[1]**

d) Wenn mein Vater hungrig wäre, würde er etwas essen. **[1]**

e) Wenn Sonja reich wäre, würde sie ein Pferd kaufen. **[1]**

f) Wenn ich mehr Geld hätte, würde ich für Kinder in Afrika spenden. **[1]**

4. a) If the teacher wasn't so boring I would learn better. **[1]**

b) If we were older we would be allowed to go into town on our own. **[1]**

c) If I had time I would do more sport. **[1]**

d) If my father was hungry he would eat something. **[1]**

e) If Sonja was rich she would buy a horse. **[1]**

f) If I had more money I would donate to children in Africa. **[1]**

Page 113

1. a) Möchtet **[1]** ihr mitkommen?

b) Wir wären **[1]** nicht geblieben.

c) Lara hätte **[1]** nicht gelacht.

d) Es wäre **[1]** schön gewesen.

2. a) Would you like to come? **[1]**

b) We would not have stayed. **[1]**

c) Lara would not have laughed. **[1]**

d) It would have been nice. **[1]**

3. a) <u>Wann</u> beginnt das Konzert? **[1]**

b) <u>Bist</u> du müde? **[1]**

c) <u>Wie viel</u> kostet dieses Buch? **[1]**

d) <u>Wer</u> bist du? **[1]**

e) <u>Was</u> hast du gekauft? **[1]**

f) <u>Wie</u> alt ist sie? **[1]**

g) <u>Warum</u> ist sie nicht hier? **[1]**

h) <u>Was für</u> Musik magst du? **[1]**

i) <u>Kommst</u> du mit? **[1]**

j) <u>Spielt</u> ihr gern Tennis? **[1]**

4. a) Ich weiß, dass **[1]** du unglücklich bist.

b) Wir haben Kuchen gegessen, aber **[1]** er war nicht gut.

c) Weißt du, ob **[1]** es draußen kalt ist?

d) Quentin war unfreundlich, als **[1]** er krank war.

e) Ich mag Grammatikübungen, weil **[1]** sie interessant sind.

f) Wir lernen Französisch, damit **[1]** wir mit unseren französischen Freunden sprechen können.

Pages 114–119 Review Questions

Page 114

1. a) Ich komme mit dir. **[1]**

b) Wie heißt du? **[1]**

c) Wie heißen Sie? **[1]**

d) Wir essen bei mir. **[1]**

e) Ist das Geschenk für mich? **[1]**

f) Mein Vater ist super. Ich mag ihn gern. **[1]**

g) Wo ist meine Handtasche? Ich habe sie verloren. **[1]**

h) Ich liebe dich. **[1]**

i) Liebst du mich? **[1]**

j) Kommst du zu uns? **[1]**

2. a) wir schwimmen **[1]**

b) ich komme **[1]**

c) sie sagen **[1]**

d) es macht **[1]**

e) du spielst **[1]**

f) ihr singt **[1]**

g) sie fliegt **[1]**

h) meine Eltern gehen **[1]**

3. a) Er verletzt sich. **[1]**

b) Sie freut sich. **[1]**

c) Ich rasiere mich. **[1]**

d) Wir interessieren uns. **[1]**

e) Sie amüsieren sich. **[1]**

4. a) Ich gehe oft ins Kino. **[1]**

b) Wir interessieren uns für Musik. **[1]**

c) Ich stehe nie vor neun Uhr auf. **[1]**

d) Sie schwimmen in der Sonne. **[1]**

e) Spielst du Tennis? **[1]**

f) Was machen Sie? **[1]**

g) Kommt ihr? **[1]**

h) Ella trinkt Kaffee. **[1]**

Page 115

1. a) du fährst **[1]**, er / sie / es fährt **[1]**

b) du schläfst **[1]**, er / sie / es schläft **[1]**

c) du isst **[1]**, er / sie / es isst **[1]**

d) du sprichst **[1]**, er / sie / es spricht **[1]**

e) du nimmst **[1]**, er / sie / es nimmt **[1]**

f) du liest **[1]**, er / sie / es liest **[1]**

2. a) Kevin isst **[1]** nicht gern Fleisch.

b) Fatima spricht **[1]** sehr gut Deutsch.

c) Benjamin fährt **[1]** nach Hause.

d) Mein Opa gibt **[1]** mir 10 Euro.

e) Nimmst **[1]** du Milch und Zucker?

f) Schläfst **[1]** du?

3. a) Meine Mutter ist nach Ibiza gefahren. **[1]**

b) Hast du mein Handy genommen? **[1]**

c) Wir haben uns um 15 Uhr getroffen. **[1]**

d) Wir sind zu Hause geblieben. **[1]**

e) Er hat ein Glas Wasser getrunken. **[1]**

f) Der Zug ist abgefahren. **[1]**

g) Marita hat Spanisch gesprochen. **[1]**

h) Meine Oma ist gestorben. **[1]**

4. a) Wir sind ausgestiegen. **[1]**

b) Ich habe ein Spiel heruntergeladen. **[1]**

c) Wann bist du aufgestanden? **[1]**

d) Der Zug ist schon abgefahren. **[1]**

Answers

e) Ich habe mich gefreut. **[1]**
f) Wir haben uns noch nicht entschieden. **[1]**

Page 116

1. a) I **[1]**, b) P **[1]**, c) P **[1]**, d) I **[1]**, e) P **[1]**, f) P **[1]**, g) P **[1]**, h) P **[1]**, i) P **[1]**, j) P **[1]**, k) I **[1]**, l) I **[1]**, m) I **[1]**, n) I **[1]**, o) I **[1]**, p) P **[1]**, q) I **[1]**, r) P **[1]**

2. Der Politiker fuhr **[1]** nach Berlin. Er kam **[1]** am Dienstag an und saß **[1]** und sprach **[1]** mit Kollegen. Er fand **[1]** die Gespräche sehr produktiv.

3. a) Wir mussten nach Hause gehen. **[1]**
   b) Sie konnten Englisch sprechen. **[1]**
   c) Wir wollten online chatten. **[1]**
   d) Sie durfte spät ins Bett gehen. **[1]**

4. a) Was wirst **[1]** du machen?
   b) Wir werden **[1]** fernsehen.
   c) Man wird **[1]** mit Mobbing ein Problem haben.
   d) Ich werde **[1]** immer recyceln.
   e) Wir werden **[1]** Ramadan feiern.

Page 117

1. a) Ich war mit dem Rad zur Schule gefahren. **[1]**
   b) Warst du früh angekommen? **[1]**
   c) Mein Vater war einkaufen gegangen. **[1]**
   d) Wir waren nach Amerika geflogen. **[1]**
   e) Wart ihr lange geblieben? **[1]**
   f) Meine Eltern waren krank gewesen. **[1]**
   g) Ich hatte zu viel gegessen. **[1]**
   h) Du hattest dein Handy vergessen. **[1]**
   i) Elise hatte zu laut gesungen. **[1]**
   j) Wir hatten Tennis gespielt. **[1]**
   k) Hattet ihr diesen Film gesehen? **[1]**
   l) Sie hatten hart gearbeitet. **[1]**

2. Change: so dass; weil; als; ob; wenn; dass; obwohl **[7]**
   No change: aber; und **[2]**

Pages 118–131 Mix it Up Questions

Reading

1. We live in the country (side) **[1]**. It is quieter / more peaceful here **[1]** than in the town **[1]** and we / you can do a lot of walking / go walking a lot **[1]**. The farm has four bedrooms, two bathrooms **[1]** and a large kitchen **[1]**. Every Saturday **[1]** there is a market **[1]** in the village **[1]**.

2. a) Fritz **[1]**, b) Agatha **[1]**, c) Ansel **[1]**, d) Petra **[1]**, e) Gabi **[1]**

3. b) **[1]**, e) **[1]**, f) **[1]**, g) **[1]**

4. a) Sabrine **[1]**, b) Bernd **[1]**, c) Jens **[1]**, d) Hans **[1]**, e) Anja **[1]**, f) Angela **[1]**

5. The first lesson begins / starts every day at 7:30 / half past 7, at 7:30 / half past 7 every day **[1]**. We are meeting in the hall / we will meet in the hall **[1]** where you will see the head(teacher) / headmistress **[1]**. You must not bring your phone (with you) **[1]** because they are forbidden / banned / not allowed **[1]**. Last week my maths teacher **[1]** saw my (mobile) phone **[1]** and I have to do a detention / I have detention this week **[1]**. That isn't good! / that's not good! **[1]**

6. a) Ahmed **[1]**, b) Kirstin **[1]**, c) Frank **[1]**, d) Sebastian **[1]**, e) Birgit **[1]**

7. a) Traditional **[1]** German food is not (particularly) healthy **[1]**.
   b) Many families **[1]** eat meat **[1]** and sausages.
   c) They are full of fat **[1]** and salt **[1]**.
   d) There are 50 calories in one slice **[1]** of sausage **[1]**.
   e) Now it's cool to be vegetarian **[1]** or vegan **[1]**.
   f) Vegans only eat food that has nothing **[1]** to do with animals **[1]**.

8. Mein Vater ist intelligent aber sehr streng. – My father is intelligent but strict. **[1]**
   Wir verstehen uns gut. – We get on well. **[1]**
   Ich streite mich nie mit meiner Schwester. – I never argue with my sister. **[1]**
   Meine Schwester ist ruhig und artig. – My sister is quiet and well-behaved. **[1]**
   Ich streite mich manchmal mit meiner Schwester. – I sometimes argue with my sister. **[1]**
   Mein Vater ist stur aber oft großzügig. – My father is stubborn but often generous. **[1]**

9. a) Bernadette **[1]**, b) Hans **[1]**, c) Michael **[1]**, d) Beate **[1]**, e) Sebastian **[1]**

10. a) Mohammed **[1]**, b) Damien **[1]**, c) Laura **[1]**, d) Bettina **[1]**, e) Rosa **[1]**, f) Aisa **[1]**, g) Cara **[1]**, h) Kevin **[1]**

11. hilfsbereit **[1]**; Kunst **[1]**; Lehrerin **[1]**; wichtiges **[1]**; klug **[1]**; leicht **[1]**

12. a) **[1]**, d) **[1]**, f) **[1]**, g) **[1]**

13. I have been married to my husband for 21 years. **[2]** We have two children, one son and one daughter. **[2]** Many marriages end in divorce but we love each other very much. **[2]** Marriage is a symbol of love. **[2]**

Writing

1. a) Ich stehe um halb sieben / sechs Uhr dreißig auf. **[2]**
   b) Meine Schwester besucht eine Grundschule. **[2]**
   c) Wir haben einen Schulhof aber er ist klein. **[2]**
   d) Morgen werde ich in der Mensa / im Speisesaal essen. **[2]**
   e) Gestern bin ich in mit dem Auto in die Schule gefahren. **[2]** (TMP rule must be accurate)

2. a) Tastatur **[1]**
   b) Startseite **[1]**
   c) WLAN **[1]**
   d) Bildschirm **[1]**
   e) herunterladen **[1]**
   f) Webseite **[1]**
   g) suchen **[1]**
   h) drucken **[1]**
   i) Nachrichten **[1]**
   j) hochladen **[1]**

3. Answers will vary. Example answer:
   Letztes Jahr während den Sommerferien sind meine Mutter und ich nach Griechenland gefahren. Wir sind jeden Tag am Strand spazieren gegangen und wir haben viel gelesen. Wir hatten viel Spaß zusammen. Es war besser, als ich dachte. Im Dezember werden wir in der Schweiz Ski laufen. **[12]**

4. a) Die Apotheke ist vor dem Bahnhof. **[2]**
   b) Ich wohne gern auf dem Lande. **[2]**
   c) Ich habe meinen Geldbeutel auf der Straße verloren. **[2]**
   d) Man kann schöne Geschenke kaufen. **[2]**
   e) Es gibt eine große Buchhandlung. **[2]**

5. In der Vergangenheit war ich nicht sehr gesund. Ich war Sklave/Sklavin vom Computer und habe zu viel ferngesehen. Jetzt esse ich mindestens fünf Portionen Obst/Frucht und Gemüse pro Tag und ich vermeide fettige Produkte. In der Zukunft werde ich bestimmt nicht rauchen und ich werde mich regelmäßig bewegen. **[12]**

6. Answers will vary. Example answers:
   Ich möchte / würde gern älteren Menschen helfen **[1]**
   Ich möchte / würde gern Geld sammeln **[1]**
   Ich möchte / würde gern Medikamente liefern / verteilen **[1]**
   Ich möchte / würde gern Mahlzeiten liefern / verteilen **[1]**
   Ich möchte / würde gern als Krankenschwester arbeiten **[1]**

7. Answers will vary. Example answers:
   I would like to help old people **[1]**
   I would like to collect money **[1]**
   I would like to deliver / distribute medicines **[1]**
   I would like to deliver / distribute meals **[1]**
   I would like to work as a nurse **[1]**

8. Answers will vary. Example answer:
   Ich arbeite seit sieben Monaten in einer Bäckerei in der Stadtmitte. Normalerweise arbeite ich samstags und sonntags und ich muss sehr früh aufstehen – ich backe Brot und ich helfe an der Kasse. Obwohl die Arbeitszeit lang ist, mag ich meinen Job, weil meine Kollegen so nett sind und das Gehalt ziemlich hoch ist. Letzte Woche haben wir einen großen Kuchen gebacken und das war super interessant, denn ich mag kreative Arbeit. In der Zukunft werde ich an die Uni gehen, um Biologie zu studieren, da ich Arzt werden will. Ich bin geduldig und ich möchte anderen Leuten helfen. **[16]**

9. a) That makes me cry. **[1]**
   b) It frightens me. **[1]**
   c) What's it about? **[1]**
   d) We prefer to download films. **[1]**
   e) It's better to stay at home. **[1]**
   f) The seats are more comfortable. **[1]**

10. Answers will vary. Example answer:
    Liebe Silke,
    Meine Stadt ist eine kleine Stadt in Süddeutschland in der Nähe vom Schwarzwald. Ich wohne gern hier, weil es viel zu tun gibt und es ziemlich ruhig ist. Letztes Wochenende sind meine Freundin und ich ins Stadtzentrum gefahren und wir sind einkaufen gegangen. Was ich nicht mag, ist die Zunahme von Obdachlosen, die um Geld bitten. Es ist traurig, das zu sehen.

Es gibt auch immer mehr Luftverschmutzung im Stadtzentrum. Um dieses Problem zu lösen, sollte man entweder zu Fuß gehen oder mit dem Zug fahren. **[16]**

11. Ich chatte mit meinen Freunden online aber ich kaufe nie online. **[2]** Meiner Meinung nach muss man vorsichtig sein. **[2]** Das Internet hilft bei meinen Hausaufgaben und ich chatte auch mit meinen Freunden. **[2]**

12. My friend Ella went out to eat with her family. **[2]** It was in an expensive restaurant in the town centre. **[2]** For a starter, Ella chose tuna salad but it didn't taste nice. **[2]** For the main course she ordered chicken but it was cold! **[2]** She didn't have a dessert and she didn't pay either. **[2]**

13. Als ich jung war, bin ich oft schwimmen gegangen **[2]**, aber heutzutage gehe ich lieber angeln. **[2]** Ich möchte Wintersport probieren **[2]**, aber sie sind oft gefährlich. **[2]**

14. Answers will vary. Example answer:
Letztes Jahr sind meine Familie und ich nach Spanien geflogen. Wir haben unseren Urlaub dort wirklich genossen, weil das Wetter immer sonnig war. Das spanische Essen war köstlich, die Leute waren auch alle so freundlich und wir haben viel gesehen und gemacht. Meiner Meinung nach war der Ausflug mit dem Bus nach Barcelona das Allerbeste. Obwohl die Reise dorthin ziemlich lang dauerte, hat es sich gelohnt. Ich fand die Restaurants in 'Las Ramblas' toll und ich werde bestimmt nochmal nach Barcelona fahren. Spanien hat mir gut gefallen und in der Zukunft möchte ich mehr vom Land sehen. Obwohl die Küste sehr schön ist, würde ich gerne in den Bergen spazieren gehen. Statt mit meiner Familie in einem Hotel zu bleiben, würde ich lieber mit Freunden in einer Jugendherberge übernachten. Das wäre auch interessanter, wenn wir mit dem Zug durch Europa fahren könnten, anstatt zu fliegen. Wenn man mit dem Zug fährt, ist das viel langsamer und dadurch kommt man viel mehr in Kontakt mit anderen jungen Leuten. **[32]**

Index

Collins

AQA GCSE 9-1
German

Workbook

with audio download

Amy Bates, Oliver Gray and Keely Laycock

Revision Tips

Rethink Revision

Have you ever taken part in a quiz and thought '*I know this!*' but, despite frantically racking your brain, you just couldn't come up with the answer?

It's very frustrating when this happens but, in a fun situation, it doesn't really matter. However, in your GCSE exams, it will be essential that you can recall the relevant information quickly when you need to.

Most students think that revision is about making sure you **know** *stuff*. Of course, this is important, but it is also about becoming confident that you can **retain** that *stuff* over time and **recall** it quickly when needed.

Revision That Really Works

Experts have discovered that there are two techniques that help with all of these things and consistently produce better results in exams compared to other revision techniques.

Applying these techniques to your GCSE revision will ensure you get better results in your exams and will have all the relevant knowledge at your fingertips when you start studying for further qualifications, like AS and A Levels, or begin work.

It really isn't rocket science either – you simply need to:

- **test yourself** on each topic as many times as possible
- **leave a gap** between the test sessions.

Three Essential Revision Tips

1. **Use Your Time Wisely**

   - Allow yourself plenty of time.
   - Try to start revising at least six months before your exams – it's more effective and less stressful.
   - Your revision time is precious so use it wisely – using the techniques described on this page will ensure you revise effectively and efficiently and get the best results.
   - Don't waste time re-reading the same information over and over again – it's time-consuming and not effective!

2. **Make a Plan**

   - Identify all the topics you need to revise (this All-in-One Revision & Practice book will help you).
   - Plan at least five sessions for each topic.
   - One hour should be ample time to test yourself on the key ideas for a topic.
   - Spread out the practice sessions for each topic – the optimum time to leave between each session is about one month but, if this isn't possible, just make the gaps as big as realistically possible.

3. **Test Yourself**

   - Methods for testing yourself include: quizzes, practice questions, flashcards, past papers, explaining a topic to someone else, etc.
   - This All-in-One Revision & Practice book provides seven practice opportunities per topic.
   - Don't worry if you get an answer wrong – provided you check what the correct answer is, you are more likely to get the same or similar questions right in future!

Visit our website to download your free flashcards, for more information about the benefits of these techniques, and for further guidance on how to plan ahead and make them work for you.

www.collins.co.uk/collinsGCSErevision

Contents

Visit our website at **www.collins.co.uk/collinsgcserevision** to download the audio material for the Listening Paper on pages 176–187 of this workbook.

Me, My Family and Friends

My Family, My Friends & Marriage and Partnerships

1 **Wähle die richtige Antwort aus dem Kästchen.** Choose the correct answer to each question from the box.

mein Onkel   mein Opa   meine Oma   meine Tante   meine Nichte
mein Stiefbruder   meine Kusine   mein Schwager   meine Stiefmutter   mein Cousin

Wer ist ...

a) der Vater von deiner Mutter? ....

b) der Bruder von deinem Vater? ....

c) die Tochter von deinem Bruder? ....

d) der Mann von deiner Schwester? ....

e) die Schwester von deinem Vater? ....

f) die zweite Frau von deinem Vater? ....

g) der Sohn von deinem Onkel? ....

h) die Tochter von deiner Tante? ....   [8 marks]

2 **Füll die Lücken mit Adjektiven aus dem Kästchen.** Complete the sentences with adjectives from the box.

peinlich   fleißig   ruhig   nervig   faul   streng
stur   frech   großzügig   intelligent   sympathisch   ruhig

a) **Er ist immer** .... (quiet) **und** .... (hard-working).

b) **Sie ist oft** .... (lazy) **und** .... (stubborn).

c) **Er ist nie** .... (cheeky) **oder** .... (irritating).

d) **Sie ist nie** .... (generous) **oder** .... (likeable).   [8 marks]

3 **Kopiere und vervollständige die Sätze über deine Familie.** Copy and complete these sentences about your family.

a) **Ich verstehe mich gut mit** .... , **weil er / sie** .... **ist.**

b) **Ich verstehe mich nicht gut mit** .... , **weil er / sie** .... **ist.**

c) **Ich streite mich oft mit** .... , **weil er / sie** .... **ist.**

[6 marks: 1 mark for each appropriate answer and 1 mark for correct use of each dative form]

4 **Verbinde die Satzteile.** Connect the two halves of the sentences.

Meine beste Freundin ist schlank und…
Sie hat blaue Augen und…
Wir kennen uns…
Sie ist immer treu und nie…
Wir haben viel….
Wir mögen…
Wir haben auch den gleichen…
Wir treffen uns immer…

die gleichen Fernsehsendungen.
neidisch oder schlecht gelaunt.
blonde Haare.
etwas kleiner als ich.
am Wochenende.
Humor.
seit fünf Jahren.
gemeinsam.

[8 marks]

5 **Beschreib deinen besten Freund / deine beste Freundin. So detailliert wie möglich bitte!** Write a description of your best friend. Include as many details as possible.

....

....

....

[10 marks]

6 **Vervollständige die Sätze mit Wörtern aus dem Kästchen. Übersetze die Sätze ins Englische.**
Complete the sentences using words from the box. Then translate the sentences into English.

verlobt   Zusammenleben   endet   bleiben
beginnt   verstehen   heiraten   verletzt

a) Ich möchte lieber ledig ....

b) Ich möchte eines Tages ....

c) Eine Ehe .... oft mit Scheidung.

d) Eine Ehe ist sicherer als ....

e) Meine Eltern sind geschieden aber sie .... sich gut.

f) Meine Freundin hat sich .... Sie heiratet bald.

[12 marks: 1 mark for each completed sentence and 1 mark for each translation]

Technology in Everyday Life

Social Media & Mobile Technology

1 **Vervollständige die Sätze mit Verben aus dem Kästchen.** Complete the sentences with verbs from the box.

> hilft   besuche   lade… herunter   schicken   empfangen   bleibt   verbringe

a) Ich _____ viel Zeit online. (I spend a lot of time online.)

b) Ich _____ täglich meine Lieblingswebseiten. (I go on to my favourite websites every day.)

c) Wir _____ und _____ E-Mails. (We send and I receive emails.)

d) Paula _____ mit ihren Freunden in Kontakt. (Paula stays in touch with her friends.)

e) Ich _____ Musik _____. (I download music.)

f) Das Internet _____ mit meinen Hausaufgaben. (The internet helps with my homework.)

[8 marks: 1 mark for each gap filled]

2 **Scheib fünf Sätze über deine Online-Aktivitäten. Beginn die Sätze mit den folgenden Ausdrücken. Wichtig: Das Verb muss immer an zweiter Stelle sein.** Write five sentences about your online activities, starting the sentences with the expressions below. Important: The verb must always come second.

Beispiel: Jeden Tag besuche ich meine Lieblingswebseiten.

a) Jeden Tag _____.

b) Oft _____.

c) Manchmal _____.

d) Einmal pro Woche _____.

e) Ab und zu _____.

[5 marks]

3 **Übersetze diese Sätze über Online-Sicherheit ins Deutsche.** Translate these sentences about online safety into German.

a) You must change your password regularly. _____

b) You mustn't give away your password. _____

c) You must be careful. _____

d) You mustn't converse with strangers. _____

e) You must install an anti-virus program. _____

[10 marks: 2 marks per sentence]

4 **Lies die Meinungen über Mobiltechnologie und beantworte die Fragen.** Read the opinions about mobile technology and answer the questions.

Peer	**Man kann online einkaufen. Das finde ich praktisch.**
Mia	**Ich rufe gern meine Freunde an, aber manchmal gibt es keinen Empfang.**
Sofia	**Die Technologie ändert sich zu schnell und es ist teuer, immer die aktuelle Version zu haben.**
Jonas	**Ich benutze mein Handy, um mich mit meinen Freunden zu verabreden.**
Leon	**Mit meinem Handy kann ich in Notfall Hilfe rufen.**
Charlotte	**Viele Leute sind stundenlang an ihrem Handy. Das finde ich doof.**
Ben	**Ich lade Musik auf mein Handy herunter und höre sie im Bus oder im Zug.**
Lena	**Das Problem ist, dass man das Gerät immer wieder aufladen muss!**

a) Who likes downloading music on a phone?

b) Who thinks some people spend too much time on their phone?

c) Who finds a mobile phone useful in an emergency?

d) Who complains about having to charge a phone all the time?

e) Who finds a phone useful for shopping online?

f) Who uses their phone to arrange meet-ups with friends?

g) Who complains that they sometimes can't get a signal?

h) Who thinks it's expensive to upgrade to the latest model?

[8 marks]

5 **Übersetze diese Sätze ins Englische.** Translate these sentences into English.

a) **Ein Vorteil der Mobiltechnologie ist, dass man sich auf dem Laufenden halten kann.**

b) **Man kann sich informieren, aber die Technologie ändert sich sehr schnell.**

c) **Ich chatte mit meinen Freunden, weil ich ihre Meinungen interessant finde.**

d) **Gestern habe ich das Internet benutzt, um mir bei meinen Hausaufgaben zu helfen.**

[8 marks: 2 marks per sentence]

Free-time Activities

Music & Cinema and TV

1 **Verbinde die Fragen mit den Antworten.** Match the questions and answers.

Hörst du oft Musik?	Mein Lieblingssänger ist James Bay und meine Lieblingssängerin ist Paloma Faith.
Was für Musik hörst du am liebsten?	Er hat eine schöne Stimme und tolle Haare und sie schreibt tolle Lieder.
Hast du einen Lieblingssänger oder eine Lieblingssängerin?	Ich interessiere mich für klassische Musik, weil ich sie so beruhigend finde.
Warum magst du ihre Musik?	Ja, ich lade jeden Tag Musik auf mein Handy herunter.
Warst du schon mal auf einem Musikfestival?	Ja, letztes Jahr war ich auf dem Lorelei-Festival in Süddeutschland.

[5 marks]

2 **Übersetze die Antworten aus Übung 1 ins Englische.** Translate all the answers from activity 1 into English.

[5 marks]

3 **Schreib fünf Sätze über deinen Musikgeschmack. Benutze die Wörter im Kästchen und dein eigenes Vokabular, wenn du willst!** Write five sentences about your musical tastes using the words in the box. Use your own vocabulary if you want! Be careful – remember that **weil** sends the verb to the end.

Rapmusik	Popmusik klassische Musik Techno Hip-hop Jazz Rockmusik sie gefällt mir sie nervt mich ich finde sie beruhigend sie macht mich glücklich die Texte sind interessant

a) Ich höre gern _____, weil _____.

b) Ich höre lieber _____, weil _____.

c) Ich höre am liebsten _____, weil _____.

d) Ich höre nicht gern _____, weil _____.

e) Ich interessiere mich nicht für _____, weil _____.

[5 marks]

4 **Füll die Lücken mit Wörtern aus dem Kästchen.** Fill in the blanks with the words from the box.

Fan	Familie	aber	finde	langweilig	Jahr	obwohl	deutsche

Schwester   Rhythmus

Meine Familie hört sehr gern Musik, _____ unser Geschmack ist unterschiedlich. Mein Vater war schon immer _____ von Bap. Das ist eine _____ Band aus Köln, aber ich _____ sie total altmodisch. Letztes _____ waren wir alle auf dem Big Gig Festival in Hamburg, aber ich habe Bap _____ gefunden und habe mit meiner _____ die Rapgruppen gehört. Wir haben den _____ viel besser gefunden. Wir sind keine musikalische _____. Meine Mutter spielt Klavier, _____ mein Vater sagt, dass sie furchtbar spielt!

[10 marks]

5 **Vervollständige die Sätze. Wähle Filme und Fernsehsendungen, die du magst und nicht magst und erkläre die Gründe mit 'weil' oder 'obwohl'. Wähle Wörter aus der Liste oder benutze deine eigenen Wörter.** Complete the sentences. Choose types of films and TV programmes you like and dislike and give reasons, using **weil** or **obwohl**. You can choose words from the list or provide your own.

Seifenopern
Spielshows
Serien
Reality-Sendungen
Krimis
Zeichentrickfilme
Kriegsfilme
Liebesgeschichten
Fantasyfilme

weil / obwohl sie mich zum Lachen / Weinen bringen.
weil / obwohl sie mir Angst machen.
weil / obwohl sie langweilig / spannend / lustig / interessant sind.
weil / obwohl die Stars / die Spezialeffekte gut / schlecht sind.

a) Ich sehe lieber _____.
b) Manchmal sehe ich gern _____.
c) Ich sehe nie _____.
d) Meine Lieblingsfilme sind _____.
e) Meine Lieblingssendungen sind _____.

[10 marks: 2 marks for each sentence]

6 **Bring die Wörter in die richtige Reihenfolge. Dann übersetze die Sätze ins Englische.** Put the words in the right order to make sentences. Then translate the sentences into English.

a) muss / die / Man / langweilige / sehen / Werbung
b) teurer / immer / Karten / Die / werden
c) Spezialeffekte / Leinwand / großen / sind / Die / besser / auf / der

[6 marks: 1 mark for each correct order and 1 mark for each translation]

Free-time Activities

Food and Eating Out, Sport & Customs and Festivals

1 **Übersetze dieses Gespräch ins Deutsche.** Translate this conversation into German.

a) I'd like one kilo of carrots please. ....

b) Of course. Here you are. ....

c) Do you have Gouda cheese as well? ....

d) Of course. How much would you like? ....

e) Eight slices please. ....

f) Anything else? ....

g) No thanks. How much is that? ....

h) That comes to two euros fifty. ....

[16 marks: 2 marks for each sentence]

2 **Lies die Speisekarte und finde die deutschen Wörter.** Read the menu and find the German words.

> **Vorspeisen**
> **Kartoffelsuppe mit Brot**
> **Thunfischsalat**
> **Lachs mit Mayonnaise**
>
> **Hauptspeisen**
> **Hähnchen mit Pommes Frites**
> **Bockwurst mit Kartoffelsalat**
> **Schweinefleisch mit Nudeln**
>
> **Nachtische**
> **Erdbeertorte**
> **Vanilleeis mit Sahne**
> **Obstsalat**

a) vanilla ice cream

b) strawberry tart

c) tuna salad

d) boiled sausage

e) cream

f) salmon

g) pork

h) potato soup

i) fruit salad

j) chicken

[10 marks]

3 **Schreib zwei Sätze im Perfekt über ein Essen, das du in einem Restaurant gegessen hast.** Write two sentences about a recent meal out, using the perfect tense.

[4 marks: 2 marks for each sentence]

4 **Übersetze die Sätze ins Englische.** Translate the sentences into English.

a) **Als ich jung war, bin ich jeden Tag gewandert.**

b) **Als ich fünfzehn war, bin ich oft in die Eishalle gegangen.**

c) **Damals bin ich immer schwimmen gegangen, aber heutzutage bleibe ich lieber zu Hause.**

d) **Früher habe ich jeden Samstag Fußball gespielt, aber jetzt bin ich zu faul!**

e) **Ich will Wintersport ausprobieren, obwohl es gefährlich ist.**

[10 marks: 2 marks for each sentence]

5 **Übersetze die Sätze ins Deutsche.** Translate the sentences into German.

a) I play hockey at the sports centre.

b) I often used to go fishing.

c) Nowadays I like going skateboarding.

d) Before, I used to go skating at the weekend, but now I find team sports better.

e) We would like to try extreme sports.

[10 marks: 2 marks for each sentence]

6 **Schreib fünf Sätze mit Meinungen über Feste mit Wörtern aus dem Kästchen. Denk daran, dass das Verb an zweiter Stelle im Satz kommt. Nach 'dass' wird das Verb ans Ende des Satzes gestellt.** Write five sentences giving your opinions on festivals and celebrations using the words in the box. Remember, the verb comes second in the sentence. After **dass**, the verb goes to the end.

> **der erste Weihnachtstag**   **der zweite Weihnachtstag**   **Ostern**
> **Fasching**   **der Ramadan [usw.]**   **altmodisch**   **lustig**
> **langweilig**   **wichtig**   **faszinierend**   **interessant [usw.]**

a) **Ich finde / glaube, dass** _____.

b) **Für mich** _____.

c) **Für andere** _____.

d) **Meiner Meinung nach** _____.

e) **Viele Leute glauben, dass** _____.

[10 marks: 2 marks for each sentence]

Environment and Social Issues

At Home, Where I Live & Town or Country

1 **Wähle die richtige Antwort auf jede Frage.** Match the questions and answers.

Wohnst du in der Stadt oder auf dem Land?	Ich liebe es, in der Stadt zu wohnen, aber ich möchte auf das Land ziehen.
Was gibt es in deiner Stadt?	Oben gibt es vier Zimmer: das Badezimmer, das Zimmer meiner Eltern, das Zimmer meines Bruders und mein Zimmer.
Wo möchtest du lieber wohnen?	Es gibt ein Einkaufszentrum und eine große Bücherei.
Wie ist das Leben auf dem Land?	Es gibt nichts für junge Leute. Wir brauchen ein Kino.
Wie viele Zimmer gibt es in deinem Haus?	Ich wohne in der Stadtmitte.
Was braucht deine Stadt?	Es ist zu ruhig und man muss mit dem Auto fahren, um Freunde zu sehen.

[6 marks]

2 **Ergänze die Sätze mit den richtigen Wörtern aus dem Kästchen. Es gibt vier Wörter zu viel.**
Complete the sentences, using the correct words from the box. There are four words too many.

neben	großes	an	gibt	große	großen	putze	in	mache	es

a) Ich wohne in einem _____ Haus.

b) Es _____ acht Zimmer.

c) Das Wohnzimmer ist _____ der Küche.

d) In meinem Zimmer habe ich eine _____ Kommode.

e) Ich _____ mein Zimmer jede Woche.

f) Es gibt Bilder _____ der Wand.

[6 marks]

3 **Schreib fünf Sätze über das, was du im Stadtzentrum gemacht hast. Benutze die Verben unten.**
Write five sentences about what you did in town. Use the verbs below.

Beispiel: Ich bin mit meiner Freundin ins Kino gegangen.

essen	gehen	kaufen	verlieren	treffen

....

....

....

....

....

[10 marks: 5 marks for conjugated verbs and 5 marks for full correct sentences]

4   **Lies die Meinungen über das Leben in der Stadt und beantworte die Fragen.** Read the opinions about life in the city and answer the questions.

Silke	**Wo ich wohne, gibt es viel Verkehr – schrecklich!**
Johannes	**Ich möchte in der Stadt wohnen, da es mehr zu tun gibt als auf dem Land.**
Brigitte	**Die Stadt ist sehr laut und die Straßen sind schmutzig. Nein danke!**
Hans	**Man kann sehr viel sehen und machen.**
Katja	**Wir brauchen dringend ein Einkaufszentrum.**
Boris	**Ich wohne gern in der Stadt, weil die öffentlichen Verkehrsmittel hier gut sind.**

a) Who points out something that their town needs? ....

b) Who is happy with the range of things to see and do? ....

c) Who finds the traffic a problem? ....

d) Who says that they would prefer to live in the town? ....

e) Who thinks the streets are dirty? ....

f) Who likes living in town due to the public transport system? ....

[6 marks]

5   **Übersetze diese Sätze ins Deutsche.** Translate these sentences into German.

a) My bedroom is always tidy.

....

b) Upstairs there are three bedrooms.

....

c) The bathroom is next to my bedroom.

....

d) There is no shopping centre but there is free parking.

....

e) There is less traffic in the countryside than in the town.

....

[10 marks: 2 marks per sentence. Award 1 mark for communication and 1 mark for precision.]

Environment and Social Issues

Charity and Voluntary Work & Healthy and Unhealthy Living

1 **Schreib fünf Sätze. Wähle ein Wort aus jedem Kästchen.** Write five sentences. Choose a word from each box.

Ich möchte	warme Mahlzeiten	helfen
Ich würde gern	Medikamente	arbeiten
Ich werde	Freiwilligenarbeit	machen
	alten Menschen	liefern
	Geld	verteilen
	als Arzt	sammeln
	Obdachlosen	

Beispiel: Ich werde als Arzt arbeiten.

_____

_____

_____

_____

_____

[5 marks]

2 **Übersetze jeden Satz, den du in Übung 1 geschrieben hast, ins Englische.** Translate each of the sentences you wrote in activity 1 into English.

Beispiel: Ich werde als Arzt arbeiten. I will work as a doctor.

_____

_____

_____

_____

_____

[10 marks: 2 marks per sentence. Award 1 mark for communication and 1 mark for precision.]

3 **Setze die Wörter in die richtige Reihenfolge.** Put the words into the correct order.

a) essen / man / gesund / soll _____

b) ziemlich / gesund / weil / und / ich / bin / Gemüse / esse / viel / ich / Obst

_____

c) fit / bleibe / da / ich / ich / treibe / Sport / genug _____

d) Gesundheit / meine / mir / wichtig / sehr / ist _____

[4 marks]

4 **Verbinde die Satzeile.** Connect the two halves of the sentences.

Ich schlafe…		Fett essen.	
Ich trainiere…		können töten.	
Ich esse viel…		zweimal pro Woche.	
Man muss wenig…		nicht rauchen.	
Zigaretten…		gut.	
Man soll…		Obst.	

[6 marks]

5 **Lies die Meinungen über Wohltätigkeit und Freiwilligenarbeit und beantworte die Fragen.** Read the opinions and comments about charity and voluntary work and answer the questions.

Samstags liefere ich warme Mahlzeiten und Trinkwasser an Obdachlose. Markus

In der Zukunft hoffe ich, nach Afrika zu fahren, um dort beim Roten Kreuz zu arbeiten. Sabine

Ich möchte etwas Nützliches machen. Vielleicht werde ich Krankenschwester sein. Julia

Ich habe dieses Wochenende Medikamente geliefert. Es war anstrengend, aber es lohnt sich. Yilmaz

a) What did Yilmaz do this weekend? _____

b) What does Sabine hope to do in the future? _____

c) What does Markus do on Saturdays? _____

[3 marks]

6 **Übersetze die Sätze ins Deutsche.** Translate the sentences into German.

a) I sleep well. _____

b) I don't eat unhealthy meals. _____

c) I drink enough water. _____

d) My dad has stopped smoking. _____

e) My sister trains in the gym every day. _____

[10 marks: 2 marks per sentence. Award 1 mark for communication and 1 mark for precision.]

Environment and Social Issues

The Environment & Poverty and Homelessness

1 Übersetze die Sätze ins Englische. Translate the sentences into English.

a) Wir dürfen unsere natürlichen Ressourcen nicht verschwenden.

_____

b) Es ist wichtig, unsere Umwelt durch Recycling zu schützen.

_____

c) Ich denke, wir sollten alle ermutigen, Müll zu sammeln, sortieren und verwerten.

_____

d) Ich finde, dass heutzutage zu viel Energie benutzt wird.

_____

e) Meiner Meinung nach ist die Wasserverschmutzung das größte Problem weltweit.

_____

[10 marks: 2 marks per sentence. Award 1 mark for communication and 1 mark for precision.]

2 Übersetze die Sätze ins Deutsche. Translate the sentences into German.

a) There is too much rubbish on the streets.

_____

b) As far as I'm concerned, deforestation is very worrying.

_____

c) We're doing what we can to protect the environment.

_____

[6 marks: 2 marks per sentence. Award 1 mark for communication and 1 mark for precision.]

3 Lies die Ergebnisse einer Umfrage und beantworte die Fragen. Read the results of a survey and answer the questions.

Was ist das beunruhigendste Problem in deiner Stadt?	
die Arbeitslosigkeit	15%
die Armut	20%
die Anzahl der Obdachlosen	25%
das Verbrechen	5%
die Verschmutzung	10%
die Anzahl der Einwanderer	2%

What percentage of people are most worried about …?

a) people who don't have enough money [   ]

b) people without a home [   ]

c) people without a job

d) problems with the environment

e) people who steal from others

[5 marks]

4 **Setze die Wörter in die richtige Reihenfolge und übersetze sie ins Englische.** Put the words in the right order and translate them into English.

a) immer mehr / Leute / die / es gibt / sind / arbeitslos

....

....

b) schnell / die Anzahl / in meiner Stadt / der Obdachlosen / wächst

....

....

c) sehen / der Armut / in meiner Stadt / eine Zunahme / man / kann

....

....

d) überall / hat / zugenommen / stark / die Kriminalität

....

....

[8 marks: 2 marks per sentence. Award 1 mark for correct order and 1 mark for correct translation]

5 **Ergänze die Lücken mit Wörtern aus dem Kästchen unten. Nur acht Wörter werden verwendet.**
Complete the gaps with words from the box below. Only eight words are used.

früher   heutzutage   weniger   fördern   mehr   steigen
waren   aktiv   sind   reduzieren   das   kein   ein   die   passiv   lösen

.... gibt es in meiner Stadt immer .... Menschen, die arbeitslos
.... und auch .... Zuhause haben. Vorher war Kriminalität
.... größte Problem. Die Polizei war sehr .... und löste das
Problem weitgehend. Leider wird die Anzahl der Arbeitslosen und Obdachlosen
...................................., wenn nichts getan wird. Ich hoffe, die Regierung kann etwas tun, um dieses
Problem zu ....

[8 marks]

Travel and Tourism

Travel and Tourism 1, 2 and 3

1 **Meine Ferien**

Lies die folgenden Sätze und wähle die richtige Person. Read the following sentences and choose the right person.

Sabine   **Während der Ferien übernachte ich oft in einem 4-Sternen Hotel.**

Jens   **Vor zwei Jahren bin ich mit meinen Freunden in die Schweiz gefahren und wir haben in einer Jugendherberge übernachtet.**

Kristina   **Ich würde gerne eines Tages in einer Berghütte übernachten - es muss sehr entspannend sein!**

Max   **Normalerweise bleiben wir bei meiner Oma, die am Meer wohnt.**

Schreib ihre Namen. Write their names.

Who...	
a) ...spends their holiday with a relative?	
b) ...is talking about a past holiday?	
c) ...goes to the seaside?	
d) ...likes good hotels?	
e) ...is talking about a relaxing holiday?	

[5 marks]

2 **Probleme im Urlaub.**

Diese fünf Leute hatten Probleme im Urlaub. Lies die Aussagen und wähle die richtige Person. These five people had problems on holiday. Read their words and choose the right person.

Ada   **Wir mussten drei Stunden am Flughafen warten! Es war wirklich frustrierend!**

Bernd   **Ich war die ganze Zeit krank! Ich hatte eine Grippe, vielleicht weil es überall so kalt war!**

Gabi   **Sie haben das Fenster eingeschlagen und unsere Pässe und Geld gestohlen!**

Georg   **Ich musste neue Klamotten kaufen, weil mein Gepäck verschwunden war.**

Nadine   **Das Essen war furchtbar und die Zimmer waren schmutzig. Nie wieder werde ich dort übernachten!**

Schreib ihre Namen. Write their names.

a) lost luggage	
b) had a delay	
c) was robbed	
d) had flu	
e) had a filthy room	

[5 marks]

3 Das Hotel mit Bergblick

Lies diese Broschüre über ein Hotel mit Bergblick. Read this brochure about a hotel with mountain views.

Hotel mit Bergblick

Das Hotel liegt in einem Dorf etwa fünfhundert Meter von den Bergen entfernt.

Fünfzehn Zimmer auf drei Etagen, einige mit Bergblick.

Freibad täglich von 09:00 Uhr bis 20:00 Uhr geöffnet (geschlossen ab 18:00 Uhr an Feiertagen).

Das Restaurant mit Terrasse befindet sich auf der zweiten Etage.

Das Hotel ist hundefreundlich.

Sind diese Sätze richtig oder falsch? Are these sentences true or false?

a) All rooms have a view of the mountains.

b) There is an indoor swimming pool.

c) The swimming pool is open every day.

d) The restaurant is on the ground floor.

e) Pets are allowed.

[5 marks]

4 **Übersetze ins Englische.** Translate into English.

a) **Nächstes Jahr möchte ich mit meinen Freunden auf dem Land zelten.**

....

b) **Normalerweise fahren meine Familie und ich für zwei Wochen nach Italien.**

....

c) **Letztes Jahr habe ich in einer Jugendherberge in München übernachtet.**

....

d) **Vor drei Jahren haben wir in einem 4-Sternen Hotel am Meer gewohnt.**

....

e) **Letzten Sommer waren wir in Spanien und sind jeden Tag am Strand spazieren gegangen.**

....

[5 marks]

Studies and Employment

My Studies and Life at School

1 **Lies die Meinungen über Schulfächer. Ergänze die Tabelle auf Deutsch.** Read the opinions about school subjects. Fill in the table in German.

Jens   **Ich habe Kunst als Wahlfach gewählt, da es mir so viel Spaß gemacht hat. Aber jetzt fallen mir die Stunden ziemlich schwer und ich lerne lieber Erdkunde als Kunst, denn es ist immer logisch und interessant.**

Rebecca   **Leider lerne ich nicht mehr Biologie oder Chemie, was echt furchtbar ist, weil ich Naturwissenschaften liebte, als ich jünger war. Heute ist mein Lieblingslehrer mein Geschichtelehrer, also lerne ich am liebsten dieses Fach.**

Zak   **Als Kind war ich sehr sportlich, deshalb nehme ich immer noch sehr gern an Sportunterricht teil. Ich war auch mathematisch begabt und ich lernte sehr gern Mathe, aber nicht mehr!**

	Lieblingsfach – jetzt	Lieblingsfach – in der Vergangenheit
Jens		
Rebecca		
Zak		

[6]

2 **Ergängze die Sätze ins Deutsche.** Complete the sentences in German.

a) I get up.   = ...   [3]

b) I wake up at 7 o'clock.   = ... **sieben** ....   [5]

c) I get dressed at 7:15.   = ... **um** .... **sieben** ....   [6]

d) I brush my teeth at half past 7.   = ... **mir** .... **acht.**   [6]

e) I go to school on foot.   = ... **zu** .... **die Schule.**   [4]

f) I never go to school by bike.   = ... **nie** .... **in die** ....   [6]

g) I get changed after school.   = ... **Schule** ....   [6]

h) I always get a lot of homework.   = ... **Hausaufgaben.**   [4]

[40]

3 **Verbinde die Fragen und die Antworten.** Match up the questions and answers.

Was ist dein Lieblingsfach?
Was lernst du nicht gern?
Wie oft hast du Mathe?
Welches Fach hast du gewählt?
Wer ist dein(e) Lieblingslehrer(in)?
Wie findest du Kunst?

Mein Wahlfach ist Religion.
Dreimal in der Woche.
Sehr kompliziert, denn ich bin nicht kreativ.
Informatik kann ich nicht leiden.
Deutsch gefällt mir sehr.
Frau Weber, da sie so gerecht ist.

[6 marks]

4 **Wähle das richtige Wort und füll die Lücken aus. Du brauchst nur acht Wörter.** Choose the correct word and fill the gaps. You only need eight words.

Musikgruppe   beginnt   Klassenzimmer   Grundschule
Fußballspiel   lang   interessant   Kantine   Lehrer
AGs   streng   Schüler   Bibliothek   Internat
freundlich   endet

Willkommen an unserer Schule! Es gibt ungefähr zweitausend _____ hier, und
da es ein _____ ist, wohnen wir alle hier zusammen, was eine Menge Spaß macht!
Obwohl der Schultag um halb vier _____, haben wir eine große Auswahl an
_____ und es gibt etwas für jeden, zum Beispiel habe ich gestern die
_____ besucht, und morgen werde ich an der Lesegruppe in der
_____ teilnehmen. Meiner Meinung nach können die Lehrer ein bisschen zu
_____ sein, aber im Großen und Ganzen ist der Unterricht sehr
_____.

[8 marks]

Studies and Employment

Education Post-16 & Career Choices and Ambitions

1 **Verbinde die Satzhälften.** Match up the sentence halves.

Man muss immer gut zuhören,
Man muss sitzenbleiben,
Wir müssen nachsitzen,
Es ist verboten,
Es ist erlaubt,
Wir müssen fragen,

wenn man schlechte Noten bekommt.
wenn wir etwas nicht verstehen.
blau zu machen.
Handys in der Pause zu benutzen.
wenn der Lehrer spricht.
wenn wir zu viel schwätzen.

[6 marks]

2 **Lies die Zukunftspläne dieser Jugendlichen. Schreib den richtigen Namen.** Read these young people's future plans. Write the correct name.

Annie   Ich habe mich um einen Ausbildungsplatz beworben. Es war ganz einfach, den Brief zu schreiben, denn ich habe einen Nebenjob und ich habe ein Arbeitspraktikum gemacht.

Fabian   Da ich keine Arbeitserfahrung habe, ist es schwierig, einen Teilzeitjob zu finden. Ich möchte arbeiten, anstatt an die Uni zu gehen, deshalb ist eine Berufsschule ideal für mich.

Elisa   Der Berufsberater hat mir einen guten Rat gegeben und ich habe mich entschieden, einen Studienplatz zu finden. Ich freue mich auf das Studentenleben!

Moritz   In der Zukunft will ich einen guten Job finden, aber es ist wichtig, mehr über die Welt zu lernen. Ich möchte deshalb ein Jahr freinehmen und im Ausland freiwillig arbeiten.

a) Who wants to volunteer?   ....

b) Who wants to go to university?   ....

c) Who has a lot of experience?   ....

d) Who has spoken to a careers adviser?   ....

e) Who would prefer a vocational education?   ....

f) Who has a part-time job?   ....

[6 marks]

3 **Übersetze ins Englische.** Translate into English.

Meine Mutter ist Beamtin, aber das ist nicht mein Traumberuf, da ich im Freien arbeiten möchte, zum Beispiel als Gärtner. Als ich jünger war, wollte ich Tierarzt werden, aber leider bin ich allergisch gegen Katzen! Nächstes Jahr werde ich einen Teilzeitjob suchen, um Geld zu verdienen.

[9 marks]

4 **Lies die Aussagen und schreib den richtigen Namen.** Read the statements and write the correct name.

Max   **Ich würde nie schwänzen, denn die Stunden sind super wichtig.**

Elise   **Hoffentlich darf ich bald versetzt werden – ich bin so fleißig!**

Tobias   **Alle meine Freunde und ich stehen bestimmt unter Notendruck.**

Christina   **Wir machen oft blau, aber nur, da die Schule so langweilig ist.**

Ben   **Mein Zeugnis kommt nächste Woche und ich denke, ich werde eine Sechs kriegen.**

Veronika   **Die Schulregeln sind sehr streng, aber zum Glück werden die Schüler nicht mehr gemobbt.**

a) Who is feeling pressured? ....

b) Who mentions bullying? ....

c) Who **does not** play truant? ....

d) Who is expecting a bad grade? ....

e) Who plays truant? ....

f) Who mentions moving up a year? ....

[6 marks]

5 **Diese Befragung zeigt, was junge Leute in drei deutschen Schulen in der Zukunft wichtig finden. Wie viel Prozent der Befragten finden diese Sachen wichtig?** This survey shows what young people from three German schools find important for the future. What percentage of those surveyed find the following things important?

Was ist dir in der Zukunft wichtig?	
den Führerschein bekommen	85%
an die Universität gehen	71%
eine Lehre finden	62%
um die Welt reisen	59%
Geld für eine Wohltätigkeitsorganisation sammeln	44%
eine Menge Geld sparen	38%
ein Jahr freinehmen	27%
ein Auto kaufen	13%

a) saving money ....

b) getting an apprenticeship ....

c) going travelling ....

d) taking a gap year ....

e) fundraising ....

f) getting a driving licence ....

[6 marks]

Grammar 1

Gender, Plurals and Articles & Cases

1 **Schreib die Pluralformen dieser Hauptwörter.** Write in the plurals of these nouns.

a) Zimmer _____

b) Tisch _____

c) Glas _____

d) Hund _____

e) Tag _____

f) Stadt _____

g) Bruder _____

h) Dorf _____

i) Hamburger _____

j) Freundin _____

k) Handy _____

l) Hand _____

m) Auto _____

n) Party _____

o) Student _____

[15 marks]

2 **Schreib den bestimmten Artikel im Nominativ.** Add the definite article in the nominative case.

a) _____ Wurst (f) **ist fettig.**

b) _____ Künstlerin (f) **spielt gut.**

c) _____ Zug (m) **ist spät angekommen.**

d) _____ Bibliothek (f) **ist voll.**

e) _____ Schrank (m) **ist braun.**

f) _____ Lehrer (m) **unterrichtet Englisch.**

g) _____ Fest (n) **ist am 14. Februar.**

h) _____ Arbeit (f) **war schwer.**

i) _____ Verkehr (m) **ist laut.**

j) _____ Stadion (n) **ist alt.**

[10 marks]

3 **Schreib den richtigen bestimmten Artikel im Akkusativ.** Add in the correct definite article in the accusative case.

a) Möchtest du _____ Butter (f)?

b) Ich finde _____ Sendung (f) furchtbar.

c) Nimmst du _____ Kartoffelsalat (m)?

d) Wer hat _____ Kreditkarte (f) verloren?

e) Hast du _____ Fernsehturm (m) gesehen?

f) Wir haben _____ Doppelzimmer (n) genommen.

g) Er hat _____ Arbeit (f) schwer gefunden.

h) Wie findest du _____ Computerspiel (n)?

i) Ich habe _____ Andenken (n) gekauft.

j) Hast du _____ Chef (m) gesehen?

[10 marks]

4 **Schreib den richtigen unbestimmten Artikel im Akkusativ.** Add in the correct indefinite article in the accusative case.

a) Ich höre _____ Vogel (m).

b) Hast du _____ Handy (n)?

c) Alex hat _____ Schwester (f).

d) Ich nehme _____ Dose (f) Erbsen.

e) Ich möchte _____ Einladung (f) zur Party.

f) Gibt es _____ Dom (m) in dieser Stadt?

g) Haben Sie _____ Hund (m)?

h) Hast du _____ Interview (n) gehabt?

[8 marks]

5 **Schreib die richtige Endung vom Possessivpronomen.** Add in the correct dative endings to the words accompanying the indirect object.

a) Er schenkt _____ Lehrer einen Apfel. (sein–)

b) Sie schenkt _____ Lehrerin eine Apfelsine. (ihr–)

c) Ich gebe _____ Mutter ein Geschenk. (mein–)

d) Schreibst du _____ Onkel? (dein–)

[4 marks]

HT **6** **Schreib die richtige Genitivform.** Insert the correct genitive form.

a) das Ende _____ Straße (f, definite article)

b) die Räder_____ Rads (n, **mein-**)

c) der Anfang _____ Sommers (m, definite article)

d) der Geschmack _____ Essens (n, definite article)

e) die Katze _____ Freundin (f, **mein-**)

f) das Büro _____ Direktors (m, definite article)

[6 marks]

Grammar 1

Adjectives and Adverbs & Prepositions

1 **Schreib die Adjektivendungen (unbestimmter Artikel).** Write in the adjective endings (indefinite article).

a) Nominative: **ein blöd__ Film** (m)

b) Accusative: **eine lang__ Pause** (f)

c) Dative: **einem groß__ Problem** (n)

d) Nominative: **ein interessant__ Fach** (n)

e) Accusative: **eine lang__ Straße** (f)

f) Dative: **einem nett__ Franzosen** (m)

g) Nominative: **ein schwer__ Betriebspraktikum** (n)

h) Accusative: **eine blau__ Handtasche** (f)

i) Dative: **einem voll__ Bus** (m)

[9 marks]

2 **Mach diese Adjektive komparativ.** Make these adjectives comparative.

a) billig   →

b) einfach   →

c) laut   →

d) gut   →

e) groß   →

f) jung   →

g) lang   →

h) schnell   →

i) cool   →

j) klein   →

[10 marks]

3 **Schreib das richtige Adverb, um diese Sätze zu vervollständigen.** Write in the correct adverb to complete these sentences.

a) **Ein Pferd läuft _____** (slow).

b) **Ein Mensch läuft _____** (slower).

c) **Eine Schildkröte läuft _____** (slowest).

d) **Ich stehe _____ auf** (early).

e) **Mutti steht _____ auf** (earlier).

f) **Vati steht _____ auf** (earliest).

[6 marks]

4 **Schreib die richtigen Endungen für diese Artikel in Akkusativform nach einer Präposition.** Write in the correct endings for these articles in the accusative after a preposition.

a) **durch d___ Stadt** (f)

b) **ohne mein___ Schwester** (f)

c) **ohne mein___ Rad** (n)

d) **um d___ Ecke** (f)

e) **für mein___ Freund** (m)

f) **für mein___ Freundin** (f)

[6 marks]

5 **Schreib diese Präpositionen in drei Kategorien in die Tabelle.** Sort these prepositions into three categories in the table.

für	aus	in	bei	vor	durch	trotz	mit	nach
seit	wegen	unter	während	auf	hinter	um		

Followed by the accusative	Followed by the dative	Followed by either the accusative or the dative	Followed by the genitive

[16 marks]

HT **6** **Schreib die richtigen bestimmten Artikel im Genitiv nach Präpositionen.** Write in the correct definite articles in the genitive after the prepositions.

a) wegen _____ Wetters (n)   b) trotz _____ Regens (m)   c) während _____ Stunde (f)

[3 marks]

HT **7** **Übersetze ins Deutsche.** Translate into German (using the words in the gender boxes to help).

Masculine	Feminine	Neuter
Ketchup	Schwester	Haus
Onkel	Straßenbahn	
	Party	
	Ecke	
	Tasche	
	Sonne	
	Stadt	

a) through a town
b) for my sister
c) in our house (no movement)
d) without ketchup
e) in the tram
f) after the party
g) from our uncle
h) round the corner
i) without his bag
j) in the sun

[10 marks]

Grammar 2

Pronouns and Present Tense Verbs 1

1 **Schreib die deutschen Pronomen im Nominativ.** Write down the German pronouns in the nominative case.

a) 'one'

b) they

c) you (formal)

d) you (two friends)

e) we

f) you (one friend)

[6 marks]

2 **Füll die Lücken mit den richtigen Dativpronomen.** Fill in the blanks with the correct dative pronouns.

a) **Kommst du zu _____ (me)?**

b) **Ich gebe _____ (him) die Hand.**

c) **Ich gebe _____ (you, formal) meine Adresse.**

d) **Unsere Freunde haben _____ (us) eine E-Mail geschickt.**

e) **Ich schicke _____ (you, familiar) eine Postkarte.**

f) **Bist du mit _____ (her) in die Stadt gegangen?**

[6 marks]

3 **Übersetze ins Deutsche.** Translate into German.

a) with him

b) with us

c) to me

d) her (accusative)

e) her (dative)

f) she

g) you (formal, nominative)

h) you (formal, dative)

[8 marks]

4 **Schreib die richtigen Endungen dieser regelmäßigen Verben im Präsens.** Write in the correct present tense endings of these regular verbs.

a) ihr spiel__

b) du mach__

c) sie bleib__

d) ihr geh__

e) Timo komm__

f) wir steig__

g) er komm__

h) sie (singular) flieg__

i) sie (plural) trink__

j) wir sag__

[10 marks]

5 **Wähle das richtige trennbare Pronomen.** Choose the correct separable pronoun.

a) Wir steigen am Bahnhof _____. (out)

b) Wir stehen früh _____. (up)

c) Was ziehst du _____? (on)

d) Ich komme _____. (with)

e) Heute sehen wir _____. (TV)

f) Ich ziehe mich _____, bevor ich ins Bett gehe. (undress)

[6 marks]

6 **Füll die Lücken mit trennbaren Verben im Präsens.** Fill in the gaps with separable verbs.

a) Wir _____ selten _____. (fernsehen)

b) Wo _____ man _____? (einsteigen)

c) Ich _____ oft Filme _____. (herunterladen)

d) Klaus _____ um 6 Uhr _____. (aufstehen)

e) Wo _____ wir _____? (umsteigen)

[5 marks]

Grammar 2

Present Tense Verbs 2 and Perfect Tense Verbs

1 **Wähle die richtigen Modalverben.** Choose the correct modal verbs.

a) they must: **sie wollen / müssen / dürfen**

b) he likes: **er muss / darf / mag**

c) I am able: **ich darf / kann / muss**

d) he's allowed: **er kann / darf / muss**

e) they want to: **sie können / müssen / wollen**

f) you like: **du magst / willst / kannst**

g) we want to: **wir dürfen / mögen / wollen**

h) you are allowed: **ihr könnt / dürft / mögt**

[8 marks]

2 **Schreib die richtigen Wörter, um diese Infinitiv-Konstruktionen zu vervollständigen.** Insert the appropriate words to complete these infinitive constructions.

a) **Ich gehe in die Stadt, ___ Essen ___ kaufen.**

b) **Wir fahren nach Ibiza, ___ Urlaub ___ machen.**

c) **Klaus bleibt zu Hause, ___ Hausaufgaben ___ machen.**

d) **Wir recyceln Plastik, ___ die Umwelt ___ schonen.**

e) **Man geht in die Schule, ___ Mathematik ___ lernen.**

f) **Du fährst mit dem Zug, ___ nach Hamburg ___ kommen.**

[6 marks]

3 **Schreib die richtige Form von 'haben' und das Partizip Perfekt.** Fill in the correct part of **haben** and the past participle.

a) _____ du meine Schwester _____? (sehen)

b) _____ du mein Handy _____? (nehmen)

c) Wir _____ uns in der Stadt _____. (treffen)

d) Oskar _____ ein neues Auto _____. (kaufen)

e) Wie _____ du das Konzert _____? (finden)

f) Meine Eltern _____ gut _____. (essen)

g) _____ Sie gut _____? (schlafen)

h) Die Mannschaft _____ gut _____. (spielen)

[8 marks]

4 **Scheib die richtigen Partizipien für diese 'sein'-Verben.** Write down the correct past participles for these **sein** verbs.

Infinitive   Past Participle

a) **fliegen**   →

b) **sterben**   →

c) **sein**   →

d) **bleiben**   →

e) **kommen**   →

f) **laufen**   →

g) **fahren**   →

h) **gehen**   →

[8 marks]

5 **Schreib die richtigen Reflexivpronomen und Partizipien, um diese Sätze zu vervollständigen.**
Insert the correct reflexive pronouns and past participles to complete these sentences.

a) **Wir haben _____ am Marktplatz _____. (treffen)**

b) **Hast du _____ schon _____? (waschen)**

c) **Ich habe _____ heute morgen nicht _____. (rasieren)**

d) **Die Kinder haben _____ _____. (amüsieren)**

[4 marks]

6 **Schreib die richtigen Partizipien, um diese Sätze zu vervollständigen.** Insert the correct past participles to complete these sentences.

a) **Wir haben noch nicht _____. (abwaschen)**

b) **Wann seid ihr _____? (ankommen)**

c) **Der Film _____ um 20 Uhr _____. (anfangen)**

d) **_____ du gestern _____? (fernsehen)**

[4 marks]

7 **Übersetze ins Deutsche mit den Verben aus dem Kasten.** Translate into German using the verbs in the box below.

ankommen   finden   sich hinsetzen   kaufen   spielen   vergessen   sagen   lesen

a) When did you (familiar) arrive?

b) What did they find?

c) We sat down.

d) I bought a cake.

e) Ergül played piano.

f) Saskia forgot her homework.

g) He said hello.

h) Have you read Harry Potter?

[8 marks]

Grammar 2

Imperfect Tense Verbs and Future Time Frame

1 **Füll die Lücken mit der Imperfekt-Form von diesen unregelmäßigen Verben.** Fill in the gaps with the imperfect tense of these irregular verbs.

a) Er _____ laut. (sprechen)

b) Wir _____ vor der Kirche. (stehen)

c) Ich _____ krank. (sein)

d) Die Teenager _____ zu viel. (trinken, plural)

e) Ich _____ meine Bruder. (sehen)

f) Sie (plural) _____ in die Berge. (fahren)

g) Wir _____ Kopfschmerzen. (haben)

h) _____ du schon oft hier? (sein)

i) Der Einbrecher _____ €1000 aus dem Geldschrank. (nehmen)

j) Ich _____ nicht gut schlafen. (können)

[10 marks]

HT **2** **Übersetze diese Sätze ins Deutsche. Benutze das Präsens für die Zukunft.** Translate these sentences into German using the present tense to express the future.

a) I'm going home soon.

b) We are going to the cinema on Friday.

c) Leon is playing table tennis this evening.

d) My parents are visiting us tomorrow.

e) I'm making breakfast at 7.30.

[5 marks]

3 **Schreib die fünf Sätze in Aufgabe 2 nochmal. Benutze das Futur.** Take the five sentences in activity 2 and put them into the official future tense.

[5 marks]

4 **Schreib diese Präsens-Sätze im Imperfekt.** Put these present tense sentences into the imperfect tense.

a) Das finde ich gut.

b) Ich sage nichts.

c) Ali kommt mit.

d) Wir haben Spaß.

e) Peter ist im Krankenhaus.

f) Es gibt viel zu sehen.

g) Sie hat keine Zeit.

h) Was musst du machen?

[8 marks]

5 **Schreib diese Modalverben im Imperfekt.** Write these modal verbs in the imperfect tense.

   a) ich muss _____

   b) wir wollen _____

   c) ihr sollt _____

   d) er mag _____

   e) du kannst _____

   f) man darf _____

   [6 marks]

6 **Entscheide, ob diese Sätze Präsens oder Futur bezeichnen. Schreib P für Präsens oder F für Futur.** Decide whether these sentences indicate the present or the future tense. Write P for present tense or F for future tense.

   a) **Wir kommen bald nach Hause.**

   b) **Werdet ihr Lasagne essen?**

   c) **Ich gehe oft ins Theater.**

   d) **Ich habe ein Problem.**

   e) **Hamburg wird das Spiel gewinnen.**

   f) **Meine Schwester heiratet morgen.**

   [6 marks]

7 **Schreib drei Sätze, um zu sagen, was du machen würdest...** Write three sentences saying what you would do...

Geld – money	**Zeit** – time	**faul** – lazy

   a) ...if you had more money.

   b) ...if you had more time.

   c) ...if you weren't so lazy.

   [3 marks]

Grammar 2

Pluperfect Tense, Subjunctive Mood and Imperative & Word Order and Conjunctions

HT **1** **Schreib die richtige Form von 'haben' oder 'sein', um die Sätze im Plusquamperfekt zu vervollständigen.** Insert the correct form of **haben** or **sein** to complete each sentence in the pluperfect tense.

a) Sie sind ins Wohnzimmer gegangen, nachdem sie gegessen _____.

b) Er _____ krank gewesen.

c) Peter _____ schon oft Muscheln gegessen.

d) Ich _____ noch nie in die Oper gegangen.

e) Birgit _____ ihre Kreditkarte vergessen.

f) Ich bin ins Bett gegangen, nachdem ich geduscht _____ .

[6 marks]

2 **Bring die Sätze in die richtige Reihenfolge.** Unjumble the words to make sentences in the correct order. Start with the underlined words.

a) Ulla / nach Spanien / nächste Woche / fährt

b) Er / in die Schule / geht / jeden Tag

c) Ich / in Kiel / letzte Woche / war

d) Letzte Woche / in Kiel / war / ich

e) Das Auto / langsam / die Straße / fuhr / entlang

f) Am Freitag / Harry / geht / zum Zahnarzt

g) Harry / am Freitag / zum Zahnarzt / geht

h) Wir / Obst / essen / gern / immer

i) Wir / gut / in Frankreich / essen / immer

j) Ich / in einem Geschäft / arbeite / jeden Tag

[10 marks]

HT **3** **Schreib diese Perfekt-Sätze im Plusquamperfekt.** Change these perfect tense sentences into the pluperfect tense.

a) Asma hat Abitur gemacht.

b) Ich habe ein Computerspiel heruntergeladen.

c) Wir sind zur Haltestelle gegangen.

d) Er ist noch nie nach Frankreich gefahren.

e) Ich habe eine E-Mail geschickt.

f) Aktar ist nicht gekommen.

g) Man hat ein Problem gehabt.

h) Wir haben Freunde eingeladen.

[8 marks]

4 Übersetze die Plusquamperfekt-Sätze, die du in Übung 3 auf Deutsch geschrieben hast, ins Englische. Translate the pluperfect sentences you have written in activity 3 into English.

[8 marks]

5 Schreib diese Sätze mit neuen Anfängen. Rewrite these sentences with new beginnings.

a) Ich fahre mit dem Bus in die Stadt.

Jeden Tag _____.

b) Meine Mutter ist krank.

Leider _____.

c) Man darf nicht parken.

Hier _____.

d) Mark ist zum Zahnarzt gegangen.

Gestern _____.

e) Wir haben Pommes mit Ketchup gegessen.

Am Freitag _____.

f) Aisa ist nach Amerika geflogen.

Letztes Jahr _____.

[6 marks]

HT **6** Übersetze diese Sätze ins Deutsche. Translate these sentences into German. Remember the TMP word order.

a) I go to school every day by bike.

b) Will you come with me to the swimming pool at the weekend?

c) We often watch TV in the living room.

d) Mehmet often plays table tennis in the youth club.

e) My father works hard every day in the office.

f) Do you want to eat pizza with me in the restaurant this evening?

[6 marks]

Collins

GCSE
German

H

Higher Tier Paper 1 Listening

Time allowed: 45 minutes
(including 5 minutes' reading time before the test)

Instructions

- Download the audio material to use with this test from
  www.collins.co.uk/collinsgcserevision
- Use black ink or black ball-point pen.

Information

- The marks for questions are shown in brackets.
- The maximum mark for this paper is 50.
- You must **not** use a dictionary during this test.

Advice

For each item, you should do the following:

- After the question number is announced, there will be a pause to allow you to read the instructions and questions.
- Carefully listen to the recording. Read the questions again.
- Listen again to the recording. Then answer the questions.
- You may write at any point during the test.
- In **Section A**, answer the questions in **English**. In **Section B**, answer the questions in **German**.
- Answer all questions in the spaces provided.
- Write down all the information you are asked to give.
- You have 5 minutes to read through the question paper before the test begins. You may make notes during this time.

Name: ....

Section A   Questions and answers in **English**

On holiday

| 0 | 1 | You are on holiday in Austria and hear three people discussing problems they have encountered. Which **three** problems have they encountered?

Write the correct letters in the boxes.

A	transport
B	luggage
C	hotel room
D	crime
E	money

[ ]   [ ]   [ ]

[3 marks]

Practice Exam Paper

My new house

Your Austrian friend Moritz is telling you about the house he has just moved to.

Answer both parts of the question in English.

0 2 . 1 What does he like best about his new house?

....

[1 mark]

0 2 . 2 Why does he like it?

....

[1 mark]

School worries

Your friends from the German exchange are telling you about their life at school.

What are they stressed about at the moment?

Answer all parts of the question in English.

0 3 . 1 Tomas is worried about...

....

[1 mark]

0 3 . 2 Josy is worried about...

....

[1 mark]

0 3 . 3 Sebastien is worried about...

....

[1 mark]

Careers

Your Swiss friend's parents are discussing their careers.

0 4   What does Sofia say about her career?

Complete the table in **English.**

Past	Present	Future
	Teacher	

[2 marks]

0 5   What does Thorsten say about his career?

Complete the table in **English.**

Past	Present	Future
		Own company

[2 marks]

Practice Exam Paper

Social media

Three teenagers explain how social media can cause problems.

What are their biggest concerns?

Write the correct letters in the boxes.

A	stranger danger
B	self image
C	bullying
D	inappropriate content
E	addiction

`0 6`·`1` Abdul ☐

[1 mark]

`0 6`·`2` Natascha ☐

[1 mark]

`0 6`·`3` Leo ☐

[1 mark]

A music festival

Your German friend Bettina is describing a music festival she recently attended.

Answer all parts of the questions in English.

`0 7`·`1` What did she like most about the event?

_____

[1 mark]

`0 7`·`2` What did she enjoy before the event?

_____

[1 mark]

`0 7`·`3` What **two** reasons did Bettina give for not being able to get tickets at first?

1. _____

2. _____

[2 marks]

`0 7`·`4` How did Bettina get tickets in the end? Give **one** detail.

_____

[1 mark]

Family relationships

You are listening to an Austrian phone-in programme on the radio.

A teenager is asking for help with a problem he has.

Answer all parts of the questions in English.

`0 8 · 1` Why has he fallen out with his father?

....

[1 mark]

`0 8 · 2` What does he find unfair?

....

[1 mark]

`0 8 · 3` What does he think of his brother? Give **one** detail.

....

[1 mark]

`0 8 · 4` What aspect of family life does he enjoy?

....

[1 mark]

`0 8 · 5` Why does he enjoy it?

....

[1 mark]

Practice Exam Paper

Mobile phones

Some students at your German exchange partner school are discussing mobile phones.

What do they think about their mobile phones?

Write **P** for a **positive** opinion.

Write **N** for a **negative** opinion.

Write **P+N** for a **positive and a negative** opinion.

Answer all parts of the question.

`0 9 · 1` Natalia

[1 mark]

`0 9 · 2` Max

[1 mark]

`0 9 · 3` Zafira

[1 mark]

`0 9 · 4` Eric

[1 mark]

Healthy and unhealthy lifestyles

You are listening to a podcast where three young people are discussing their health.

What is said about each person's lifestyle?

Answer all parts of the question.

Write the correct letters in the boxes.

1 0 · 1 Tabitha is...

A	not getting enough sleep.
B	sleeping too much.
C	falling asleep at work.

[1 mark]

1 0 · 2 Stephan is...

A	an ex-smoker.
B	trying to stop smoking.
C	not worried about smoking.

[1 mark]

1 0 · 3 Nicole is...

A	happy with her weight.
B	trying to gain weight.
C	trying to lose weight.

[1 mark]

Practice Exam Paper

Local area

Your German exchange partner Lianne is telling you about her local area before you go to visit.

Answer all parts of the question.

Write the correct letters in the boxes.

`1` `1` · `1` She lives in a…

A	farmhouse.
B	flat.
C	semi-detached house.

[1 mark]

`1` `1` · `2` The area is…

A	quiet.
B	clean.
C	pretty.

[1 mark]

Answer the following question in English.

`1` `1` · `3` What advantage does she think a town has over a village?

[1 mark]

Social issues

1 2 At a school event in Germany, Michael is giving a presentation about social issues.

What social issue is he talking about?

Write the correct letter in the box.

A	poverty
B	homelessness
C	unemployment rates

[1 mark]

Global problems

You hear three radio adverts aiming to raise awareness about environmental problems across the world.

What problem does each advert mention?

Write the correct letters in the boxes.

A	climate change
B	over population
C	species extinction
D	water shortage
E	food shortage

1 3 · 1

[1 mark]

1 3 · 2

[1 mark]

1 3 · 3

[1 mark]

Practice Exam Paper

Section B Questions and answers in **German**

Freizeit

Eine Studie hat junge Leute über ihre Hobbys befragt.

Schreib die richtigen Zahlen.

Beantworte alle Teile der Frage.

Example: *72%*   *spielen ein Instrument.*   [1 mark]

1 4 · 1 _____% lesen gern.   [1 mark]

1 4 · 2 _____% gehen gern ins Kino.   [1 mark]

1 4 · 3 _____% benutzen keine soziale Netzwerke.   [1 mark]

1 4 · 4 _____% treiben regelmäßig Sport.   [1 mark]

Die Ehe

Drei Jugendliche in deiner Partnerschule sprechen über die Ehe.

Für eine positive Meinung, schreib P

Für eine negative Meinung, schreib N

Für eine positive und negative Meinung, schreib P + N.

Beantworte alle Teile der Frage.

1 5 · 1 Rafael

[1 mark]

1 5 · 2 Elisa

[1 mark]

1 5 · 3 Julian

[1 mark]

Fernsehen

1 6 **Du sprichst mit deiner Freundin Isabel aus Österreich über Fernsehen.**

Welche drei Aussagen sind richtig?

Schreib die richtigen Buchstaben ins Kästchen.

A	Isabel sieht gern die Nachrichten im Fernsehen.
B	Isabel sieht gern Dokumentarfilme im Fernsehen.
C	Isabel sieht selten fern.
D	Isabel geht nicht gern ins Kino.
E	Isabel sieht mit ihrer Schwester fern.

[3 marks]

Collins

GCSE
German

H

Higher Tier Paper 2 Speaking

Candidate's material – Role-play
Candidate's material – Photo card

Time allowed: **12 minutes**
(+ 12 minutes' preparation time)

Instructions

- During the preparation time, you are required to prepare **one** Role-play card and **one** Photo card.
- During the General Conversation, you are required to ask at least one question.

Information

- The test will last a maximum of 12 minutes and will consist of a Role-play card (approximately 2 minutes) and a Photo-card (approximately 3 minutes), followed by a General Conversation. The General Conversation is based on two out of the three Themes (5 – 7 minutes).
- You must **not** use a dictionary, either in the test or during the preparation time.

Name: ....

Role-play

Prepare your <u>spoken</u> answers to this Role-play.

Instructions to candidates

Your teacher will play the part of a German hotel receptionist and will speak first.

You should address the receptionist as 'Sie'.

When you see this – ! – you will have to respond to something you have not prepared.

When you see this – ? – you will have to ask a question.

Sie sind in einem Hotel in Deutschland. Sie sprechen mit der Person an der Hotelrezeption.

- Zimmer – wie viele Personen.
- Was für ein Zimmer (**zwei** Details).
- !
- Ihr letzter Besuch nach Deutschland.
- ? Restaurant.

Practice Exam Paper

Photo card

- Look at the photo.
- Prepare your <u>spoken</u> answers to the three questions that follow.

- **Was sieht man auf dem Foto?**
- **Ist es wichtig, Feste zu feiern? Warum (nicht)?**
- **Wie hast du letztes Jahr Weihnachten gefeiert?**

In the examination, your teacher will ask you **two** further questions, which you have not prepared.

Think of other questions you might be asked on the topic of 'Customs and festivals' and prepare answers to those, too.

General Conversation

The questions on the Photo card are followed by a General Conversation. The first part of this conversation will be from your nominated Theme and the second part on a Theme chosen by the examiner. The total time of the General Conversation will be between five and seven minutes and a similar amount of time will be spent on each Theme.

Themes for this example General Conversation are:

- Local, national, international and global areas of interest
- Current and future study and employment

Remember! It is a requirement for you to ask at least **one** question during the General Conversation; this can happen at any time during this section of the test.

Collins

GCSE
German
Higher Tier Paper 3 Reading

H

Time allowed: 1 hour

Instructions

- Use black ink or black ball-point pen.
- Answer **all** questions.
- You must answer the questions in the spaces provided.
- In **Section A**, answer the questions in **English**. In **Section B**, answer the questions in **German**. In **Section C**, translate the text into **English**.

Information

- The marks for questions are shown in brackets.
- The maximum mark for this paper is 60.
- You must **not** use a dictionary during this test.

Name: ....

Section A — Questions and answers in **English**

0 1 **Family relationships**

You read this magazine article where three teenagers are discussing their family life.

Write the first letter of the correct name in the box.
Write **A** for **Alex**.
Write **B** for **Bettina**.
Write **C** for **Carlotta**.
Write **D** for **Daniel**.

Mein Vater arbeitet viel, also sehen wir uns nicht so oft, was mich oft traurig macht. Zum Glück habe ich drei Geschwister und wir sind gute Freunde – wir streiten uns selten und das finde ich schön.
Alex

Meine Eltern gehen mir wirklich auf die Nerven, denn sie geben mir keine Freiheiten. Ich habe zwei ältere Brüder aber keine Schwester, was nicht gut ist.
Bettina

Ich habe eine Zwillingsschwester und wir verstehen uns ganz gut. Wir streiten uns nicht so oft, aber manchmal gibt es Probleme, weil wir ein Zimmer teilen müssen. Sie ist so unordentlich!
Carlotta

Ich habe keine Geschwister aber das stört mich nicht. Meine Eltern sind seit einem Jahr geschieden und ich wohne mit meiner Mutter und unserem Hund in einem kleinen Haus.
Daniel

0 1 · 1 Who has strict parents?

[1 mark]

0 1 · 2 Whose parents are no longer married?

[1 mark]

0 1 · 3 Who has arguments about an untidy bedroom?

[1 mark]

0 2 Social networks

You read this newspaper interview where two teenage girls have been asked their opinions about social networks.

Complete the grid in **English**.

Soziale Netzwerke sind äußerst nützlich, wenn man mit Freunden, Familie und Bekannten in Kontakt bleiben will. Ich liebe es, dass ich immer informiert bleiben kann. Aber in der Schule habe ich leider gesehen, dass Cybermobbing immer öfter passiert, weil sowohl die Täter als auch die Opfer anonym sind.

Alya

Für mich gibt es mehr Nachteile als Vorteile, zum Beispiel wissen Kinder nicht immer, mit wem sie chatten. Ich muss aber zugeben, dass es nützlich ist, wenn man Informationen teilen kann, um anderen zu zeigen, was man macht oder wofür man sich interessiert. Ich benutze gern soziale Neztwerke aber ich habe natürlich gesehen, dass sie zu Gesundheitsprobleme führen können – man kann sehr schnell süchtig und faul werden!

Marlene

	One advantage	One disadvantage
Alya		
Marlene		

[4 marks]

Practice Exam Paper

Life at school

You are doing research for a presentation about school in Germany and you come across a school website, where there is an article written by a student called Ralf.

Which **four** statements are true? Write the correct letters in the boxes.

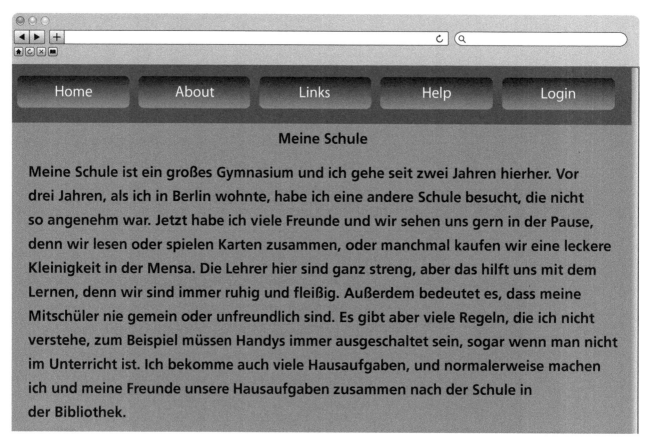

Home   About   Links   Help   Login

Meine Schule

Meine Schule ist ein großes Gymnasium und ich gehe seit zwei Jahren hierher. Vor drei Jahren, als ich in Berlin wohnte, habe ich eine andere Schule besucht, die nicht so angenehm war. Jetzt habe ich viele Freunde und wir sehen uns gern in der Pause, denn wir lesen oder spielen Karten zusammen, oder manchmal kaufen wir eine leckere Kleinigkeit in der Mensa. Die Lehrer hier sind ganz streng, aber das hilft uns mit dem Lernen, denn wir sind immer ruhig und fleißig. Außerdem bedeutet es, dass meine Mitschüler nie gemein oder unfreundlich sind. Es gibt aber viele Regeln, die ich nicht verstehe, zum Beispiel müssen Handys immer ausgeschaltet sein, sogar wenn man nicht im Unterricht ist. Ich bekomme auch viele Hausaufgaben, und normalerweise machen ich und meine Freunde unsere Hausaufgaben zusammen nach der Schule in der Bibliothek.

A	Ralf prefers his new school to his old school.
B	Ralf lives in Berlin.
C	There is a large gym at this school.
D	Most students eat lunch at school.
E	Ralf likes having strict teachers.
F	There are no bullying issues.
G	Ralf may only use his phone at break and lunch.
H	You can do your homework at school.

[4 marks]

0 4 Holidays

You are on a flight to Vienna and read this article in a magazine about holidays.

Answer the questions **in English**.

> Urlaub bedeutet für viele vor allem etwas Anderes zu machen als in dem normalen Alltag. Viele Europäer reisen in Nachbarstädte und andere Länder. Aber leider sind solche Reisen nicht besonders gut für die Umwelt, wegen der Abgase von Autos und Flugzeugen und des Mülls, den große Hotels produzieren. Außerdem kosten weite Reisen oft viel Geld. Das ist der Hauptgrund, warum viele Österreicher ihren Urlaub in ihrem eigenen Land verbringen. Sogar zu Hause kann man tolle Ausflüge machen, direkt vor der Haustür. Immer mehr Leute, die früher keine Interesse an einem Heimaturlaub hatten, planen dieses Jahr, zu Hause zu bleiben.

0 4 · 1 What do holidays mean for many people? Give **one** detail.

....

[1 mark]

0 4 · 2 Where do many Europeans go on holiday?

....

[1 mark]

0 4 · 3 Name **one** environmental problem caused by travelling to holiday destinations.

....

[1 mark]

0 4 · 4 What is the main reason why many Austrians are choosing to holiday at home?

....

[1 mark]

0 4 · 5 This year, more and more people are...

A	against 'staycations'
B	interested in 'staycations'
C	planning 'staycations'

[1 mark]

Practice Exam Paper

0 5   Health

You read an interview in an Austrian magazine with four people about their health and lifestyles.

How would you describe these people's lifestyles **at present**?

Write **H** for **healthy**.

Write **U** for **unhealthy**.

Write **H + U** for **healthy and unhealthy**.

Sonia:	Vor einem Jahr war ich total unfit – ich habe zu viel gegessen und ich habe sehr schnell zugenommen. Jeden Abend habe ich zwei oder drei Stunden beim Fernsehen verbracht. Ich dachte, "das reicht!". Jetzt esse ich viel gesünder und ich gehe zweimal pro Woche ins Fitnessstudio.
Peter:	Seitdem ich mit dem Rauchen aufgehört habe, habe ich zu viele Süßigkeiten und Bonbons gegessen. Es freut mich (und meinen Arzt!), dass ich nicht mehr nach Rauch stinke und dass das Lungenkrebs-Risiko nicht so hoch ist, aber ich bin trotzdem zu dick und zu ungesund.
Amy:	Mein Mann geht jeden Tag laufen und das ist zu viel für mich, aber ich versuche, einmal pro Woche mitzumachen. Ich habe eine stressige Arbeit und ich finde es besser, wenn ich viele Obst und Gemüse esse. Es macht mein Leben einfacher, denn ich habe mehr Energie. Ich muss jetzt weniger Alkohol trinken.
Thorsten:	Meine Oma ist vor zehn Jahren an einer Leberkrankeit gestorben, also trinke ich keinen Tropfen Alkohol. Das bedeutet nicht, dass ich immer super gesund bin. Ich rauche ab und zu, zum Beispiel auf Partys, und ich könnte nie auf Schokolade verzichten. Alles in Maßen!

0 5 · 1 Sonia

[1 mark]

0 5 · 2 Peter

[1 mark]

0 5 · 3 Amy

[1 mark]

0 5 · 4 Thorsten

[1 mark]

0 6 Social problems

You are researching charities in Germany and come across the website for a homeless charity based in Berlin.

Write **T** if the statement is **true**.

Write **F** if the statement is **false**.

Write **NT** if the information is **not in the text**.

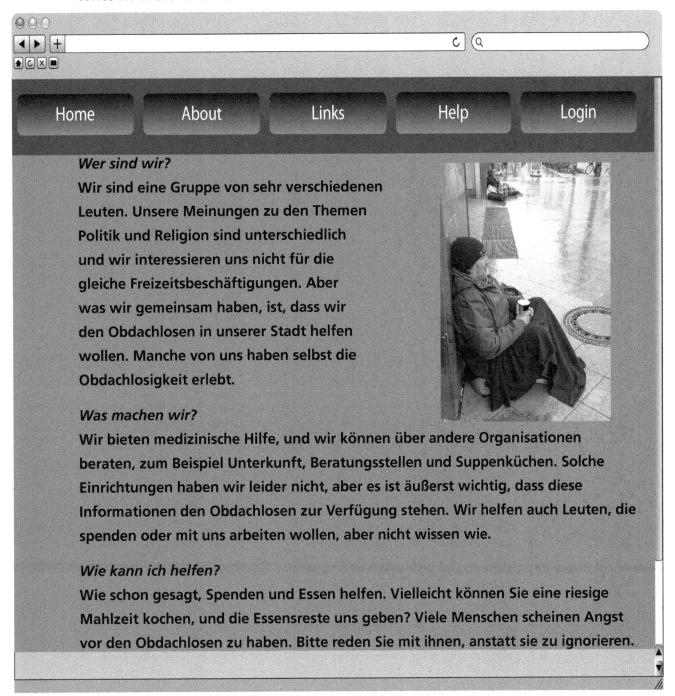

Home   About   Links   Help   Login

Wer sind wir?

Wir sind eine Gruppe von sehr verschiedenen Leuten. Unsere Meinungen zu den Themen Politik und Religion sind unterschiedlich und wir interessieren uns nicht für die gleiche Freizeitsbeschäftigungen. Aber was wir gemeinsam haben, ist, dass wir den Obdachlosen in unserer Stadt helfen wollen. Manche von uns haben selbst die Obdachlosigkeit erlebt.

Was machen wir?

Wir bieten medizinische Hilfe, und wir können über andere Organisationen beraten, zum Beispiel Unterkunft, Beratungsstellen und Suppenküchen. Solche Einrichtungen haben wir leider nicht, aber es ist äußerst wichtig, dass diese Informationen den Obdachlosen zur Verfügung stehen. Wir helfen auch Leuten, die spenden oder mit uns arbeiten wollen, aber nicht wissen wie.

Wie kann ich helfen?

Wie schon gesagt, Spenden und Essen helfen. Vielleicht können Sie eine riesige Mahlzeit kochen, und die Essensreste uns geben? Viele Menschen scheinen Angst vor den Obdachlosen zu haben. Bitte reden Sie mit ihnen, anstatt sie zu ignorieren.

`0 6` · `1` The team at the charity don't have much in common.

[1 mark]

`0 6` · `2` The team at the charity have all been homeless at some point.

[1 mark]

`0 6` · `3` The charity collects clothes donations.

[1 mark]

`0 6` · `4` The charity runs a soup kitchen.

[1 mark]

`0 6` · `5` The charity will not accept leftover food.

[1 mark]

`0 6` · `6` The charity wants the public to interact more with homeless people.

[1 mark]

07 **Future plans**

You are considering studying abroad in future and email your Swiss friend Marie-Elisabeth for advice. She sends you this reply.

deine Zukunftspläne   Inbox ×

Marie-Elisabeth Schroeder   10:36 AM (8 minutes ago)   reply ▾
to: Me

Hallo!

Die Idee, eine Zeit lang im Ausland zu leben und zu studieren, gefällt mir sehr gut. Es ist eine gute Möglichkeit, ein neues Land zu sehen, eine andere Kultur kennenzulernen und eine andere Sprache zu lernen. Gleichzeitig kann man viele Menschen kennenlernen und neue Freunde finden. Ich kenne einige Leute, die im Ausland studiert haben und die meisten hatten eine tolle und lustige Zeit.

Im Ausland zu studieren kann aber auch Nachteile haben. Zum einen kostet es oft viel Geld. Zweitens ist es manchmal nicht so leicht, im Studium weiterzukommen, wenn man die Sprache nicht so gut versteht. Außerdem lassen sich einige Studenten durch viele Partys vom Studium ablenken.

Schreib mir bald!

M.E. ☺

07·1 Give **two** advantages of studying abroad according to Marie-Elisabeth.

1. ....

[1 mark]

2. ....

[1 mark]

07·2 Give **two** disadvantages of studying abroad according to Marie-Elisabeth.

1. ....

[1 mark]

2. ....

[1 mark]

Practice Exam Paper

0 8   **Free time**

You read a blog entry where the writer is discussing their attitude towards sport and exercise.

Answer the questions in **English**.

> Ich treibe super gern Sport im Freien, nicht nur weil es mich fit hält, sondern auch weil ich es genieße, die frische Luft einzuatmen. Trotz der vielen Vorteile haben viele junge Leute keine Lust auf Sport, weil sie lieber Zeit vor einem Bildschirm verbringen. Es kann schwierig sein, mit Sport oder Bewegung anzufangen, wenn man ein lebenslanger Stubenhocker ist. Ich schlage vor, einmal pro Woche wandern zu gehen – es ist einfach, sehr schön und braucht nicht so viel Energie.

0 8 · 1 Apart from keeping fit, why does the writer play sport?

_____

[1 mark]

0 8 · 2 Why do many young people not play sport?

_____

[1 mark]

0 8 · 3 What does the writer suggest doing if you are not very sporty?

_____

[1 mark]

Section B   Questions and answers in **German**

09   ## Die Welt in 100 Jahren

Lies diesen Teil aus dem Buch 'die Welt in 100 Jahren', geschrieben von Arthur Brehmer im Jahre 1909.

Beantworte die Fragen.

Schreib **R**, wenn die Aussage richtig ist.

F, wenn die Aussage falsch ist.

NT, wenn die Aussage nicht im Text ist.

Der Sport der Zukunft wird unbeschränkt in den Geschwindigkeiten* werden, aber mit der Erhöhung der Geschwindigkeit* wachsen die Gefahren des Sports, denn die Geschwindigkeit* kennt keine Grenzen.

Unsere kommenden Sportarten werden sich hauptsächlich im Wasser, unter Wasser und in der Luft abspielen, rund um die Welt und in vierundzwanzig Stunden. Wir werden in Zukunft mit der Geschwindigkeit* eines Torpedobootes den schnellsten Fisch in seinem Element überholen können.

Unser Körper wird sich den neuen Lebensverhältnissen anpassen. Die Menschen werden kleiner und leichter werden. Auch die Möglichkeit von Tauch- und Flugkombinationen ist nicht ausgeschlossen.

In der Zukunft...

09 · 1 **wird es keinen Wassersport mehr geben.**

[1 mark]

09 · 2 **wird Sport nicht gefährlich sein.**

[1 mark]

09 · 3 **wird es keinen Teamsport mehr geben.**

[1 mark]

09 · 4 **werden Menschen anders aussehen.**

[1 mark]

09 · 5 **wird man immer und überall Sport treiben.**

[1 mark]

0 9 · 6 wird man fliegen können.

[1 mark]

0 9 · 7 werden Fische schneller als Menschen schwimmen.

[1 mark]

0 9 · 8 wird es keine Torpedoboote mehr geben.

[1 mark]

Geschwindigkeit = speed

1 0 ## Die Heinzelmännchen zu Köln

Lies den Text basierend auf dem Gedicht „Die Heinzelmännchen zu Köln" von August Kopsich.

Beantworte die Fragen auf **Deutsch**.

Es war einmal eine reiche, schöne und große Stadt namens Köln. Vor langer Zeit gab es in der Stadt Köln kleine Männer, die „Heinzelmännchen" hießen. Sie halfen den Leuten in Köln bei der Arbeit, aber nur als es dunkel war, und als die Leute in der Stadt schliefen. Sie halfen den Leuten, die keine Zeit hatten, zum Beispiel für den Koch im Restaurant machten sie Suppen und Soßen, und für den Bäcker backten sie das Brot.

1 0 · 1 Wie beschreibt man Köln? Gib **zwei** Details.

[2 marks]

1 0 · 2 Wann kommen die Heinzelmännchen?

[1 mark]

1 0 · 3 Was machen die die Heinzelmännchen, um den Leuten zu helfen? Gib **ein** Beispiel.

[1 mark]

1 1 **Problemseite**

Du liest einen Brief in einem „Kummerkasten". Felix schreibt über seine Probleme.

Beantworte die Fragen **auf Deutsch**.

Ich bin ganz traurig, weil es zwischen meinen Eltern und mir die ganze Zeit Krach gibt. Sie arbeiten viel, deshalb muss ich immer zu Hause helfen, zum Beispiel gestern habe ich gebügelt und abgespült. Es sind nur kleine Aufgaben, aber meine Freunde machen überhaupt nichts und ich finde es ganz unfair. Meine Eltern sagen, dass es Teil des Erwachsenenlebens ist. Außerdem sind meine Noten nicht gut genug – dank der Hausarbeit fehlt es mir an Zeit, meine Hausaufgaben zu machen. Ich kann nicht schlafen, denn ich habe Angst vor den Prüfungen, deshalb bin ich oft krank und ich bin zu oft abwesend. Obwohl mein Leben zu Hause nicht immer schön ist, komme ich toll mit meiner älteren Schwester aus – wir verstehen uns gut und besprechen alles. Ich habe Glück, dass sie da ist.

1 1 · 1 Was macht Felix unglücklich?

....

[1 mark]

1 1 · 2 Warum hilft Felix zu Hause?

....

[1 mark]

1 1 · 3 Wie oft helfen Felixs Freunde zu Hause?

....

[1 mark]

1 1 · 4 Warum hat Felix Probleme mit der Schularbeit?

....

[1 mark]

1 1 · 5 Warum geht Felix manchmal nicht in die Schule?

....

[1 mark]

1 1 · 6 Zu wem hat Felix eine gute Beziehung?

....

[1 mark]

Practice Exam Paper

Section C   Translation into **English**

1 2   You have asked your German exchange partner about their local area for a school website article. You receive this reply. Translate it into **English** for your headteacher.

Obwohl es ruhig und ziemlich klein ist, liebe ich mein Dorf. Vor zwei Jahren waren die öffentlichen Verkehrsmittel furchtbar, und ich bin oft spät in die Schule gekommen, aber jetzt bin ich immer pünktlich. Ich werde in den Bergen bei Wien wohnen, wenn ich achtzehn bin.

....

....

....

....

....

....

....

....

....

....

....

....

[9 marks]

END OF QUESTIONS

Collins

GCSE
German

Higher Tier Paper 4 Writing

H

Time allowed: 1 hour 15 minutes

Instructions

- Use black ink or black ball-point pen.
- You must answer **three** questions.
- Answer all questions in **German**.
- Answer the questions in the spaces provided.

Information

- The marks for questions are shown in brackets.
- The maximum mark for this paper is 60.
- You must **not** use a dictionary during this test.
- In order to score the highest marks for Question 1 you must write something about each bullet point. You must use a variety of vocabulary and structures and include your opinions.
- In order to score the highest marks for Question 2 you must write something about both bullet points. You must use a variety of vocabulary and structures and include your opinions.

Name: ....

Practice Exam Paper

Question 1

Du schreibst einen Artikel zum Thema Familie für die Schulzeitung.

Schreib:

- über deine Familienmitglieder
- warum Familie dir wichtig ist
- was du letztes Wochenende mit deiner Familie gemacht hast
- über deine Familiepläne für die Zukunft

Du musst ungefähr 90 Wörter auf Deutsch schreiben. Schreib etwas über alle Punkte der Aufgabe.

[16 marks]

Question 2

Du hast gerade Deutschland besucht und schreibst ein Blog darüber.

- Schreib etwas über deinen Besuch
- Vergleich die deutsche Stadt und deine Gegend

Du musst ungefähr 150 Wörter auf Deutsch schreiben. Schreib etwas über beide Punkte der Aufgabe.

[32 marks]

Question 3

Translate the following passage into **German**.

We must try to protect the environment, and recycling is important in order to be more environmentally friendly. The inhabitants of my town have learnt to separate rubbish, although we throw away too much. In future I will not use plastic bags and I want to use public transport more often.

[12 marks]

END OF QUESTIONS

Answers

Me, My Family and Friends
Pages 144–145: My Family, My Friends & Marriage and Partnerships

1. a) mein Opa [1]
   b) mein Onkel [1]
   c) meine Nichte [1]
   d) mein Schwager [1]
   e) meine Tante [1]
   f) meine Stiefmutter [1]
   g) mein Cousin [1]
   h) meine Kusine [1]

2. a) Er ist immer ruhig [1] und fleißig [1]
   b) Sie ist oft faul [1] und stur [1]
   c) Er ist nie frech [1] oder nervig [1]
   d) Sie ist nie großzügig [1] oder sympathisch [1]

3. Answers will vary. Example answers:
   a) Ich verstehe mich gut mit meinem / meiner xxx weil er / sie xxx ist. [2]
   b) Ich verstehe mich gut mit meinem / meiner xxx weil er / sie xxx ist. [2]
   c) Ich streite mich oft mit meinem / meiner xxx weil er / sie xxx ist. [2]

4. Meine beste Freundin ist schlank und etwas kleiner als ich. [1]
   Sie hat blaue Augen und blonde Haare. [1]
   Wir kennen uns seit fünf Jahren. [1]
   Sie ist immer treu und nie neidisch oder schlecht gelaunt. [1]
   Wir haben viel gemeinsam. [1]
   Wir mögen die gleichen Fernsehsendungen. [1]
   Wir haben auch den gleichen Humor. [1]
   Wir treffen uns immer am Wochenende. [1]

5. Answers will vary. Example answer:
   Meine beste Freundin heißt Molly. Sie hat braune Augen und kurze Haare. Sie ist immer freundlich und nicht schüchtern. Wir haben viel gemeinsam. (More details welcome!) [10]

6. a) Ich möchte lieber ledig bleiben. [1] I'd prefer to stay single. [1]
   b) Ich möchte eines Tages heiraten. [1] I'd like to get married one day. [1]
   c) Eine Ehe endet oft mit Scheidung. [1] A marriage often ends in divorce. [1]
   d) Eine Ehe ist sicherer als Zusammenleben. [1] Marriage is more secure than living together. [1]
   e) Meine Eltern sind geschieden aber sie verstehen sich gut. [1] My parents are divorced but they get on well. [1]
   f) Meine Freundin hat sich verlobt. Sie heiratet bald. [1] My friend has got engaged. She's getting married soon. [1]

Technology in Everyday Life
Pages 146–147: Social Media & Mobile Technology

1. a) Ich verbringe [1] viel Zeit online.
   b) Ich besuche [1] täglich meine Lieblingswebseiten.
   c) Wir schicken [1] und empfangen [1] E-Mails.
   d) Paula bleibt [1] mit ihren Freunden in Kontakt.
   e) Ich lade [1] Musik herunter [1].
   f) Das Internet hilft [1] mit meinen Hausaufgaben.

2. Answers will vary but check that the verb is second. Example answer: Jeden Tag lade ich Musilk herunter. [5]

3. a) Man muss regelmäßig das Passwort ändern. [2]
   b) Man darf das Passwort nicht verraten. [2]
   c) Man muss vorsichtig sein. [2]
   d) Man darf sich nicht mit fremden Leuten unterhalten. [2]
   e) Man muss ein Virenschutzprogramm installieren. [2]

4. a) Ben [1]
   b) Charlotte [1]
   c) Leon [1]
   d) Lena [1]
   e) Peer [1]
   f) Jonas [1]
   g) Mia [1]
   h) Sofia [1]

5. a) One advantage of mobile technology is that you can keep up to date. [2]
   b) You can find out information but the technology changes quickly. [2]
   c) I chat with my friends because I find their opinions interesting. [2]
   d) Yesterday I used the internet to help me with my homework. [2]

Free-time Activities
Pages 148–149: Music & Cinema and TV

1. Hörst du oft Musik? – Ja, ich lade jeden Tag Musik auf mein Handy herunter. [1]
   Was für Musik hörst du am liebsten? – Ich interessiere mich für klassische Musik, weil ich sie so beruhigend finde. [1]
   Hast du einen Lieblingssänger oder eine Lieblingssängerin? – Mein Lieblingssänger ist James Bay und meine Lieblingssängerin ist Paloma Faith. [1]
   Warum magst du diese Musik? – Er hat eine schöne Stimme und tolle Haare und sie schreibt tolle Lieder. [1]
   Warst du schon mal auf einem Musikfestival? – Ja, letztes Jahr war ich auf dem Lorelei-Festival in Süddeutschland. [1]

2. Yes, I download music onto my phone every day. [1]
   I'm interested in classical music because I find it so calming. [1]
   My favourite male singer is James Bay and my favourite female singer is Paloma Faith. [1]
   He has a nice voice and good hair and she writes great songs. [1]
   Yes, last year I was at the Lorelei Festival in South Germany. [1]

3. Answers will vary. Example answers:
   a) Ich höre gern [Musik], weil … (verb at end) [1]
   b) Ich höre lieber [Musik], weil … (verb at end) [1]
   c) Ich höre am liebsten [Musik], weil … (verb at end) [1]
   d) Ich höre nicht gern [Musik], weil … (verb at end) [1]
   e) Ich interessiere mich nicht für [Musik], weil … (verb at end) [1]

4. Meine Familie hört sehr gern Musik, *aber* [1] unser Geschmack ist unterschiedlich. Mein Vater war schon immer *Fan* [1] von Bap. Das ist eine *deutsche* [1] Band aus Köln, aber ich *finde* [1] sie total altmodisch. Letztes *Jahr* [1] waren wir alle auf dem Big Gig Festival in Hamburg, aber ich habe Bap *langweilig* [1] gefunden und habe mit meiner *Schwester* [1] die Rapgruppen gehört. Wir haben den *Rhythmus* [1] viel besser gefunden. Wir sind keine musikalische *Familie* [1]. Meine Mutter spielt Klavier, *obwohl* [1] mein Vater sagt, dass sie furchtbar spielt!

5. Answers will vary. Example answers:
   a) Ich sehe lieber [Filme], weil / obwohl … (verb at end) [2]
   b) Manchmal sehe ich gern [Sendungen], weil / obwohl … (verb at end) [2]
   c) Ich sehe [Filme / Sendungen] nie, weil / obwohl … (verb at end) [2]
   d) Meine Lieblingsfilme sind [Filme], weil / obwohl … (verb at end) [2]
   e) Meine Lieblingssendungen sind [Sendungen], weil / obwohl … (verb at end) [2]

6. a) Man muss die langweilige Werbung sehen. [1] You have to watch the boring adverts. [1]
   b) Die Karten werden immer teurer. [1] The tickets are getting more and more expensive. [1]
   c) Die Spezialeffekte sind besser auf der großen Leinwand. [1] The special effects are better on the big screen. [1]

Pages 150–151: Food and Eating Out, Sport & Customs and Festivals

1. a) Ich möchte ein Kilo Karotten bitte. [2]
   b) Gerne. Bitte schön. [2]
   c) Haben Sie auch Gouda-Käse? [2]
   d) Natürlich. Wie viel möchten Sie? [2]
   e) Acht Scheiben bitte. [2]
   f) Sonst noch etwas? [2]
   g) Nein danke. Was macht das? [2]
   h) Das macht zwei Euro fünfzig. [2]

2. a) Vanilleeis [1]
   b) Erdbeertorte [1]
   c) Thunfischsalat [1]
   d) Bockwurst [1]
   e) Sahne [1]
   f) Lachs [1]
   g) Schweinefleisch [1]
   h) Kartoffelsuppe [1]
   i) Obstsalat [1]
   j) Hähnchen

3. Answers will vary. Make sure the perfect tense has been used. Example answer: Wir haben Hähnchen gegessen, aber es hat nicht geschmeckt. [4]

4. a) When I was young I went hiking every day. [2]
   b) When I was fifteen I often went to the ice rink. [2]
   c) Back then I always went swimming but nowadays I prefer to stay at home. [2]
   d) I used to play football every Saturday but now I'm too lazy! [2]
   e) I want to try winter sports, even though they are dangerous. [2]

5. a) Ich spiele Hockey im Sportzentrum. [2]
   b) Früher bin ich oft angeln gegangen. [2]
   c) Heutzutage fahre ich gern Skateboard. [2]
   d) Früher bin ich am Wochenende Schlittschuh gelaufen, aber jetzt finde ich Mannschaftssport besser. [2]
   e) Wir möchten Extremsport probieren. [2]

6. Answers will vary. Check that the verb comes second in the sentence and that, after **dass**, the verb is at the end. Example answer: Ich finde, dass Fasching altmodisch, aber auch lustig ist. [10]

Environment and Social Issues
Pages 152–153: At Home, Where I Live & Town or Country

1. Wohnst du in der Stadt oder auf dem Land? – Ich wohne in der Stadtmitte. [1]
   Was gibt es in deiner Stadt? – Es gibt ein Einkaufszentrum und eine große Bücherei. [1]
   Wo möchtest du lieber wohnen? – Ich liebe es, in der Stadt zu wohnen, aber ich möchte auf das Land ziehen. [1]
   Wie ist das Leben auf dem Land? – Es ist zu ruhig und man muss mit dem Auto fahren, um Freunde zu sehen. [1]
   Wie viele Zimmer gibt es in deinem Haus? – Oben gibt es vier Zimmer: das Badezimmer, das Zimmer meiner Eltern, das Zimmer meines Bruders und mein Zimmer. [1]
   Was braucht deine Stadt? – Es gibt nichts für junge Leute. Wir brauchen ein Kino. [1]

2. a) Ich wohne in einem großen [1] Haus.
   b) Es gibt [1] acht Zimmer.
   c) Das Wohnzimmer ist neben [1] der Küche.
   d) In meinem Zimmer habe ich eine große [1] Kommode.
   e) Ich putze [1] mein Zimmer jede Woche.
   f) Es gibt Bilder an [1] der Wand.

3. Answers will vary. Example answers:
   Ich habe bei McDonalds gegessen. [2]
   Ich bin in die Bücherei gegangen. [2]
   Ich habe ein Kleid gekauft. [2]
   Ich habe meine Tasche verloren. [2]
   Ich habe mich mit meinen Freunden getroffen. [2]

4. a) Katja [1]
   b) Hans [1]
   c) Silke [1]
   d) Johannes [1]
   e) Brigitte [1]
   f) Boris [1]

5. a) Mein Zimmer ist immer ordentlich. [2]
   b) Oben gibt es drei Schlafzimmer. [2]
   c) Das Badezimmer ist neben meinem Zimmer / Schlafzimmer. [2]
   d) Es gibt kein Einkaufszentrum, aber das Parken ist kostenlos. [2]
   e) Es gibt weniger Verkehr auf dem Land als in der Stadt. [2]

Pages 154–155: Charity and Voluntary Work & Healthy and Unhealthy Living

1. Answers will vary. Example answers:
   Ich möchte Obdachlosen helfen. [1]
   Ich würde gern Freiwilligenarbeit machen. [1]
   Ich werde alten Menschen helfen. [1]
   Ich möchte warme Mahlzeiten liefern. [1]
   Ich würde gern Medikamente verteilen. [1]

2. Answers will vary. Example answers:
   Ich möchte Obdachlosen helfen. [1] I would like to help the homeless. [1]

Ich würde gern Freiwilligenarbeit machen. [1] I would like to do voluntary work. [1]

Ich werde alten Menschen helfen. [1] I will help old people. [1]

Ich möchte warme Mahlzeiten liefern. [1] I would like to deliver warm meals. [1]

Ich würde gern Medikamente verteilen. [1] I would like to distribute medicines. [1]

3. a) Man soll gesund essen. [1]
   b) Ich bin ziemlich gesund, weil ich viel Obst und Gemüse esse. [1]
   c) Ich bleibe fit, da ich genug Sport treibe. [1]
   d) Meine Gesundheit ist mir sehr wichtig. [1]

4. Ich schlafe gut. [1]
   Ich trainiere zweimal pro Woche. [1]
   Ich esse viel Obst. [1]
   Man muss wenig Fett essen. [1]
   Zigaretten können töten. [1]
   Man soll nicht rauchen. [1]

5. a) distributed medicines [1]
   b) help the Red Cross in Africa [1]
   c) delivers warm meals and drinking water to the homeless [1]

6. a) Ich schlafe gut. [2]
   b) Ich esse keine ungesunde Mahlzeiten. [2]
   c) Ich trinke genug Wasser. [2]
   d) Mein Vater hat aufgehört zu rauchen. [2]
   e) Meine Schwester trainiert jeden Tag im Fitnessstudio. [2]

Pages 156–157: The Environment & Poverty and Homelessness

1. a) We must not waste our natural resources. [2]
   b) It is important to protect our environment through recycling. [2]
   c) I think we should encourage everyone to collect, sort and recycle waste. [2]
   d) I think that we use too much energy nowadays/ I think too much energy is used nowadays. [2]
   e) In my opinion, water pollution is the biggest problem globally. [2]

2. a) Es gibt zu viel Müll auf den Straßen. [2]
   b) Soweit es mich betrifft, ist die Abholzung sehr beunruhigend. [2]
   c) Wir machen, was wir können, um die Umwelt zu schützen. [2]

3. a) 20% [1]
   b) 25% [1]
   c) 15% [1]
   d) 10% [1]
   e) 5% [1]

4. a) Es gibt immer mehr Leute, die arbeitslos sind. [1] There are more and more people who are unemployed. [1]
   b) Die Anzahl der Obdachlosen in meiner Stadt wächst schnell. [1] The number of homeless people in my town is growing quickly. [1]
   c) In meiner Stadt kann man eine Zunahme der Armut sehen. [1] In my town, you can see an increase in poverty. [1]
   d) Die Kriminalität hat überall stark zugenommen. [1] Crime has increased a lot everywhere. [1]

5. Heutzutage [1] gibt es in meiner Stadt immer mehr [1] Menschen, die arbeitslos sind [1] und auch kein [1] Zuhause haben. Vorher war Kriminalität das [1] größte Problem. Die Polizei war sehr aktiv [1] und löste das

Problem weitgehend. Leider wird die Anzahl der Arbeitslosen und Obdachlosen steigen [1], wenn nichts getan wird. Ich hoffe, die Regierung kann etwas tun, um dieses Problem zu lösen [1].

Travel and Tourism
Pages 158–159: Travel and Tourism 1, 2 and 3

1. a) Max [1]
   b) Jens [1]
   c) Max [1]
   d) Sabine [1]
   e) Kristina [1]

2. a) Georg [1]
   b) Ada [1]
   c) Gabi [1]
   d) Bernd [1]
   e) Nadine [1]

3. a) F [1]
   b) F [1]
   c) R [1]
   d) F [1]
   e) R [1]

4. a) Next year, I would like to go camping in the countryside with my friends. [1]
   b) Usually, my family and I go to Italy for two weeks. [1]
   c) Last year, I stayed in a youth hostel in Munich. [1]
   d) Three years ago, we stayed in a 4-star hotel by the sea. [1]
   e) Last summer, we were in Spain and we went walking on the beach every day. [1]

Studies and Employment
Pages 160–161: My Studies and Life at School

1.

	Lieblingsfach – jetzt	Lieblingsfach – in der Vergangenheit
Jens	Erdkunde [1]	Kunst [1]
Rebecca	Geschichte [1]	Naturwissenschaften [1]
Zak	Sport [1]	Mathe [1]

2. a) Ich [1] stehe [1] auf [1].
   b) Ich [1] wache [1] um [1] sieben Uhr [1] auf [1].
   c) Ich [1] ziehe [1] mich [1] um Viertel [1] nach [1] sieben an [1].
   d) Ich [1] bürste [1] mir die [1] Zähne [1] um [1] halb [1] acht.
   e) Ich [1] gehe [1] zu Fuß [1] in [1] die Schule.
   f) Ich [1] fahre [1] nie mit [1] dem [1] Fahrrad [1] in die Schule [1].
   g) Ich [1] ziehe [1] mich [1] nach [1] der [1] Schule um [1].
   h) Ich [1] bekomme [1] immer [1] viel [1] Hausaufgaben.

3. Was ist dein Lieblingsfach? – Deutsch gefällt mir sehr. [1]
   Was lernst du nicht gern? – Informatik kann ich nicht leiden. [1]
   Wie oft hast du Mathe? – Dreimal in der Woche. [1]
   Welches Fach hast du gewählt? – Mein Wahlfach ist Religion. [1]
   Wer ist dein(e) Lieblingslehrer(in)? – Frau Weber, da sie so gerecht ist. [1]
   Wie findest du Kunst? – Sehr kompliziert, denn ich bin nicht kreativ. [1]

4. Willkommen an unserer Schule! Es gibt ungefähr zweitausend Schüler **[1]** hier, und da es ein Internat **[1]** ist, wohnen wir alle hier zusammen, was eine Menge Spaß macht! Obwohl der Schultag um halb vier endet **[1]**, haben wir eine große Auswahl an AGs **[1]** und es gibt etwas für jeden, zum Beispiel habe ich gestern die Musikgruppe **[1]** besucht, und morgen werde ich an der Lesegruppe in der Bibliothek **[1]** teilnehmen. Meiner Meinung nach können die Lehrer ein bisschen zu streng **[1]** sein, aber im Großen und Ganzen ist der Unterricht sehr interessant **[1]**.

Studies and Employment

Pages 162–163: Education Post-16 & Career Choices and Ambitions

1. Man muss immer gut zuhören, wenn der Lehrer spricht. **[1]**
   Man muss sitzenbleiben, wenn man schlechte Noten bekommt. **[1]**
   Wir müssen nachsitzen, wenn wir zu viel schwätzen. **[1]**
   Es ist verboten, blau zu machen. **[1]**
   Es ist erlaubt, Handys in der Pause zu benutzen. **[1]**
   Wir müssen fragen, wenn wir etwas nicht verstehen. **[1]**

2. a) Moritz **[1]**
   b) Elisa **[1]**
   c) Annie **[1]**
   d) Elisa **[1]**
   e) Fabian **[1]**
   f) Annie **[1]**

3.

	Accept	Reject	Mark
Meine Mutter ist Beamtin,	My mum / mother is a civil servant		1
aber das ist nicht mein Traumberuf,	but that is not my dream job		1
da ich im Freien arbeiten möchte,	because I would like to work outside / outdoors		1
zum Beispiel als Gärtner.	for example / e.g. as a gardener.		1
Als ich jünger war,	When I was younger,		1
wollte ich Tierarzt werden,	I wanted to work as / become / be a vet		1
aber leider bin ich allergisch gegen Katzen!	but unfortunately I am allergic to cats!	allergic against	1
Nächstes Jahr werde ich einen Teilzeitjob suchen,	Next year I will / am going to look for a part time job	seek	1
um Geld zu verdienen.	(in order) to earn money.		1

4. a) Tobias **[1]**
   b) Veronika **[1]**
   c) Max **[1]**
   d) Ben **[1]**
   e) Christina **[1]**
   f) Elise **[1]**

5. a) 38% **[1]**
   b) 62% **[1]**
   c) 59% **[1]**
   d) 27% **[1]**
   e) 44% **[1]**
   f) 85% **[1]**

Grammar 1

Pages 164–165: Gender, Plurals and Articles & Cases

1. a) Zimmer **[1]**, b) Tische **[1]**, c) Gläser **[1]**, d) Hunde **[1]**, e) Tage **[1]**, f) Städte **[1]**, g) Brüder **[1]**, h) Dörfer **[1]**, i) Hamburger **[1]**, j) Freundinnen **[1]**, k) Handys **[1]**, l) Hände **[1]**, m) Autos **[1]**, n) Partys **[1]**, o) Studenten **[1]**

2. a) Die **[1]** Wurst ist fettig.
   b) Die **[1]** Künstlerin spielt gut.
   c) Der **[1]** Zug ist spät angekommen.
   d) Die **[1]** Bibliothek ist voll.
   e) Der **[1]** Schrank ist braun.
   f) Der **[1]** Lehrer unterrichtet Englisch.
   g) Das **[1]** Fest ist am 14. Februar.
   h) Die **[1]** Arbeit war schwer.
   i) Der **[1]** Verkehr ist laut.
   j) Das **[1]** Stadion ist alt.

3. a) Möchtest du die **[1]** Butter?
   b) Ich finde die **[1]** Sendung furchtbar.
   c) Nimmst du den **[1]** Kartoffelsalat?
   d) Wer hat die **[1]** Kreditkarte verloren?
   e) Hast du den **[1]** Fernsehturm gesehen?
   f) Wir haben das **[1]** Doppelzimmer genommen.
   g) Er hat die **[1]** Arbeit schwer gefunden.
   h) Wie findest du das **[1]** Computerspiel?
   i) Ich habe das **[1]** Andenken gekauft.
   j) Hast du den **[1]** Chef gesehen?

4. a) Ich höre einen **[1]** Vogel.
   b) Hast du ein **[1]** Handy?
   c) Alex hat eine **[1]** Schwester.
   d) Ich nehme eine **[1]** Dose Erbsen.
   e) Ich möchte eine **[1]** Einladung zur Party.
   f) Gibt es einen **[1]** Dom in dieser Stadt?
   g) Haben Sie einen **[1]** Hund?
   h) Hast du ein **[1]** Interview gehabt?

5. a) Er schenkt seinem **[1]** Lehrer einen Apfel.
   b) Sie schenkt ihrer **[1]** Lehrerin eine Apfelsine.
   c) Ich gebe meiner **[1]** Mutter ein Geschenk.
   d) Schreibst du deinem **[1]** Onkel?

6. a) das Ende der **[1]** Straße
   b) die Räder meines **[1]** Rads
   c) der Anfang des **[1]** Sommers
   d) der Geschmack des **[1]** Essens
   e) die Katze meiner **[1]** Freundin
   f) das Büro des **[1]** Direktors

Pages 166–167: Adjectives and Adverbs & Prepositions

1. a) Nominative: ein blöder **[1]** Film
   b) Accusative: eine lange **[1]** Pause
   c) Dative: einem großen **[1]** Problem
   d) Nominative: ein interessantes **[1]** Fach

e) Accusative: eine lange [1] Straße
f) Dative: einem netten [1] Franzosen
g) Nominative: ein schweres [1] Betriebspraktikum
h) Accusative: eine blaue [1] Handtasche
i) Dative: einem vollen [1] Bus

2. a) billiger [1]
   b) einfacher [1]
   c) lauter [1]
   d) besser [1]
   e) größer [1]
   f) jünger [1]
   g) länger [1]
   h) schneller [1]
   i) cooler [1]
   j) kleiner [1]

3. a) Ein Pferd läuft langsam. [1]
   b) Ein Mensch läuft langsamer. [1]
   c) Eine Schildkröte läuft am langsamsten. [1]
   d) Ich stehe früh [1] auf.
   e) Mutti steht früher [1] auf.
   f) Vati steht am frühsten [1] auf.

4. a) durch die [1] Stadt
   b) ohne meine [1] Schwester
   c) ohne mein [1] Rad
   d) um die [1] Ecke
   e) für meinen [1] Freund
   f) für meine [1] Freundin

5. Followed by the accusative: für, durch, um [3]
   Followed by the dative: aus, bei, mit, seit, nach [5]
   Followed by either the accusative or the dative:
   in, vor, unter, auf, hinter [5]
   Followed by the genitive: trotz, wegen, während [3]

6. a) wegen des [1] Wetters
   b) trotz des [1] Regens
   c) während der [1] Stunde

7. a) durch eine [1] Stadt
   b) für meine [1] Schwester
   c) in unserem [1] Haus
   d) mit keinem Ketchup / ohne [1] Ketchup
   e) in der [1] Straßenbahn
   f) nach der [1] Party
   g) von unserem [1] Onkel
   h) um die [1] Ecke
   i) ohne seine [1] Tasche
   j) in der [1] Sonne

Grammar 2
Pages 168–169: Pronouns and Present Tense Verbs 1
1. a) man [1], b) sie [1], c) Sie [1], d) ihr [1],
   e) wir [1], f) du [1]

2. a) Kommst du zu mir [1]?
   b) Ich gebe ihm [1] die Hand.
   c) Ich gebe Ihnen [1] meine Adresse.
   d) Unsere Freunde haben uns [1] eine E-Mail geschickt.
   e) Ich schicke dir [1] eine Postkarte.
   f) Bist du mit ihr [1] in die Stadt gegangen?

3. a) mit ihm [1]
   b) mit uns [1]
   c) zu mir [1]
   d) sie [1]
   e) ihr [1]
   f) sie [1]

g) Sie [1]
h) Ihnen [1]

4. a) ihr spielt [1]
   b) du machst [1]
   c) sie bleibt [1]
   d) ihr geht [1]
   e) Timo kommt [1]
   f) wir steigen [1]
   g) er kommt [1]
   h) sie fliegt [1]
   i) sie trinken [1]
   j) wir sagen [1]

5. a) Wir steigen am Bahnhof aus [1].
   b) Wir stehen früh auf [1].
   c) Was ziehst du an [1]?
   d) Ich komme mit [1].
   e) Heute sehen wir fern [1].
   f) Ich ziehe mich aus [1], bevor ich ins Bett gehe.

6. a) Wir sehen selten fern. [1]
   b) Wo steigt man ein? [1]
   c) Ich lade oft Filme herunter. [1]
   d) Klaus steht um 6 Uhr auf. [1]
   e) Wo steigen wir um? [1]

Pages 170–171: Present Tense Verbs 2 and Perfect Tense Verbs
1. a) sie müssen [1]
   b) er mag [1]
   c) ich kann [1]
   d) er darf [1]
   e) sie wollen [1]
   f) du magst [1]
   g) wir wollen [1]
   h) ihr dürft [1]

2. a) Ich gehe in die Stadt, um Essen zu kaufen. [1]
   b) Wir fahren nach Ibiza, um Urlaub zu machen. [1]
   c) Klaus bleibt zu Hause, um Hausaufgaben zu machen. [1]
   d) Wir recyceln Plastik, um die Umwelt zu schonen. [1]
   e) Man geht in die Schule, um Mathematik zu lernen. [1]
   f) Du fährst mit dem Zug, um nach Hamburg zu kommen. [1]

3. a) Hast du meine Schwester gesehen? [1]
   b) Hast du mein Handy genommen? [1]
   c) Wir haben uns in der Stadt getroffen. [1]
   d) Oskar hat ein neues Auto gekauft. [1]
   e) Wie hast du das Konzert gefunden? [1]
   f) Meine Eltern haben gut gegessen. [1]
   g) Haben Sie gut geschlafen? [1]
   h) Die Mannschaft hat gut gespielt. [1]

4. a) geflogen [1]
   b) gestorben [1]
   c) gewesen [1]
   d) geblieben [1]
   e) gekommen [1]
   f) gelaufen [1]
   g) gefahren [1]
   h) gegangen [1]

5. a) Wir haben uns am Marktplatz getroffen. [1]
   b) Hast du dich schon gewaschen? [1]
   c) Ich habe mich heute morgen nicht rasiert. [1]
   d) Die Kinder haben sich amüsiert. [1]

6. a) Wir haben noch nicht abgewaschen. [1]
   b) Wann seid ihr angekommen? [1]
   c) Der Film hat um 20 Uhr angefangen. [1]
   d) Hast du gestern ferngesehen? [1]

7. a) Wann bist du angekommen? [1]
   b) Was haben sie gefunden? [1]
   c) Wir haben uns hingesetzt. [1]
   d) Ich habe einen Kuchen gekauft. [1]
   e) Ergül hat Klaviert gespielt. [1]
   f) Saskia hat ihre Hausaufgaben vergessen. [1]
   g) Er hat hallo gesagt. [1]
   h) Hast du Harry Potter gelesen? [1]

Pages 172–173: Imperfect Tense Verbs and Future Time Frame

1. a) Er sprach [1] laut.
   b) Wir standen [1] vor der Kirche.
   c) Ich war [1] krank.
   d) Die Teenager tranken [1] zu viel.
   e) Ich sah [1] meinen Bruder.
   f) Sie fuhren [1] in die Berge.
   g) Wir hatten [1] Kopfschmerzen.
   h) Warst [1] du schon oft hier?
   i) Der Einbrecher nahm [1] €1000 aus dem Geldschrank.
   j) Ich konnte [1] nicht gut schlafen.

2. a) Ich gehe bald nach Hause. [1]
   b) Wir gehen am Freitag ins Kino. [1]
   c) Leon spielt heute Abend Tischtennis. [1]
   d) Meine Eltern besuchen uns morgen. [1]
   e) Ich mache um 7.30 Frühstück. [1]

3. a) Ich werde bald nach Hause gehen. [1]
   b) Wir werden am Freitag ins Kino gehen. [1]
   c) Leon wird heute Abend Tischtennis spielen. [1]
   d) Meine Eltern werden uns morgen besuchen. [1]
   e) Ich werde um 7.30 Frühstück machen. [1]

4. a) Das fand ich gut. [1]
   b) Ich sagte nichts. [1]
   c) Ali kam mit. [1]
   d) Wir hatten Spaß. [1]
   e) Peter war im Krankenhaus. [1]
   f) Es gab viel zu sehen. [1]
   g) Sie hatte keine Zeit. [1]
   h) Was musstest du machen? [1]

5. a) ich musste [1]
   b) wir wollten [1]
   c) ihr solltet [1]
   d) er mochte [1]
   e) du konntest [1]
   f) man durfte [1]

6. a) F [1]
   b) F [1]
   c) P [1]
   d) P [1]
   e) F [1]
   f) F [1]

7. Answers will vary. Example answers:
   a) Wenn ich mehr Geld hätte, würde ich… [1]
   b) Wenn ich mehr Zeit hätte, würde ich… [1]
   c) Wenn ich nicht so faul wäre, würde ich… [1]

Pages 174–175: Pluperfect Tense, Subjunctive Mood and Imperative & Word Order and Conjunctions

1. a) Sie sind ins Wohnzimmer gegangen, nachdem sie gegessen hatten [1].
   b) Er war [1] krank gewesen.
   c) Peter hatte [1] schon oft Muscheln gegessen.
   d) Ich war [1] noch nie in die Oper gegangen.
   e) Birgit hatte [1] ihre Kreditkarte vergessen.
   f) Ich bin ins Bett gegangen, nachdem ich geduscht hatte [1].

2. a) Ulla fährt nächste Woche nach Spanien. [1]
   b) Er geht jeden Tag in die Schule. [1]
   c) Ich war letzte Woche in Kiel. [1]
   d) Letzte Woche war ich in Kiel. [1]
   e) Das Auto fuhr langsam die Straße entlang. [1]
   f) Am Freitag geht Harry zum Zahnarzt. [1]
   g) Harry geht am Freitag zum Zahnarzt. [1]
   h) Wir essen immer gern Obst. [1]
   i) Wir essen immer gut in Frankreich. [1]
   j) Ich arbeite jeden Tag in einem Geschäft. [1]

3. a) Asma hatte Abitur gemacht. [1]
   b) Ich hatte ein Computerspiel heruntergeladen. [1]
   c) Wir waren zur Haltestelle gegangen. [1]
   d) Er war noch nie nach Frankreich gefahren. [1]
   e) Ich hatte eine E-Mail geschickt. [1]
   f) Aktar war nicht gekommen. [1]
   g) Man hatte ein Problem gehabt. [1]
   h) Wir hatten Freunde eingeladen. [1]

4. a) Asma had done A-levels (Abitur). [1]
   b) I had downloaded a computer game. [1]
   c) We had gone to the bus stop. [1]
   d) He had never travelled to France. [1]
   e) I had sent an email. [1]
   f) Aktar hadn't come. [1]
   g) There had been a problem. [1]
   h) We had invited friends. [1]

5. a) Jeden Tag fahre ich mit dem Bus in die Stadt. [1]
   b) Leider ist meine Mutter krank. [1]
   c) Hier darf man nicht parken. [1]
   d) Gestern ist Mark zum Zahnarzt gegangen. [1]
   e) Am Freitag haben wir Pommes mit Ketchup gegessen. [1]
   f) Letztes Jahr ist Aisa nach Amerika geflogen. [1]

6. a) Ich fahre jeden Tag mit dem Rad zur Schule. [1]
   b) Wirst du am Wochenende mit mir zum Schwimmbad kommen? [1]
   c) Wir sehen oft im Wohnzimmer fern. [1]
   d) Mehmet spielt oft im Jugendklub Tischtennis. [1]
   e) Mein Vater arbeitet jeden Tag hart im Büro. [1]
   f) Willst du heute Abend mit mir im Restaurant Pizza essen? [1]

Pages 176–187
Higher Tier Paper 1 Listening – Mark Scheme
Section A Questions and answers in English

01	In any order: A		[1]
	B		[1]
	D		[1]
02.1	The conservatory		[1]
02.2	It's always light / the windows / light (not lights) make(s) his photos better		[1]
03.1	(low) grades / pressure to achieve good grades		[1]
03.2	undecided / (lack of / no) future plans		[1]
03.3	bullying / mean classmates		[1]
04	Past:	Secretary	[1]
	Future:	Lawyer	[1]
05	Past:	Fireman / fighter	[1]
	Present:	Businessman	[1]
06.1	B		[1]
06.2	E		[1]

06.3	A	[1]
07.1	She was near the front / She had a good view	[1]
07.2	Chatting to / Meeting her favourite group	[1]
07.3	One from: The cheap tickets were sold out	
	She couldn't afford expensive tickets	[1]
07.4	Her mum's friend got (2) tickets	[1]
	Her mum gave her them as a birthday gift	[1]
08.1	His father won't let him see his girlfriend	[1]
08.2	His brother is treated differently / his brother can	
	do what he wants [even though he is younger]	[1]
08.3	One from: he is selfish / mean	[1]
08.4	Holidays together	[1]
08.5	They never argue	[1]
09.1	N	[1]
09.2	P	[1]
09.3	P+N	[1]
09.4	P	[1]
10.1	A	[1]
10.2	C	[1]
10.3	A	[1]
11.1	C	[1]
11.2	C	[1]
11.3	There is more / lots to do	[1]
12	B	[1]
13.1	C	[1]
13.2	D	[1]
13.3	A	[1]

Section B Questions and answers in German

14.1	82	[1]
14.2	57	[1]
14.3	5	[1]
14.4	66	[1]
15.1	P	[1]
15.2	N	[1]
15.3	P+N	[1]

16 In any order: B **[1]**, C **[1]**, D **[1]**

Pages 188–190
Higher Tier Paper 2 Speaking – Mark Scheme
Role-play
Your teacher will start the role-play by saying an
introductory text such as:
Sie sind in einem Hotel in Deutschland. Ich bin die Person
an der Hotelrezeption.

1. Teacher: **Guten Tag, wie kann ich Ihnen helfen?**
   Hello, how can I help you?
   Student: **Ich möchte ein Zimmer für zwei Personen,
   bitte.**
   I would like a room for two people, please.
2. Teacher: **Was für ein Zimmer möchten Sie?**
   What sort of room would you like?
   Student: **Ein Doppelzimmer mit Bad, bitte.**
   A double room with a bathroom, please.

Tip
Make sure you include two elements as required in
the question.

3. Unprepared question
   Teacher: **Wie lange bleiben Sie hier?**
   How long will you be staying here?
   Student: **Wir bleiben vier Nächte.**
   We are staying for four nights.

4. Teacher: **Und haben Sie schon Deutschland besucht?**
   And have you visited Germany before?

Student: **Ja, letztes Jahr bin ich nach Berlin geflogen,
es war super.**
Yes, I flew to Berlin last year, it was great.

Tip
Make sure you use the correct tense and take care
with the auxiliary verb.

5. Asking a question
   Student: **Gibt es ein gutes Restaurant hier in der
   Nähe?**
   Is there a good restaurant nearby?
   Teacher: **Ja, wir haben ein tolles italienisches
   Restaurant hier im Hotel.**
   *Yes, we have a great Italian restaurant here
   in the hotel.*

Tip
There will always be a question to ask, so ensure that
you know to form open and closed questions.

Preparation tips
When you are preparing for your role-play consider:
• Whether you are using 'du' or 'Sie' (both in questions
  and answers)
• If you need to use a different tense
• What sort of '!' question could be possible in the
  context you are given

Photo Card
Example answers:
1st question
Auf dem Bild sehe ich eine große Familie in einem
schönen Haus (vielleicht sind sie in der Küche oder
im Esszimmer). In dieser Familie gibt es Eltern, Kinder
und Großeltern. Sie sehen sehr glücklich aus, und
im Hintergrund sieht man einen geschmückten
Weihnachtsbaum, also muss es Winter und Weihnachtszeit
sein. Es gibt viel Essen, zum Beispiel Gemüse und Pute.
Meiner Meinung nach werden sie nach dem Essen
Weihnachtsgeschenke austauschen.

Tip
Always give as much information as you can,
using key phrases such as **'es gibt'**, **'ich sehe'**,
'man sieht' etc. You can also make (educated!)
guesses using words such as **'vielleicht'**
(maybe) and **'meiner Meinung nach'** (in my
opinion). For this photo, many words will start
with some form of the word **'Weihnachten'**
(Christmas) such as **'Weihnachtsbaum'** (Christmas
tree), **'Weihnachtszeit'** (Christmas time) and
'Weihnachtsgeschenke' (Christmas presents).

2nd question
Ich finde es sehr wichtig, Feste zu feiern. Man kann Zeit
mit Freunden und Familie verbringen, was immer schön
ist. Viele Leute müssen nicht arbeiten, also ist man nicht so
gestresst und man kann sich entspannen. Jedoch glauben
manche, dass Feste zu kommerzialisiert sind und sie zu
viel Geld kosten. Ich finde, dass Feste wie Halloween nur
für Kinder sind und ich glaube, dass Valentinstag super
langweilig ist.

3rd question

Letztes Jahr war Weihnachten prima! Ich habe viel Zeit mit meiner Familie verbracht. Wir haben meine Großeltern in London besucht und meine Cousins sind auch gekommen. Es macht immer viel Spaß, denn wir sind sehr gute Freunde. Ich habe viele Geschenke bekommen, zum Beispiel ein neues Handy und ein tolles Buch, das ich sofort gelesen habe. Ich hatte zwei Wochen Schulferien also konnte ich viel schlafen!

You will be asked two further questions, on the same topic. Other questions you might be asked are:
- Wie feierst du normalerweise deinen Geburtstag?
- Wie findest du Ostern?
- Was ist dein Lieblingsfest?
- Was isst du normalerweise zum Weihnachten?
- Ist es wichtig, Geschenke zu kaufen? Warum (nicht)?

Prepare your answers to these questions, too!

General Conversation
Theme 2: Local, national, international and global areas of interest
Aimed at Foundation level candidate – 3–5 minutes

Wo wohnst du?

Ich wohne mit meinen Eltern und meinem Bruder in einem Doppelhaus in Nantwich – das ist eine mittelgroße Stadt in Nordwestengland. Ich liebe unser Haus, denn es ist gemütlich und ordentlich, obwohl es ein bisschen klein ist. Wir haben einen riesigen Garten, wo ich Fußall spiele, und das ist echt toll.

Was kann man in deiner Gegend machen?

Hier gibt es nicht so viel für junge Leute. Obwohl meine Gegend super sauber ist, ist es leider ziemlich ruhig und langweilig. Man kann schwimmen gehen oder in den Cafés essen und trinken, und es gibt eine schöne Kirche, aber es gibt keine guten Geschäfte. Wir haben ein Kino, aber das ist nicht im Stadtzentrum. Schade!

Wo wirst du in der Zukunft wohnen?

In der Zukunft möchte ich in einer großen Stadt wohnen, da es viel mehr zu tun gibt. Ich habe vor, im Ausland zu wohnen, denn ich mag reisen. Ich werde an die Uni gehen und danach will ich einen guten Job in Deutschland oder in der Schweiz finden. Ich plane, in einer Wohnung mit meiner besten Freundin zu wohnen.

Bist du gesund?

Nein! Ich esse zu viele Süßigkeiten und ich bin nie aktiv. Als ich jünger war, war ich sehr fit, und ich habe viel Sport getrieben, aber jetzt bin ich ein Stubenhocker! In der Zukunft will ich abnehmen, also werde ich zweimal in der Woche schwimmen gehen und mehr Obst und Gemüse essen.

Was hast du neulich gemacht, um umweltfreundlich zu sein?

Ich denke, ich bin sehr umweltfreundlich. Gestern habe ich den Müll getrennt, weil Recycling sehr wichtig ist. Letzte Woche bin ich mit dem Bus zur Schule gefahren, denn die öffentlichen Verkehrsmittel sind umweltfreundlicher. Meine Familie kauft immer Energiesparlampen und wir benutzen keine Plastiktüten mehr.

Willst du in der Zukunft freiwillig arbeiten?

Ja, denn es ist sehr wichtig, anderen Leuten zu helfen. Ich möchte in einem Kindergarten freiwillig arbeiten, weil ich Kinder mag. Ich werde später als Lehrer arbeiten und freiwillige Arbeit ist eine gute Erfahrung. Ich will auch den Obdachlosen in meiner Stadt Geld spenden.

Theme 3: Current and future study and employment
Aimed at Higher level candidate – 5–7 minutes

Was ist dein Traumberuf?

> **Tip**
> This is a good opportunity to use the conditional. Your answer here should include a lot of opinions, so make sure you explain them too.

Als ich jung war, war es immer mein Traum, als Feuerwehrmann / -frau zu arbeiten, denn es ist ein sehr interessanter Beruf. Aber jetzt ist das zu gefährlich für mich, deshalb will ich Geschäftsmann / -frau werden, und da ich sehr gern Deutsch spreche, möchte ich im Ausland arbeiten. Das wäre toll und hoffentlich würde ich viel Geld verdienen.

Sind Fremdsprachen wichtig?

> **Tip**
> If you get a question about language learning or speaking German, it's a good idea to be positive! Even if you find the subject hard, mention the advantages too.

In meiner Schule müssen wir eine Fremdsprache lernen, und ich habe Deutsch gewählt, denn es ist sehr nützlich und es fällt mir leichter als Spanisch oder Französisch. Ich finde Fremdsprachen äußerst wichtig, um mit Leuten rund um die Welt zu kommunizieren. Ich liebe Fremdsprachen!

Wirst du an die Uni gehen?

> **Tip**
> You may not have decided about future plans, but you will be expected to use the future tense and this type of question elicits this. Learn some more unusual set phrases such as 'ich habe vor' (I plan), 'ich habe die Absicht' (I have the intention) or 'ich beabsichtige' (I intend).

Ich habe vor, an die Uni zu gehen, obwohl es ein bisschen teuer ist. Meine Eltern sagen, dass ich Mathe studieren soll, aber ich würde lieber Arzt / Ärztin werden und deshalb werde ich Naturwissenschaften studieren. Ich habe die Absicht, ein Jahr vor der Uni freizunehmen und ich beabsichtige, ein Arbeitspraktikum in einem Krankenhaus zu finden.

Wie findest du das Schulleben in Deutschland?

> **Tip**
> This question involves you demonstrating some cultural knowledge. You don't have to know loads about each topic, but where there are important differences (for example the school system or recycling in Germany) you are expected to be familiar with them.

Ich finde sitzenbleiben nicht gut! Es ist zu stressig für die Schüler. Zum Glück haben wir das hier in England nicht. Es gibt viele verschiedene Schulen in Deutschland und das ist sehr interessant. Sie müssen keine Schuluniform tragen und das ist bestimmt bequemer und einfacher als in meiner Schule. Auch gibt es manchmal keinen Unterricht nachmittags – das wäre toll!

Beschreib deine Schule.

> **Tip**
> This is a very vague, open-ended question, but don't fall into the trap of a simple, list-style answer. You must still develop your answer and use as much advanced language as possible.

Da wir viele neue Gebäude haben, sieht unsere Schule sehr modern aus. Natürlich gibt es viele Klassenzimmer und so weiter, aber was mir am besten gefällt, ist die Bibliothek, weil ich stundenlang dort lesen oder Hausaufgaben machen kann. Die Mensa in meiner Grundschule war echt mies, aber das Essen hier schmeckt mir viel besser – gestern habe ich Hähnchen mit Gemüse und Kartoffeln gegessen: super gesund und lecker!

Was sind die Vor- und Nachteile von Hausaufgaben?

> **Tip**
> If you are asked about advantages and disadvantages, it is important to cover both points of view. It doesn't matter which one you agree with, but you can include your own opinion and contrast it with other people's, using connectives such as '**jedoch**' (however) or phrases such as '**einerseits / andererseits**' (on the one hand/on the other hand).

Das ist eine interessante Frage! Es gibt viel Leistungsdruck in meiner Schule, und der Direktor und die Lehrer glauben, dass Hausaufgaben sehr wichtig sind. Es stimmt, dass die Hausaufgaben mir helfen, jedoch kann ich manchmal gestresst werden. Einerseits lernen wir viel mehr, aber andererseits haben wir nicht genug Freizeit und keine Zeit zum Entspannen. Ich finde, dass zu viele Hausaufgaben keine gute Sache ist.

Pages 191–204
Higher Tier Paper 3 Reading – Mark Scheme
Section A Questions and answers in English

01.1	B	[1]
01.2	D	[1]
01.3	C	[1]

02

	One advantage	One disadvantage
Alya	any **one** from: • stay in contact with people / friends / family / acquaintances etc. • stay informed **[1]**	cyberbullying **[1]**
Marlene	any **one** from: • can share information • can show others your interests **[1]**	any **one** from: • children don't always know who they are speaking to • can lead to health problems • can become addictive • can make you lazy **[1]**

03 In any order: A [1], E [1], F [1], H [1]

04.1 A chance to do something different / something outside of the ordinary [1]

04.2 To neighbouring / nearby countries or cities / towns [1]

04.3 Any one from: (plane / car) emissions, (plane / car) exhaust fumes, rubbish / waste from hotels [1]

04.4 It is too expensive / costs too much to travel [far from home / abroad], it's cheaper to stay at home [1]

04.5 C [1]

05.1 H [1]

05.2 U [1]

05.3 H+U [1]

05.4 H+U [1]

06.1 T [1]

06.2 F [1]

06.3 NT [1]

06.4 F [1]

06.5 F [1]

06.6 T [1]

07.1 Any two from: see a new country, get to know a new culture, learn a new language, make new friends, get to know new people [2]

07.2 Any two from: can cost a lot of money, can have language difficulties, can struggle with the classes, can become distracted e.g. through parties [2]

08.1 He / she / they enjoy(s) (breathing) the fresh air [1]

08.2 They prefer to spend time in front of a screen (accept reference to computer / TV etc.) [1]

08.3 Go for a walk (once a week) [1]

Section B Questions and answers in German

09.1 F [1]

09.2 F [1]

09.3 NT [1]

09.4 R [1]

09.5 R [1]

09.6 R [1]

09.7 F [1]

09.8 NT [1]

10.1 Any two from: reich / schön / groß [2]

10.2 Nachts / wenn es dunkel ist / wenn die Leute schlafen [1]

10.3 Any one from: Sie kochen / sie backen [1]

11.1 Er streitet mit den Eltern / es gibt Krach/Streit mit den Eltern [1]

11.2 Seine Eltern arbeiten / um Verantwortung zu lernen / Die Eltern sagen, dass ein Teil des Erwachsenlebens ist [1]

11.3 (Sie helfen) nie [1]

11.4 Er hat keine / nicht genug Zeit für Hausaufgaben / um Hausaufgaben zu machen [1]

11.5 Er ist krank / er hat nicht (gut) geschlafen [1]

11.6 (Zu) (seiner) Schwester [1]

Section C Translation into English
12

Obwohl es ruhig und ziemlich klein ist,	Although it is quiet and rather / quite small, [1]
liebe ich mein Dorf.	I love my village. [1]
Vor zwei Jahren	2 / two years ago [1]
waren die öffentlichen Verkehrsmittel furchtbar,	the public transport was dreadful / awful, [1]
und ich bin oft	and I was often / and I often arrived / came / got (if 'late' is at end of next sentence), [1]
spät in die Schule gekommen,	late to school, [1]
aber jetzt bin ich immer pünktlich.	but now I am always punctual / on time. [1]
Ich werde in den Bergen bei Wien wohnen,	I will live in the mountains around / near Vienna. [1]
wenn ich achtzehn bin.	when I am 18 / eighteen. [1]

Pages 205–208
Higher Tier Paper 4 Writing – Mark Scheme
Question 1
Example answer:
Ich liebe meine Familie und wir verstehen uns sehr gut. Meine Mutter ist sehr nett und sympatisch und ich verbringe gern Zeit mit meinem Vater, denn wir spielen Fußball und Schach zusammen. Familie ist mir super wichtig, weil meine Eltern immer Unterstützung geben und sie mir bei Problemen helfen. Letztes Wochenende sind wir nach London gefahren und wir haben viele interessante Sehenswürdigkeiten besucht – es war ein tolles Erlebnis. In der Zukunft will ich heiraten und dann drei Kinder haben, und ich werde ein riesiges Haus auf dem Land kaufen. [16]

Question 2

> **Tip**
> Even if the question doesn't specifically elicit tenses and opinions, you can presume that this is what the examiner is looking for to award high marks. Remember to include a range of time frames, and always justify your opinions.

Example answer:
Ich habe neulich eine Woche in Köln verbracht, und es hat mir sehr viel Spaß gemacht. Ich war mit meiner Schule dort, da ich an dem Schulaustausch teilgenommen habe, und mein Austauschpartner war zum Glück super freundlich. Köln habe ich sehr schön gefunden, und es gab viel zu tun und zu sehen. Obwohl es kalt und windig war, haben wir viele Weihnachtsmärkte besucht, und ich habe dort viele Andenken für meine Familie gekauft. Natürlich musste ich auch viel Deutsch sprechen, was manchmal schwierig war.
Da ich in einem kleinen Dorf wohne, war meine Woche in einer großen Stadt sehr interessant! Ich finde, dass Köln besser ist, weil die Busse und Züge immer pünktlich kommen und das passiert hier nicht. Es war auch sehr gut, viele Museen in der Nähe zu haben. Ein Nachteil war, dass es so viele Leute in der Stadtmitte gab, denn es ist hier viel ruhiger. [32]

Question 3
Example answer:
Wir müssen versuchen, die Umwelt zu schützen, und das Recycling / die Wiederverwertung ist wichtig, um umweltfreundlicher zu sein. Die Einwohner in meiner Stadt haben gelernt, den Müll zu trennen, obwohl wir zu viel wegwerfen. In der Zukunft werde ich keine Plastiktüten benutzen, und ich will die öffentlichen Verkehrsmittel öfter benutzen. [12]

Collins

GCSE
German

H

Higher Tier Paper 1 Listening Test Transcript

Section A   Questions and answers in **English**

01   **F1**   Wir wollten gestern die Burgruinen besuchen, und wir hatten alles im Voraus gebucht. Leider hatten wir eine Panne auf der Autobahn – wie schade!

M1   Die Fluglinie hat meinen Koffer verloren und noch nicht gefunden. Zum Glück war unser Fünf-Sterne-Hotel super einfach zu finden und die Zimmer sind riesig und sauber.

F1   Als ich im Zug war, hat jemand meine Reisetasche gestohlen. Meinen Ausweis, meine Fahrkarten, meine Straßenkarte – alles geklaut! Zum Glück war mein Geld in meiner Handtasche.

02   **M**   Mein altes Haus war in einer wunderbaren Stadt, aber wir sind neulich umgezogen und ich muss zugeben, dass unser neues Haus viel größer und schöner ist. Was ich am liebsten mag ist der Wintergarten, denn ich fotografiere gern und in diesem Zimmer gibt es viele Fenster, deshalb ist es immer hell und meine Fotos sind besser.

03   **M1**   Mensch, ist das Schulleben stressig! Was ich am schwierigsten finde, ist der Notendruck. Ich habe neulich eine Vier in allen meinen Fächern bekommen, obwohl ich auf eine Zwei gehofft hatte. Es war keine gute Überraschung.

F1   Meine Noten sind eigentlich ganz gut, aber ich bin momentan sehr gestresst, weil ich keine festen Pläne für die nächsten zwei Jahre habe. Ich hatte einen Termin mit der Berufsberaterin, aber sie hat mir nicht geholfen.

	M2	Meine Eltern machen sich Sorgen darüber, dass ich unglücklich in der Schule bin. Ich habe gute Freunde, aber Mobbing ist ein großes Problem in meiner Schule und es gibt viele Schüler, die sehr gemein und unfreundlich sind.
04	F1	Bevor ich Kinder hatte, habe ich als Sekretärin in Deutschland gearbeitet. Jetzt bin ich Lehrerin und das passt mir gut, wegen der langen Ferien. Eines Tages will ich eine Ausbildung als Rechtsanwältin machen.
05	M1	Bald werde ich meine eigene Firma gründen, was super sein wird! Als Geschäftsmann habe ich gelernt, ein guter Chef zu sein und mit Kollegen effektiv zu arbeiten. Als ich jünger war, war ich Feuerwehrmann, aber es war zu gefährlich für mich.
06	M1	Soziale Netzwerke gehen mir wirklich auf die Nerven. Die Fotos und Statusmeldungen sind so unrealistisch und junge Leute denken, dass sie im Vergleich ein langweiliges oder unglückliches Leben haben. Sie fühlen sich deshalb weniger selbstbewusst.
	F1	Als ich jünger war, habe ich mit meinen Freunden im Freien gespielt – wir sind radgefahren, wir haben die frische Luft genossen ... Jetzt verbringen handysüchtige Kinder zu viel Zeit vor dem Bildschirm und sie spielen stundenlang auf Apps.
	M2	Ich liebe soziale Medien, aber ich weiß, dass das Leben online gefährlich sein kann. Man weiß nie, mit wem man spricht. Viele Nutzer können persönliche Daten und Bilder teilen und sehen, aber sie sind nicht immer gute Leute.
07	F	Ich war neulich bei einem Konzert in Nürnberg und es war ein tolles Erlebnis, vor allem weil ich ganz vorne war und ich den perfekten Blick auf alle Musiker hatte. Ich musste sehr früh aufstehen, um einen guten Platz zu finden, aber es lohnte sich, denn vor dem Konzert hatte ich die Gelegenheit, mit meiner Lieblingsgruppe zu plaudern, als sie angekommen ist!
	F	Ich konnte keine Karten kaufen, denn die billigen Karten waren ausverkauft, und ich konnte mir die teuren Karten nicht leisten. Zum Glück arbeitet eine Freundin meiner Mutter beim Fest und hat ihr zwei Karten gegeben, die Mama mir für meinen letzten Geburtstag geschenkt hat.
08	M	Ich weiß, dass alle Familien streiten, aber ich fühle mich immer so traurig, wenn es in meiner Familie Krach gibt. Mein Vater hat letzte Woche gesagt, dass ich wegen schlechter Noten meine Freundin nicht mehr sehen darf und seitdem haben wir nicht gesprochen.

M Jetzt bin ich fast 16 Jahre alt und ich habe einen Teilzeitjob, also warum werde ich von meinen Eltern wie ein Kind behandelt? Mein Bruder kann machen, was er will, obwohl er jünger ist als ich – das ist so ungerecht. Wir sind keine guten Freunde, da ich ihn egoistisch und gemein finde.

M Ich hoffe, dass meine Beziehung zu meinem Vater besser wird. Nächstes Wochenende fährt die ganze Familie in den Urlaub und ich freue mich trotz unserer Probleme sehr darauf. Ich liebe unsere Ferien zusammen, denn wir streiten nie. Vielleicht weil wir alle so entspannt sind?

09 **F1** Man ist mit einem Handy immer erreichbar, und ich denke, das ist nervig. Ich will nicht immer in Kontakt mit der ganzen Welt bleiben! Manchmal will ich einfach mich entspannen, ohne mein Handy immer anzugucken.

M1 Meine Freunde finden es ziemlich lustig, dass ich immer noch kein Smartphone habe, aber für mich ist es nicht wichtig, das neuste Modell zu haben. Mit meinem Handy kann ich simsen und anrufen und das reicht – es hat alles, was man braucht.

F2 Obwohl mein Handy mir auf die Nerven geht, wenn es immer klingelt, könnte ich ohne es nicht leben. Das heißt, dass ich handysüchtig bin, was ungesund sein kann. Ich habe neulich eine App heruntergeladen, die mir bei dieser Sucht helfen kann.

M2 Meine Eltern finden es viel sicherer, wenn ich mein Handy dabei habe. Sie haben nicht nur mein neues Handy gekauft, sondern sie zahlen auch meine Handyrechnung, und sie denken, dass man in der heutigen Welt immer erreichbar sein muss. Ich stimme zu!

10 **F1** Es macht keinen Spaß, wenn man Schlafprobleme hat. Ich versuche immer, früh ins Bett zu gehen, aber wenn mein Wecker morgens klingelt, bin ich immer müde. Ich habe eine stressige Arbeit, und ich schreibe und schicke E-Mails, wenn ich im Bett bin – das hilft nicht!

M1 Als ich 14 war, habe ich angefangen zu rauchen. Zwei Monate später habe ich versucht, aufzuhören, aber ich hatte keinen Erfolg. Jetzt mache ich mir keine Sorgen darüber. Natürlich gibt es Gesundheitsrisiken, aber es fällt mir zu schwer, aufzugeben.

F2 Viele Frauen und Mädchen sind heute unter Druck von den Medien, dünn zu sein und abzunehmen. Wenn man übergewichtig ist, ist es ohne Zweifel gesundheitsschädlich, aber viele junge Leute sehen unrealistische Bilder. Es ist mir völlig egal, wieviel ich wiege.

11   **F**   Ich freue mich sehr auf deinen Besuch! Ich wohne mit meiner Mutter und meinem Stiefvater in einem Doppelhaus in einem kleinen Dorf. Meine Gegend ist sehr hübsch und die Nachbarn sind alle ganz freundlich, aber es kann auch langweilig sein. Mein Vater wohnt in einem Bauernhaus zwanzig Kilometer von uns entfernt, also vielleicht besuchen wir ihn am Wochenende, denn alles ist dort so sauber und ruhig. Meine Schwester hat eine Wohnung in der Stadt, da sie an der Uni studiert, und ich besuche sie gern, da es so viel dort zu tun gibt, und es ist immer viel los.

12   **M**   Es ist eine Kette von schlechten Ereignissen, die uns allen passieren könnte. Man verliert den Job, deshalb ist man pleite, deshalb kann man die Miete nicht bezahlen, deshalb muss man auf der Straße leben. Dann beginnt der Teufelskreis – man hat keinen festen Wohnsitz, deshalb kann man keine Arbeit finden, deshalb kann man kein Geld verdienen … Es gibt leider nicht genug Sozialwohnungen, um allen Obdachlosen hier zu helfen, aber ich denke, jeder hat das Recht auf ein Zuhause. Was können wir tun?

13   **F**   Stellen Sie sich vor, Sie sind im Regenwald. Sie sehen grüne Blätter, Sie riechen tropische Blumen, Sie fühlen die Sonne auf der Haut. Aber Lärm gibt es nicht – keine Vögel, keine Insekten. Immer mehr Tierarten sterben aus, und wir müssen sie retten.

         M   Haben Sie genug zu essen? Haben Sie heute vor der Arbeit geduscht? Haben Sie Medikamente? Vielen Leuten rund um die Welt stehen diese Sachen nicht zur Verfügung, denn es gibt einen Mangel an Wasser. Wir müssen aufhören, unser Wasser zu verschwenden.

         F   Wir fliegen alle gern in Urlaub und wir verbringen gern zwei Wochen in einem heißen, sonnigen Land. Aber wenn die Temperaturen wegen des Klimawandels steigen, steigt auch der Meeresspiegel. Die Zukunft der Erde liegt in unseren Händen.

Section B   Questions and answers in **German**

14   **M**   Unsere Studie hat gezeigt, dass viele junge Leute Leseratten sind – 82% der Befragten verbringen gern Zeit mit einem guten Buch und einer Tasse Tee oder Kaffee – wie schön! Sie sind auch musikalisch – 72% haben gesagt, dass die Klavier oder Gitarre spielen. Kinobesuche sind nicht so beliebt, und zwar sehen nur 57% gern Filme auf der großen Leinwand. Sehen sie lieber Filme im Internet? Keine Ahnung, aber im Internet benutzen sie sicher super gern soziale Netzwerke, denn nur 5% haben keine Profile online. Stubenhocker sind diese Jugendlichen nicht – 66% sind aktiv, indem sie Sport ein- oder zweimal pro Woche machen.

15   **M1**   Ich will nicht immer ledig bleiben, deshalb will ich bestimmt heiraten. Es ist besser für die Kinder, wenn die Eltern verheiratet sind. Meine Eltern sind seit zwanzig Jahren zusammen und sie haben mir die Vorteile einer Ehe gezeigt.

    F1   Meiner Meinung nach ist die Liebe wichtiger als ein Blatt Papier. Ich finde die Ehe altmodisch und heute unnötig und meine Karriere hat Vorrang. Mein Freund hat versucht, mich zu überzeugen, aber das hat er nicht geschafft!

    M2   Ein modisches Kleid, schöne Blumen, lange Flitterwochen – lohnt es sich? Aus religiösen Gründen will ich heiraten und es ist mir sehr wichtig. Aber es scheint mir, dass es bei der Ehe für viele Leute um eine teure Hochzeit geht, und das macht mich traurig.

16   **F**   Persönlich verbringe ich fast keine Zeit vor der Glotze, denn ich habe bessere Sachen zu tun, zum Beispiel Hausaufgaben oder Tanzstunden. Es ist wichtig, die Nachrichten zu sehen, um die Welt besser zu verstehen, aber das mache ich im Internet oder ich lese Zeitungen. Allerdings schwärme ich für Dokumentarfilme, weil sie so faszinierend sind, vor allem wenn sie von Geschichte oder Natur handeln. Meine Schwester geht gern ins Kino, aber ich finde die Karten sind nicht preiswert und es lohnt sich nicht.

[END OF TEST]

Acknowledgements

The authors and publisher are grateful to the copyright holders for permission to use quoted materials and images.

All images © Shutterstock.com

Every effort has been made to trace copyright holders and obtain their permission for the use of copyright material. The authors and publisher will gladly receive information enabling them to rectify any error or omission in subsequent editions. All facts are correct at time of going to press.

Published by Collins
An imprint of HarperCollins*Publishers* Ltd
1 London Bridge Street
London SE1 9GF

HarperCollins*Publishers*
1st Floor, Watermarque Building,
Ringsend Road, Dublin 4, Ireland

© HarperCollins*Publishers* Limited 2020

ISBN 9780008292034

First published 2018
This edition published 2020

10 9 8 7

British Library Cataloguing in Publication Data.

A CIP record of this book is available from the British Library.

Authored by: Amy Bates, Oliver Gray and Keely Laycock
Commissioning Editor: Kerry Ferguson
Project Manager and Editorial: Chantal Addy
Indexing: Simon Yapp
Cover Design: Sarah Duxbury and Kevin Robbins
Inside Concept Design: Sarah Duxbury and Paul Oates
Text Design and Layout: Jouve India Private Limited
Production: Natalia Rebow

Printed and Bound in the UK using 100% Renewable Electricity at CPI Group (UK) Ltd

MIX
Paper from
responsible source
FSC
www.fsc.org
FSC™ C007454

This book is produced from independently certified FSC™ paper to ensure responsible forest management.

For more information visit:
www.harpercollins.co.uk/green